YOUR GUIDE TO
A LIFE OF BALANCE,
ENERGY, AND VITALITY

ON
TARGET
LIVING

Chris Johnson

WILEY

Library of Congress Cataloging-in-Publication Data:

Johnson, Chris, 1957-
   On target living : your guide to a life of balance, energy, and vitality / Chris Johnson.
     pages cm
   ISBN 978-1-118-43529-8 (pbk.); ISBN 978-1-118-63297-0 (ebk);
ISBN 978-1-118-63296-3 (ebk); ISBN 978-1-118-63295-6 (ebk)
   1. Health behavior–Popular works. 2. Health promotion–Popular works. 3. Industrial hygiene–Popular works. I. Title.
   RA776.9.J64 2013
   613–dc23

                                                                        2012049823

Printed in the United States of America

20 19 18 17 16 15 14 13 12 11

Contents

Acknowledgments

There are so many people who were instrumental in the development and completion of this book. I'd like to begin by thanking many of my teachers. To Miss Ellis, my sixth-grade teacher, who believed in me. To my college professors, Dr. Louis Junker, Dr. Wayne Van Huss, Dr. William Heusner, and Dr. Kwok Ho. Thank you for sharing your passion and vision and opening my eyes to a life's work in health and fitness.

To my mentor Al Arens, your guidance and support made a huge impact on my life!

To my colleagues Phil Nuernberger, Bena Long, Matthew Cross, Diana Doroftei, and Anna Callori, who I have learned from and been supported by; they inspired me to keep learning and growing.

Thanks to all my wonderful friends and family who have supported me from the beginning.

To all our faithful On Target Living readers, followers, whose letters, phone calls, e-mails, and testimonials motivate and drive me everyday—I thank you!

To our wonderful team at On Target Living, Matt, Dawn, Sherri, Tab, Toni, Regie, and CJ: you are truly changing lives every day!

To brother, sister, and Annette: your love over the years has been a guiding force in my life.

And to my wife, Paula; my daughter, Kristen and her friend Sean, my son, Matt, daughter-in-law, Holly, and my dog, Dolly, for all your love and support.

To my mom and dad—thank you for your guidance,
support, and most of all your love!

Introduction

Why On Target Living?

What makes On Target Living different from other health and fitness programs? The answer is Balance! With over 46,000 diet and nutrition books on the market today, and countless exercise DVDs, books, and programs, don't we have enough information to keep us healthy and performing at our best? The answer is yes! But what most people are missing for better health and performance is balance!

The On Target Living philosophy is centered around balance. Helping people understand how quality nutrition, proper rest and rejuvenation, along with regular exercise, keep the mind and body working in harmony. For over 30 years, I have watched people work hard in the gym and get little results. Or follow a strict nutritional program only to abandon ship only after a month or two.

Each year I receive hundreds of e-mails and phone calls from people all over the world who may be struggling with their health, energy, or performance. I try to help them understand that the answer to their high cholesterol, type 2 diabetes, or getting a good night's sleep does not come from a prescription pad. That losing weight does not need to be a low calorie diet tied to intense exercise. Or the solution to erectile dysfunction or low testosterone may not be a pill or hormone replacement therapy, but learning how to control stress.

What do performance, productivity, and success mean to you? I believe many people view this as a financial description. If you are successful, you make a lot of money; if you are a top performer, you earn the most income; if you have the most productive sales team, you get the largest commission. What if I told you none of this matters if you don't have your health, or better yet, you can have greater performance, be more productive and have more success in your life, if you take control of your health!

How can being overweight affect your work? How can being on multiple medications affect your relationships? Is your energy not what it used to be? Why are my kids overweight? These are a few questions to think about. Each one is related to performance in some way, shape or form.

I have witnessed the positive change that comes when people adopt a mentally and physically healthy lifestyle. A better understanding of simple nutrition has not only improved their health, but changed their life. An important, though often overlooked, part of lasting success is finding the energy and vitality to complete your goals. Companies are spending a significant amount of money and resources to find solutions that will help their employees overcome the challenges of daily fatigue. The first step to solving these problems is a system of health and energy strategies.

Peak Performance: Something I have and something you want!

As I have evolved throughout my career, I have made some dramatic changes in my teachings, but the one thing that really stands out is how nutrition, rest, and exercise relate to PEAK performance. What I call PEAK performance is not something you compare to others, but your ability to perform, you being your best. Being your best as a parent, spouse, friend, boss, employee, athlete, grandparent, neighbor, or volunteer—all aspects of your life. If you are not feeding your body, resting properly, or exercising enough, you can never reach your full potential. As you read further in this book, think about where you want to go. Is your health and fitness where you want it to be? Are you on a path to greater success in your life? How do you want to be remembered? Let *On Target Living* help you bring greater health, energy, and vitality into your life!

Peak Performance: Learn it and earn it!

You may be asking yourself what "taking care of your health" has to do with my business or performance.

Traveling the world helping high performers and companies with time, money, and risk is my passion. I engage, educate, and motivate people on the benefits of eating healthy and exercising efficiently, and the reasons why getting proper rest is critical for peak performance. I reach thousands of people each year through my live On Target Living seminars and through this book I am now bringing this information to you! The goal is for you to walk away with the knowledge and practical applications to immediately implement into daily life.

- Build momentum into your business with more energy.
- Increase your productivity as you increase your vitality.
- Understand stress and how to manage it.
- Unlock the secrets to why we lose momentum and the keys to getting it back.
- Learn how your health relates to your wealth.
- Learn how to set realistic goals.
- Gain insight on how your brain takes on new habits.
- Find out the key metrics for optimal health and how to stay focused.
- Be your peak performer.

At the end of this book, you will be asking yourself, *Why isn't this taught in the top business schools all over the country?*

Raised by Wolves!

I usually begin most of my seminars by asking the audience if they were "raised by wolves." Some people laugh, some nod yes, but many are not sure what I mean when I ask this question. Let me explain: If you drank out of a garden hose, rode a bike without a helmet, or rode in the backseat of a car without a seatbelt and survived, you were most likely "raised by wolves" too!

I want to begin your journey by giving you a little background on the author (that's me!) to help you understand where this guy is coming from. I was born in Lansing, Michigan, on November 22, 1957. I have truly enjoyed living in the Midwest—I like the change of seasons, the Great Lakes, and the pace of life in Michigan, and by connecting the dots in my life; I hope to give you a deeper understanding of the man behind the curtain!

When I ask the audience about being "raised by wolves," I'm not criticizing my two wonderful parents, but like most baby boomers, it was an era of "freedom"—rode my bike across town, played in the woods all day, and our only rule was to come home when the streetlights came on. I was told not to fight with my brother or sister, no swearing allowed, and I had to be home for Sunday dinner. There may have been a few more rules, but not many. It was a simple time, playing outside from morning till dark, spending summers at Douglas Lake, building tree forts, and playing games. My family loved to play games: Croquet, tennis, golf, ping-pong, cards, board games, if you could bet on it, we were playing it!

As my grandmother and dad used to say, I grew up eating the Food of the Gods. I don't believe we had any whole food in the house except maybe a banana, apple, or orange once in awhile. I grew up eating processed everything: Captain Crunch, Alpha Bits, Golden Grahams, Lucky Charms, Little Debbie Oatmeal Pies, Hostess Snowballs, Snickers, Three Musketeer bars, Heath bars, bologna sandwiches on white bread with Miracle Whip, Stouffer's broccoli with cheese, Beefaroni, McDonald's, Jon's Country Burger, Yankee Cone Shop, A&W Hot Dogs and Root Beer, Famous Recipe Chicken, DeMarco's Pizza, margarine, whole milk, Kool-Aid, Coke, Pepsi, and the list went on. I drank little water, except when playing sports, and the food I ate became a game changer in my life.

For most of my life, from ages 5 to 21, I had major skin rashes, dandruff, and psoriasis. Doctors prescribed topical creams, cortisone, and oral medications to help my skin, but nothing seemed to make a difference. Finally, the doctors told my parents their son just had "sensitive skin."

During my college years, my "sensitive skin" continued until I enrolled in my junior year economics class with Dr. Louis Junker (a man way ahead of his time). One day, Dr. Junker explained the profitability of processed foods. He stated that there was little profit to be made selling whole foods such as a tomato, but if you took that tomato and turned it into catsup or tomato paste, then the profitability would go through the roof.

He continued his lecture, discussing digestion and drinking cow's milk. This was one of my greatest aha moments (have you ever had one of those moments when everything makes sense?). Dr. Junker was not a big fan of cow's milk. He began by saying that the protein molecule in cow's milk is very difficult for the human body to digest and absorb correctly—remember this was in the late 1970s. He went on to say poor digestion of cow's milk could lead to many problems such as asthma and skin rashes. Skin rashes? I was a poor college student drinking two gallons of cow's milk per week and had terrible skin. My doctors never mentioned anything about what I was eating or drinking and how that could affect my skin. After this discussion in class, I cut back on my consumption of cow's milk (a lot!) and my skin immediately started to improve. It turns out I did not have "sensitive skin"; what I had was a horrible diet. What I was eating and drinking was causing havoc to my skin.

After I graduated from college with a business degree, an economics minor, and better skin, I went to work for Butternut Bread selling white bread and Dolly Madison cakes and cupcakes. This was my first experience working in grocery stores, observing the buying habits of consumers, and learning how the grocery stores get consumers to buy. After one year of sleep deprivation and working more than 70 hours per week, it was time for me to move on from the Butternut Bread gig.

Next on my job list was Frito-Lay where I spent my days selling Doritos, Ruffles, Munchos, and Funyons. This time the hours and pay were much better, and I had options for future growth within the company if I desired. Again I was back in the grocery stores and was amazed at the volume of snack foods people were buying. Some of the larger stores would take over five hours to service (just one store). Each day on my route, I would pack my lunch, extra snacks, water, and find myself talking to co-workers, people in grocery stores, friends and family about fitness, nutrition, and health. After two years at Frito-Lay, my interest continued to grow and so I decided to pursue other career options.

I really did not know what direction to turn. I was thinking about going back to school to study physical therapy, sports medicine, or start a career teaching, and although I had a lot of options, I knew whatever I decided, I wanted more.

After many phone calls and interviews, I finally struck gold when I met with Dr. Kwok Ho at Michigan State University. Dr. Ho was a professor in the School of Education, and he had his doctorate in Exercise Physiology. We had never met before, and it amazed me that he was willing to spend over two hours with a person that was not yet a student. He asked all the right questions: What was driving me? How did I want to help people? Was I looking for a job, career, or a calling? This question was deep: I never once thought of finding work that would turn into my calling. I was just trying to make a living and have some fun along the way.

As we talked, I could feel his passion and his belief that what he did was very important work. When our meeting ended, I stood up and gathered my notes, and he said something I will never forget. He said, "Chris, you are a prevention guy and the world needs you!" The next day, I began the enrollment process as a graduate student at Michigan State University in Exercise Physiology, and in the fall of 1985 I began my journey, or as Dr. Ho would say, my calling.

So when you begin to read and learn more about cod liver oil, chia seeds, sweet potatoes, cacao, macadamia nuts, hemp seeds, flaxseed, wheatgrass, hydration, bone health, hormones, weight loss, pH balance, cellular health, spirulina/chlorella, almond, hemp or coconut milk, diaphragmatic breathing, how to get a good night's sleep, medications, rejuvenation strategies, body alignment, and posture exercises, remember I wasn't raised on this stuff: I was "raised by wolves"!

I hope you enjoy your journey!

Health and Happiness!

—Chris

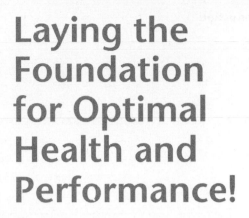

Laying the Foundation for Optimal Health and Performance!

1

What's Possible in Your Life?

Our life is what our thoughts make it.

—Marcus Aurelius

The question, "What's possible in your life?" can be fascinating and yet a little scary. Have you ever taken the time to dream, step back, and truly contemplate "what is possible in your life"? Is it possible to be medication-free for the rest of your life? Climb the Grand Canyon rim to rim? Ski with your great-grandkids? How about owning your own business? Lose 100 pounds and keep it off for the rest of your life? Have a great night's sleep? Get into the best shape of your life? Have greater stamina in your professional and personal lives? And live life with greater balance?

During some of my experiential events, I have the audience participate in this new way of thinking. I set up two walls: the Wall of Possibilities and the Wall of Doom. I have the audience write on separate sticky notes what they believe is possible, this is the Wall of Possibilities, and also what may be holding them back, Wall of Doom. They start thinking about their possibilities and their fears at the beginning of the event and add to the wall throughout the day.

At first, both walls usually receive an equal number of sticky notes, but as the event goes on, the Wall of Possibilities continues to grow and grow and grow! (See Figure 1.1.) This exercise is fun, thought provoking, and creates lots of powerful energy in the room. I believe most of us need that little nudge to uncover what may be possible, and then the curious questions begin. What wall are you filling up on a daily basis?

FIGURE 1.1 Wall of Possibilities

"Real responses from people participating in a new way of thinking at my seminars!"

I believe lifelong learning and growth are key factors for a healthy and happy life.

With growth comes change, and for most people, change only occurs when you let yourself get uncomfortable. If you stay in your comfort zone, seldom will change occur. In over 25 years in the health and fitness industry and more than 17,000 one-on-one personal training sessions, one thing I have learned is how challenging change can be!

Developing new lifestyle habits that are sustainable can be difficult for almost anyone. Too often attempts to change start with New Year's resolutions, goals to lose weight and increase exercise, and you say "this is my year to get healthier and into better shape," but the next thing you know your good intentions are a thing of the past. For sustainable change to take hold, let's begin with five basic steps.

Step 1: Self-Awareness That Change Must Occur

Nothing will change until you recognize the need for change. Have you ever been on a long car or plane ride and at the end of the trip you can hardly sit still? No matter how many times you readjust your position in the seat, it is just not working; you need to make a change. How many times have you heard about the person who has a heart attack or is put on oxygen and after all this still does not believe it's necessary to quit smoking? Or what about the person with type 2 diabetes, high blood pressure, and acid reflux, is 100 pounds overweight—and continues to eat fast food and drink diet soda? Self-awareness that you must change is step one in your pursuit to being your best!

Step 2: What Do You Want?

What do you truly want? Is it to get off some of your medications or decrease the dosage? Run or walk your first 5K? Play with your great-grandkids? Lose 25 pounds? Run for political office? Do you want to perform like a professional athlete? Have more energy, greater stamina, or life balance? What about greater health? Being your best? Once you have decided what you want, get laser beam specific and write it down!

Step 3: Finding Your WHY

The longer I am in the health and fitness industry, the more I realize the importance of finding your "WHY." Your "WHY" is your desire, your need; it is your fuel for change to take place. Finding your WHY can occur as a result of a major event in your life, such as the death of a family member, divorce, a poor report from your doctor, some major trigger that gets you to decide *now* is the time, your moment of truth, that you must change and change now!

Finding your WHY can also be an ongoing process including goals for your future like taking a hiking trip to Mt. Kilimanjaro, skiing with your grandkids, competing in a senior bodybuilding competition, having a small wager with your co-worker to lose a few pounds (and keep it off!), or lowering your blood glucose or blood pressure. Your WHY is something that gets you excited, something or someone to focus on.

As I travel around the world, speaking to thousands of people each year, I continually challenge my audiences to find their WHY. Every time I hear from someone who has made changes I always ask the same questions, "What was your WHY?" and "What steps did you take along the way?" I always get the same answer; they had one major WHY or many smaller WHYs.

A few years ago, I received a phone call from one of my longtime colleagues and good friend, Mike Combes. Mike is the Executive Director of three large health clubs with the Mercy Health System in Cincinnati, Ohio. I had presented my On Target Living seminar there in the past, and I had the privilege to meet Joan Barber, one of their shining stars. Joan is 68 years young, has lost over 150 pounds, and decreased her prescription medications from 16 to 3 all over a three-year time period (WOW)! Joan told me how she came to one of my events, read my book, and received wonderful help from the Mercy Health System team. She told me how she took "baby steps" and kept making small improvements and never gave up. I was thinking the entire time she was telling me her story that her WHY must have been powerful for her to start on this journey at age 65, and it was!

Joan has been married to her husband Clarence for over 40 years, and they are still very much in love. Clarence has two major loves in his life, first for his wife Joan and second for motorcycles, but because of Joan's poor health, Clarence and Joan had stopped riding motorcycles. Listening to Joan, I could feel her love for Clarence. She knew how much he loved riding his motorcycle with his wife at his side. Joan decided it was time to start riding again, and today Clarence and Joan are in a motorcycle club and ride together on a regular basis. Joan's story is a great reminder that your "WHY" must be bigger than your "BUT" in order to make change happen!

Step 4: One Small Step at a Time

We all know making change can be challenging and even extremely difficult at times, especially when making healthier lifestyle changes. Most sustainable change occurs by taking **One Step at a Time**! This success model works because:

1. The prefrontal cortex of the brain can only handle one step at a time. If you become too busy or stressed, and are trying to do too much all at once, then you can easily fall right back into your old habits.

2. Do you remember the old phone cords that had a soft rubber coating surrounding the phone lines? This same type of protective coating or insulation of every nerve fiber throughout the human body is called the myelin sheath. The myelin sheath is built one strand at a time and is essential for every thought, emotion, and movement throughout

the entire body. The thicker the myelin sheath, the faster and stronger the signal, and the stronger and more powerful habits become. (See Figures 1.2 and 1.3.)

How would you teach someone how to ride a bike, play a musical instrument, or do a triple flip off a high dive? People need to be taught by breaking the activity down into small steps, because building the myelin

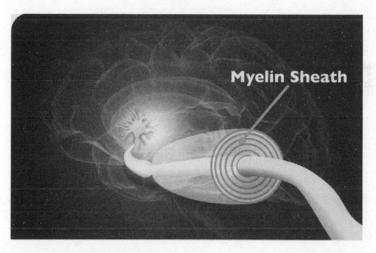

FIGURE 1.2 Myelin Sheath

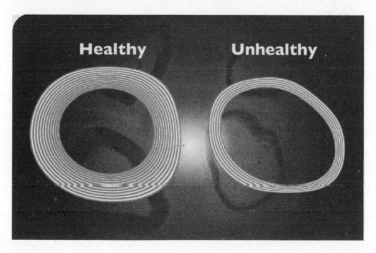

FIGURE 1.3 Healthy and Unhealthy Myelin Sheaths

sheath takes repetition and time! If one of your goals is to have better health, then building solid, sustainable habits is all about building your myelin sheath.

Once a habit is built into your myelin sheath, you have that habit for a lifetime and to break this habit you must consciously think about undoing your behavior until a new habit takes hold. This takes time, focus, and energy, and that is why when we become stressed or too busy we go right back to our old comfortable habits (and also why taking small steps, one at a time, is critical for developing new, healthier habits)!

When I began in the personal training business many years ago, I couldn't wait to share with my clients everything that would make them healthy. I educated them about the wonderful benefits of wheatgrass, cod liver oil, flaxseeds, spirulina/chlorella, hydration, body alignment, strength training, progressions, stretching . . . the list was long. This was a huge mistake on my part because I did not understand that, in most cases, **information does not create transformation**.

To help others build sustainable habits, I had to think about how to help them begin a journey of habit building.

In Shawn Achor's 2010 book *The Happiness Advantage*, published by Crown Business, Shawn states that we are "mere bundles of habits." A habit is an activity we repeat on a regular basis, and we typically don't think twice about the building of our myelin sheath. When brushing your teeth, what side of the mouth do you begin on? Putting on your socks, do you begin with the left or right foot? How many different ways can you get dressed?

Shawn states that building habits is centered on "energy activation," the amount of energy needed to begin any activity. If you get home from a long day at work and the remote is staring at you, we all know it is extremely easy to sit on the couch and turn on the television, but if you took the batteries out of the remote, and placed them upstairs in a drawer, you probably wouldn't walk upstairs and go through this entire process because of the amount of energy you would have to activate. If your goal is to build a new habit, you need to make the activity as easy as possible and then repeat it over and over. If your goal is to change a poor habit into a healthier habit, then you should make your current habit more difficult to perform.

For example, a question I receive on a regular basis is "how do I break the habit of drinking diet soda?" I ask, "What do you enjoy about drinking diet soda?" People usually say they enjoy the sweetness, the carbonation, and the energy boost. So let's put the diet soda in the basement and replace it with mineral water mixed with a shot of organic pomegranate or cherry juice! The mineral water has the carbonation, and the juice adds sweetness and is very refreshing. Then repeat this behavior over and over until it takes little energy to activate.

A few years ago, prior to speaking at a large dental conference for dentists and dental hygienists, I had an appointment with my dentist. While sitting in the dental chair, I asked my dental hygienist if she could give me the inside scoop about some of her challenges at work. She immediately started talking about prevention and the challenges she had with getting her patients to floss on a regular basis. Something that is so simple, takes little time, and yet only about 10 to 15 percent of her patients add flossing to their regular routines. I then took a big gulp because I was part of that group that did not floss on a regular basis, and we all know you can't lie about flossing to your dental hygienist. So I asked the magic question, "How many days a week should I floss?" She said, "Let's start with flossing two times per week," and I asked, "Is that enough?" She told me, "You don't floss at all now, so yes, two times per week is a good place to start!"

Following her recommendation, I started flossing, and at first it was something I had to plan. It took energy to floss, but truly very little time, and I knew it was something that would give me great benefits in the future. The day arrived when I was speaking in front of a large group of dentists and dental hygienists, and I opened up with a story about my new flossing experience. After telling my story, feeling proud of my newfound habit, a dentist in the front row said, "Flossing two to three times a week is not enough." For a few seconds I didn't know what to say, and then I asked him, "How often are you exercising?" The entire room became still, and he responded by saying he was not exercising on a regular basis. I said, "What if you went for a walk twice a week for 10 minutes; do you think this would be a good place to start?" After the presentation he approached me and said I had inspired him to start exercising! Three months later I received an e-mail saying he is now exercising three to four times per week and has also hired a health and fitness coach that he meets with every two weeks. At age 72, he said, he hasn't felt this good in years!

So, start slowly and build your habits, one step at a time! Understand that your journey comes with every change you make along the way. Focus on what you are gaining, not what you are giving up. How can you ask better questions? How can you make the change journey more enjoyable?

Your journey does not have to be painful, and it won't be if you take it one step at a time. One step always leads you to another, and it's time to get ready for that next step.

Step 5: Monitoring Your Success

With every successful change and new habit, there is usually some form of monitoring system in place. Feedback is the breakfast of champions, and you need some way to measure your new habits to see if they are working. If your goal is to lose weight, get off some of your medications, run a personal best in a 5K, or have greater energy throughout the day, you need simple tools to measure your progress and success! Whether you are tracking your water intake, nutrition, exercise habits, quality of sleep, belt size, how tight your pants fit, the numbers on your scale, blood work, skin, hair, nails, blood pressure, resting heart rate, or strength, there are hundreds of ways to monitor your success.

While working out the other day, I began talking to a guy who was asking me about the benefits of eating healthy fats. As we talked more, he asked me what I thought of the Weight Watchers program. I told him I thought Weight Watchers was terrific and a great way to help people stay focused. I asked him what he liked about the program, and he said he liked the camaraderie of the members along with the group's ability to keep him focused because he knew he was going to weigh in each week. Regular monitoring is an essential component to keep the momentum going; it helps determine if your plan is working and allows you to have small celebrations along the way. Celebrating even the smallest success is critical for supporting your commitment to change!

The importance of making changes and keeping momentum over time really hit home for me when I was watching an interview from one of the past winners of the television show *The Biggest Loser*. This gentleman began his journey weighing over 416 pounds when he came to the Biggest Loser Ranch and by the end of the show he weighed 198 pounds—he lost 218 pounds! He won the $250,000 first-place prize money and became an instant celebrity overnight. During an interview they asked him how much he currently weighed, and he said he had no idea. He had not weighed himself in over a year. He knew he had regained a great deal of weight but truly did not know. He guessed he now weighed around 300 pounds, but only 18 months after his first-place finish he stepped on the scale and was shocked that he now weighed over 400 pounds! The look on his face was heartbreaking. How could he fall so quickly?

As the interview went on it was clear that he did not believe he could continue the lifestyle activities he learned at the Biggest Loser Ranch on his own. He said he could not continue the regimen of exercising three to four hours per day along with eating only 1,500 to 1,800 calories per day, so he went back to his old habits. I don't believe any of the trainers from *The Biggest Loser* recommended exercising three to four hours per day or an eating plan so limited. From this interview, I learned how powerful a person's beliefs may be. It's important to set up realistic goals. Was it possible for him to weigh 198 pounds 24/7? How much exercise is enough? Did he understand that he could never out-exercise a poor diet? What was his WHY? Was he truly taking one step at a time and building sustainable habits? Did he have a monitoring system in place to track his progress and to celebrate his successes along the way? Are your goals sustainable?

What's Possible in Your Life?

Whenever you feel like you are stuck, having a difficult time making the changes necessary for your future growth, keep coming back to this chapter. Making sustainable changes can be hard work and difficult for almost everyone. Climbing that mountain begins by taking that first step!

THE BOTTOM LINE

1. What is possible in your life can be a fascinating yet scary question to ask yourself.
2. Making lifestyle changes can be difficult for almost everyone.
3. It takes five steps for sustainable change to take hold. Your On Target Living Journey begins with self-awareness, focus, finding your WHY, one step at a time, and monitoring your success!

2

The Elephant in the Room

Prevention is so much better than healing.

—Thomas Adams

One of my great friends and colleagues, Phil Nuernberger, PhD, a leading expert on stress and how we use our mind, wrote a newsletter article titled "Getting Rid of the Elephant." He explained that the term *health care* is being discussed everyday by our politicians, our businesses, and our society at large. Health care costs are rising at an alarming rate, and as he argued, we cannot fix the problem by simply making our health care system more efficient. The cost of treating disease is the "elephant in the room" that must be discussed. Imagine if everyone looked at health care from a new perspective? I personally look at health care as a security blanket, it is there if I need it, but I rarely use it. Having more healthy people should be our goal, not more health care options!

With all that we have learned and all the resources at our disposal, it's sad to say this is true and only getting worse. Obesity levels are growing extremely fast here in the United States while obesity continues to grow into a major global problem; it even has a new name—*Globesity*! In 1973 we did not have an obesity problem in the United States; in fact, less than 10 percent of the population was obese. Today, obesity levels have grown to over 30 percent of the population nationwide, and one of the worst statistics of all shows that this obesity rate is still climbing and will continue to climb in years to come. By the year 2020 experts are predicting our entire nation will have more than 35 to 40 percent obesity, and by 2030, we will be looking at 45 percent obesity levels in the United States!

You don't have to be a math magician to figure out we just can't afford to keep going down this road of self-destruction. What about genetics, have our genetics changed? What role has genetics played in America's increasing levels of obesity? One point I want to make crystal clear is that our genetic footprint has not changed over the past 40 to 50 years. In 1970, roughly 500,000 Americans were diagnosed with type 2 diabetes and today we have more than 26 million, along with over 50 million prediabetics waiting in the wings! Our kids don't have a chance if we keep going down this unhealthy path.

Why Are We Moving in an Unhealthy Direction?

In almost every one of my seminars I talk about why we are moving in the wrong direction when it comes to our health. Even with greater advances in medicine, more highly trained health professionals, more medical procedures to choose from medications to choose from, and an overwhelming amount of information on the benefits of proper rest, nutrition, and exercise to keep our bodies healthy, we are doing a lousy job when it comes to managing our health!

It is estimated that more than 175 million Americans now live with at least one chronic disease or disability. According to the Centers for Disease Control and Prevention, chronic illness accounts for more than 80 percent of all money spent on health care in the United States. Obesity, type 2 diabetes, high blood pressure, Alzheimer's, MS, heart disease, and cancer continue to rise! More than 25 percent of women over the age of 50 have thyroid problems, and poor bone health is a common concern among women. Acid reflux, gluten intolerance, and irritable bowel syndrome are everyday problems for many adults, and over one-third of our children are overweight or obese! It is not a pretty picture and we all need to get into the game! So why are we moving in the wrong direction?

Poor-Quality Food and Beverages

The food environment in which we live has changed dramatically over the past 40 to 50 years. In the mid-1970s we consumed approximately 2,800 calories per person, per day, in the United States. Today we are consuming over 4,100 calories per person. As you can probably guess, we are not consuming more whole foods, such as fruits, vegetables, whole grains, high-quality proteins, and healthy fats. Unfortunately, we are producing (and consuming) unhealthier, refined, nutrient-deficient **Junk Food!**

Everywhere we turn we are faced with large quantities of cheap, low-quality food and beverages—in airports, vending machines, fast food restaurants, gas stations, grocery stores, and schools. This is not just a problem in the United States, but also a global problem as more and more countries adopt our convenient, processed food and beverage mentality. Last year, I traveled to Guadalajara, Mexico, to work with a large cookware company. I was shocked as I was driving through their beautiful city to see all the fast food restaurants; I felt as though I could have been driving through any large city in the United States. It is no accident that Mexico is now ranked number two, second only to the United States, in the world's leading nations of type 2 diabetics. Sadly, it was less than 10 years ago that Mexico was not even on the radar screen for type 2 diabetes!

We have grown into convenience-food consumers across the globe. In most cases, convenience translates into highly processed, poor-quality food and beverages. As our lives speed up, so does the demand for convenience, fast, available food (actually, I'm not always sure this is truly food). Food and beverage companies are continuing to expand their lines of cheap, low-quality food and beverages. How many energy drinks were on the market 10 years ago? Today there are over 100!

Working multiple grocery stores for over eight years, I learned that almost all grocery stores are set up with the main items people are coming to buy—whole foods like fruits, vegetables, meat—surrounding the entire perimeter of the store. These food items are strategically placed to get you to walk around the entire store. Then, down the center aisles, the big profits lay waiting! Next time you are going down the center aisles of the grocery store, look at the food and beverages offered at the beginning of each aisle. All the best sellers are placed to get you to walk down the aisle, but as consumers become more educated and experience the amazing benefits of eating higher-quality foods and beverages, the demand for better options in the center aisles will increase.

Lack of Movement

The human body is meant to move daily and the benefits are truly amazing, but most people choose not to make time to move their bodies on a daily basis. Less than 25 percent of American adults exercise regularly, and the time we spend being physically active continues to decline. Our kids seldom walk to school or just play outside. They sit in the classroom and then sit behind the computer, video games, television, and cell phones. Physical education classes have been cut from many school systems, and yet if you could put exercise in a bottle it would be the most prescribed medication on the planet! We need to change this, not only for ourselves, but also for the well-being of generations to come.

Poor Information

Many different approaches to nutrition, physical activity, rest and rejuvenation are advocated through popular culture, the media, books, magazines, Internet, friends, and family. This overwhelming environment of information overload leave the consumer in a state of flux and confusion, and even when we want to live healthier lives through better nutrition, exercise, and rest and rejuvenation, it can be extremely difficult to know what path to follow. At times I get confused with all of the mixed messages, and I have been in this business for over 25 years!

Dieting Mentality

When I began working with my publisher, John Wiley & Sons, one of our first conversations was about what this book was to become. I told them I wanted to write a book on performance—being the best you can be! They strongly agreed and also pointed out that they were not interested in having me write a book about dieting, due to the large volume of diet books already on the market—to the tune of 46,000! Over the past 40 to 50 years, hundreds of fad diets and trendy ways to eat, rest, and move, have bombarded Americans and others around the world. New books, magazines, supplements, celebrity testimonials, reality television shows, Internet sensations, and infomercials all bring the promise of instant weight loss and greater fitness. With each empty promise, it's easy to see why many of us will try any new diet that comes along if the marketing claims are powerful enough.

Your Time Has Arrived

Okay, enough of the gloom and doom. I had to tee it up to help you understand it is "Go Time" for all of us. We are at the tipping point and change needs to happen now! One of my strongest beliefs is how truly amazing the human body is in its ability to heal itself. If you cut your hand it will start to heal itself in just a few days. If you struggle with your weight, have low energy, poor health, or would just like to feel better and be your best, help has arrived! I have seen tremendous life changes in many people in my more than two decades of work in the health and fitness industry, and I would like to help you as well.

A few years ago, Sally Bonta contacted me about doing some one-on-one health and fitness coaching. She had recently moved back to Michigan from California and her sister had referred her to me. In our first meeting, Sally and I went over her health history, her current situation, and, most importantly, her future. At age 57, Sally was on 24 medications—yes, 24! Sally had little energy, her heart was empty, and her eyes were dull. We talked for over an hour, and I truly believed Sally wanted a better life. I explained to her how we would tackle her needs one step at a time and slowly build a solid foundation for better health. Step by step, Sally started making amazing progress and three years later, at age 60, Sally went from 24 medications to just 3! Sally is a new person, with lots of "juice," and every time I run into her at the health club she makes me smile. Sally has not only improved her fitness and health, but more importantly her mind-set that prevention is her only option and she must be the driver in her journey toward greater well-being!

As a society we all need to start focusing on prevention! Prevention is our only way out and we all need to come together and fight back. Start slowly and help everyone you know take one step towards a healthier lifestyle.

THE BOTTOM LINE

1. We are facing a serious health crisis, not only in the United States, but also around the world.
2. Over 175 million Americans now live with at least one chronic disease or disability.
3. Obesity has risen to over 30 percent in the United States and continues to grow worldwide.
4. We are moving in a very unhealthy direction due to our toxic food environment, lack of movement, poor information, and dieting mentality.
5. The good news is that the human body is truly amazing in its ability to heal itself if given the right ingredients!

3

Let Food Be Your Medicine

Why treat an illness from a medicine bag versus curing it with food.

—Hippocrates

In my more than 25 years of health and fitness coaching experience and speaking across the country in my On Target Living Seminars, an alarming message comes through: the United States has become an overmedicated society.

Why are so many people looking for medications as a means to improve their health? Is it because we have more medications available? Are our doctors prescribing more medications? Do we have stronger advertising by the pharmaceutical companies? We don't know of any other options? Or maybe we are not willing to make the necessary lifestyle changes to improve our health; it's just easier to take a pill or pills?

Much of the increase in medication consumption has to do with having an unhealthy lifestyle. Lack of sleep, poor nutrition, too much stress, and lack of movement, is it our unhealthy lifestyles that may be causing the problem? For many health issues, medications can be lifesavers for people. I just want to create awareness and give people more options when it comes to improving your health. Taking more medications in most cases is not the answer!

Over the past 25 years I have personally seen a steady rise in the amount of medications people are taking. Whether it's reviewing a health history questionnaire from a health and fitness–coaching client, receiving an e-mail from someone who has recently attended one of my seminars, or just talking

18

to friends and family, **people are flat out taking more medications than ever!** I am always curious as to how this medication process began. Did it start with a stomach medication to help with their occasional bout of acid reflux? Was their cholesterol level slowly creeping up? The pain in their muscles and joints was becoming more of a constant problem? Getting a good night sleep was a thing of the past? Or their blood glucose was too high? This medication train in most cases starts slowly, but quickly can get out of control!

Just like obesity epidemic, medication growth has now become a global problem, emotionally, physically, and financially.

One of the most important things you can learn from *On Target Living* is to be curious and start asking better questions. If you had a plant that was wilted and not doing well, what would you do? Does your plant need water, sunlight, or better-quality soil? It sounds so simple, but most of the time we are programmed not to be curious. If you have high cholesterol the answer does not begin with a statin medication to lower your cholesterol. This may be an option, but in most cases it is not the answer. Your first question should be why, why do I have high cholesterol or why is my cholesterol out of balance? Do you lack sleep, have a boatload of stress, drink too much soda pop, alcohol, or coffee? Is exercise a thing of the past, do you have poor nutritional habits, are you deficient in essential minerals or healthy fats? Could your poor lifestyle habits be the cause of your out-of-balance cholesterol or other health challenges?

A few years ago while working with a large group of financial advisers, I was approached by one of the male members of the group. We had just completed an early morning workout together on the beach in southern California; this was our first morning together of a three-day training program. The sun was shining, the ocean breeze was warm, it was a beautiful morning, and everyone was full of excitement. As the group headed to breakfast, this guy asks, "Can I speak with you privately?" I said, "Sure, how can I help?" He said, "You are 52 and so am I. What do you know about erectile dysfunction (ED)?" I said I knew quite a bit about ED. So I began our conversation by asking better questions. I asked him, "How long have you been taking a statin medication to lower your cholesterol?" He said, "How did you know I was on a statin med?" I said, "One of the side effects of statin medications is that it blocks the production of cholesterol, and cholesterol is the backbone of all steroidal hormones, your sex hormones, including the production of testosterone." With low testosterone levels, there can be an increase in belly fat, drop in sex drive, decrease in muscle mass, low energy, and erectile dysfunction! Statin meds also block the production of CoQ10, which improves the health of your heart, improves blood pressure, heart palpitations, and your energy level. CoQ10 is critical for not only a healthy heart, but also your overall health. Why would you want to begin a medication that is supposed to lower your risk of what? Having a healthier heart?

My second question was, "How long have you been taking an acid reflux medication?" Now he was really confused! "How did you know I was taking an acid reflux medication?" I said, "I just took an educated guess." Acid reflux medications leach out the valuable trace mineral zinc. You need zinc in order to hear, see, taste, and have sex. Zinc also is extremely important for building a strong and healthy immune system. Men need one-third more zinc than women because this mineral helps make testosterone: back to the testosterone issue! Combine the statin medications with the acid reflux medications, and you are asking for low testosterone, which in many cases may lead to male challenges, including ED. Erectile dysfunction medications have exploded to the tune of $10 billion per year in the United States. I wonder why.

The rest of the story: For the next few months we talked on the phone, exchanged e-mails, and he slowly began taking one step after another on his quest to become a healthier person. Eight months go by and the entire group is back for stage two of this personal development program. The program begins by sharing success stories between the group, before I know it this guy stands up and starts spilling his guts. He tells the mixed audience about his erectile dysfunction, high cholesterol, and acid reflux. He gladly states that he is now off his cholesterol and acid reflux medications, no longer has erectile dysfunction, has lost over 30 pounds, his wife has lost over 20 pounds, and then he says his relationship with his wife has never been better! Wow, was this cool to hear!

I am not here to beat up medications; some medications can be extremely helpful and necessary in some situations. One of my strongest beliefs is how powerful the human body can be in its ability to heal itself. If given enough time and the right ingredients, the mind and body will try to heal itself. Why not give your body that opportunity?

I find that many people have a difficult time speaking openly with their physician or health care provider about their health care needs. You always have to remember you are their customer. Ask and you shall receive, so ask! Next time you see your physician or health care provider, begin a dialogue about your goals and how they can help you. Take an active role in working with your physician or health care provider. Your health care provider wants his or her patients to be interested in having a healthy and happy life. **Before accepting or using prescription medications, ask your physician a few tough questions**:

1. What is the cause of my problem?
2. Are there non-drug approaches I can try first?
3. Exactly what condition is this medication supposed to treat?
4. What is my risk?
5. How much will this medication lower my risk?
6. What are the side effects of this medication?
7. Is it possible to decrease my dosage or eliminate this medication by making healthier lifestyle choices?

Medications may be extremely helpful in some situations, especially when used in the short run. Work closely with your physician and take an active role in your health. **Start slowly** by making healthier food and drink choices, and think about what your medicine cabinet could look like in the future.

THE BOTTOM LINE

1. The United States along with many countries around the world has become overmedicated.
2. The cost of prescription drugs is driving the cost of health care out of sight.
3. We all need to take more responsibility for our own health.
4. Work closely with your physician and health care professionals.
5. Let food be your medicine!
6. Start by making small changes and develop these changes into daily habits.

4 The World Is Flat?

Every problem has in it the seeds of its own solution.
—Norman Vincent Peale

For centuries many people thought the world was flat. If you sailed a ship out into the open seas and went too far, your ship would sail off the end of earth and monsters were waiting for you! When did people stop believing the world was flat? It was not until the fifteenth century that the knowledge the world was round became widespread, even though Ancient Greece and many other earlier philosophers knew the world was not flat. This was mainly because people who went against beliefs of the time sometimes got killed!

One of my earliest beliefs was my belief in Santa Claus. My sister and I would leave out a few cookies and milk every Christmas Eve. The excitement around our house was electric: Santa was on his way! But as much as I wanted to believe in Santa Claus, I slowly realized my belief was not true. My older brother didn't help my belief along with me questioning "how could Santa really deliver all those toys around the world in just one night?"

So what is a belief? A belief is some level of certainty. What shapes our beliefs? Experiences, information, family, friends, media, we all have our own beliefs, and this is what makes the world go round and life interesting. Have you ever had a strong belief and later you realized it was not true? I think we all have had a few of those beliefs; I know I have! A key component when talking to people about their health and fitness is to explore their beliefs.

22

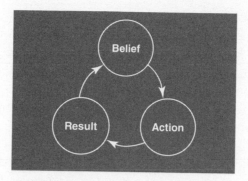

FIGURE 4.1   Belief—Action—Result Circle

If I don't tackle their beliefs, they may take actions that don't get them the results they are looking for. (See Figure 4.1.) I call these limiting beliefs that someone may have that may be blocking their success: Many people believe fat makes you fat. Carbs make you fat. The best way to lose weight is long-duration cardiovascular exercise. Eating healthy does not taste good. Exercise has to be painful to be beneficial. A high protein diet makes you lean. Energy drinks are your ticket to better energy. The best way to lose weight is to decrease calories. A calorie = a calorie. Think about the volume of diet books on the market, information on the Internet, from friends, family, and co-workers; each day you are bombarded with the next best thing. With the sheer volume of information at our fingertips, confidence drops and confusion rises, making it extremely difficult to know what to believe!

How many remember the first human being to break the four-minute mile? In 1954 Great Britain's Roger Bannister broke the four-minute mile with a time of 3:59.4. Many people believed that it was not humanly possible to break this marker! Over the next two years the four-minute mile marker was broken over 30 times! Why? Because people now believed it was possible. So what is possible in your life and what limiting beliefs may be holding you back?

In many of my seminars when talking on the subject of beliefs, I ask the audience, "How many of you believe cod liver oil tastes bad? Please raise your hand." Most of the hands go up! Then I ask, "How many of you believe cod liver tastes bad, but have never tried it?" Everyone begins to laugh because they realize they have fallen into the trap of not truly knowing something but believing it to be true! Then I explain to the audience the benefits of taking cod liver oil, how cod liver oil improves your skin, hair, nails, makes your cells soft, improves your lipid profile, hormonal balance, brain health, weight control, increases energy, decreases inflammation, the number of health benefits are powerful! Then I ask the audience, "Would you be willing to try something so amazing that tastes like a lemon drop?" This is why I ship cod liver oil to every one of my events around the world because I know the audience needs to experience tasting the cod liver oil themselves so they can dispel their current belief about the taste. I place the cod liver oil on ice, and at the end of each event almost everyone comes over to take their shot—and almost every time I hear the same response, "It tastes like a lemon drop," or "It has very little taste," or "I can do this, this is nothing!" My goal is to create amazing results for the audience, and I know the impact cod liver oil can make to improve one's health!

Changing a person's mind-set is critical to one's success. What beliefs do you have that may be holding you back? Maybe you believe cardiovascular exercise is the best way to lose weight? Fats make you fat? A calorie = a calorie? Eating healthy is too restricting or costs too much? You need to exercise an hour a day? You can out-exercise a poor diet? Proteins make you lean? Eating healthy does not taste good? Exercise is boring? Getting more rest and rejuvenation into your life is a luxury not a necessity? You will be heavily medicated as you age? Changing beliefs can be challenging, but is critical for your success.

Is it possible to lose weight and keep it off for a lifetime?. Now is your time, greatness is in you, you just need to believe!

THE BOTTOM LINE

1. A belief is some level of certainty.
2. Your beliefs are directly tied to your results. Beliefs—Action—Results!
3. Roger Bannister broke the four-minute mile in 1954, and this record was broken over 30 times during the next two years!
4. Cod liver oil has amazing health benefits and tastes like a lemon drop.
5. What limiting beliefs may be holding you back in your life? Now is your time, greatness is in you, you just need to believe!

5 Aging Well versus Anti-Aging!

The future belongs to those who believe in the beauty of their dreams.
—Eleanor Roosevelt

Every time you turn around you hear the next fountain of youth solution. Berries grown on the highest mountaintop, water coming down from the purest glacier, or some magical skin cream that makes wrinkles disappear—all promising to slow down the aging process. Think about the term "anti-aging"; do people really believe they can stop the aging process? I personally don't like the term "anti-aging"; I believe it sends a signal that there is something wrong with aging. We are all aging; this is part of life, and nobody is going to elude the aging process.

What I do believe with all my heart is you truly have a choice on how you age; I call it "Aging Well"! Aging is commonly thought to be a process of degeneration. Although aging usually involves physical decline, there is a fast-growing group of people who are maintaining high levels of physical and mental health throughout their entire life. Many people may want to live a long time, I am in this category too, but what I believe most people are interested in is the quality of their years, Aging Well!

In 2004, Dan Buettner teamed up with National Geographic and hired the best longevity researchers to identify pockets around the world where people lived measurably longer and healthier lives. In these "Blue Zones," they found that people reach age 100 at rates 10 times greater than in the United States. The five regions identified and discussed by Buettner in his 2008 book *Blue Zones*, published by National Geographic:

1. Okinawa, Japan
2. Sardinia, Italy
3. Loma Linda, California
4. Nicoya, Costa Rica
5. Ikaria, Greece

After identifying the world's Blue Zones, Buettner and his team of scientists went to each location to identify lifestyle characteristics that might explain this health and longevity phenomenon. They found that the lifestyles of residents in the Blue Zones shared multiple specific characteristics:

- Happy—Most of these people are happy. If you are grumpy, things aren't looking good!
- Family—Focus on family.
- Plant-based diet—Meat is more of a condiment than a staple. Eating legumes was also a common staple in these groups.
- No smoking—I don't think the Marlboro Man lived in a Blue Zone.
- Active lifestyles—Daily moderate physical activity. These people are moving their bodies daily!
- Low stress—Pace of life is more relaxed and balanced.
- Eat to 80 percent full—Stop meals when you are 80 percent full. No "Supersize Me" for this crowd!
- Wine—Moderate drinking has some positive benefits. This is going to make many people happy! Maybe wine drinking makes people happy?
- Sense of purpose and belonging.

I don't see wheatgrass on the list; maybe we will have our own Blue Zone in 50 years?

So what should we expect as we age? Nerve conduction, lung function, strength, mobility, and flexibility, all slowly drop as we age, but the key is at what speed. From age 20 to 90, there is little decline if you live a healthy lifestyle. But what if your lifestyle is not so healthy? Many people who live an unhealthy lifestyle may begin to see a rapid decline between the ages of 50 and 60—I call this "The Cliff" (see Figure 5.1).

Blood pressure starts to creep up, type 2 diabetes may set in, joint pain is a daily problem, cholesterol is up, energy is down, hormones are out of

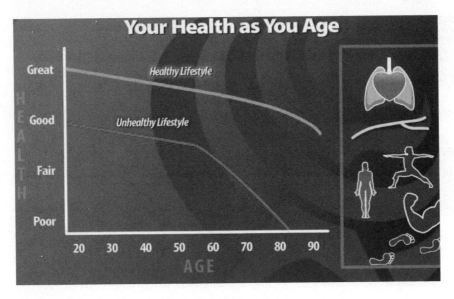

FIGURE 5.1 Your Health as You Age

balance, flexibility diminishes along with an increase in poor balance and mobility. Here is the good news: The human body is amazing in its ability to heal itself. If you feel like you may have fallen, there is hope and you can get better, much better. Start slowly and take that next step.

What is possible in your life (see Figure 5.2)?

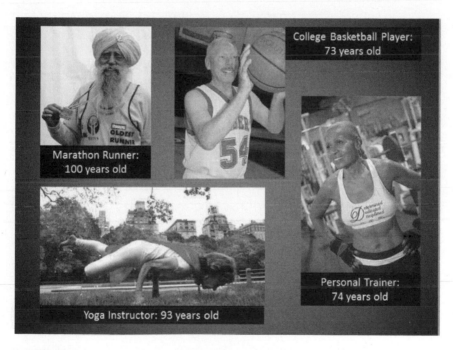

FIGURE 5.2 Some Examples of Aging Well

THE BOTTOM LINE

1. We all have a choice on how we age—I call it "Aging Well."
2. Blue Zones are pockets around the world where people live long and healthy lives.
3. Blue Zone lifestyles include being happy, family-focused, eating a plant-based diet, slow-paced lifestyle, and a sense of purpose and belonging.

6

Cellular Health

Everything Begins at the Cellular Level!

If the world is cold, make it your business to build fires.

—Horace Traubel

For years we have been influenced to focus on **calories** as the most important factor around food. Most people believe to lose weight they just need to eat fewer calories. This may be true when starting a diet, but over time calorie restriction can lead to a feeling of deprivation, making the diet difficult to sustain. Imagine shifting your beliefs away from calories and focusing on feeding your cells with higher-quality food that retains all its nutrients! For many this can be difficult at first. We have been influenced for years to focus on calories. The question I hear over and over is "How many calories should I be eating per day? Is it 1,200 calories, 1,800 calories, 2,500 calories, or more?" My response is, it depends. It depends on many factors, but most of all it depends on the **quality** of the calories you are consuming.

When people begin to "get" this concept, the way they look at food changes forever. No longer are they concerned about adding an extra 100 to 200 calories per day of healthy fat to their diets. Their attention has shifted away from calories and losing weight, to feeding their cells high-quality foods and getting healthier! Their skin begins to look better, energy improves, clothes fit differently, inflammation begins to disappear, cholesterol improves, blood glucose improves, their cells are slowly transforming, and the body is getting healthier!

One comment I hear on a regular basis from many seminar attendees or health and fitness coaching clients is how their skin is softer, their nails are growing faster, and their hair and scalp are much healthier due to their eating higher-quality foods and beverages. Consuming higher-quality foods and beverages creates healthier cells.

What about taste, you ask? Do you need to eat wheatgrass, cod liver oil, micro-algae, or sea vegetables to keep your cells in good shape? You may want to do this in the future, but for now you don't need to worry about it. Whew. Okay, back to the cell. Our focus now turns to how we get healthy cells that result in a healthy mind and body.

The human body has over 100 trillion cells. One of the most beautiful aspects of the human body is its ability to adapt and heal itself. Each day the cells in the human body are going through constant change. **In fact, the human body turns over 3 to 4 trillion cells per day**. Each and every day you have a wonderful opportunity to improve your cellular health! I am going to give you two major concepts throughout this entire book: concept number one is cellular health and concept number two is pH balance, which is discussed in the next chapter. If you begin to grasp these two concepts your energy, health, and performance will greatly improve! Here is concept number one, the cell.

The Cell Membrane

Let's begin with a better understanding of the cell. Every cell has an outer crust called the cell membrane. The main job of the cell membrane is to control what goes in and out of the cell. Keeping the cell membrane soft and permeable is critical to the overall health of every cell. **The goal is to not only get your cell membranes soft and permeable, but to also keep them soft and permeable as you age**.

Consuming high-quality foods and beverages, especially the right types of fats, is essential in keeping the cell membranes soft and healthy. If you are consuming foods that contain trans fats (partially hydrogenated oils), the cell membrane starts to become hard and brittle. Remember the M&M candy: hard on the outside, soft on the inside. That's what your cells may become if you don't take care of them. As the cell membrane becomes hard and brittle, it makes it difficult for nutrients to enter the cell and the cells to be fed correctly.

When we eat, our blood glucose begins to rise and the hormone insulin is secreted to allow the cells to be fed. Insulin's job is to open the cell for feeding. If the cell is hard and stiff due to too much trans fat and processed food, the hormone insulin has difficulty opening the cell to be fed. Over time the cell may become desensitized to insulin, leading to elevated blood glucose and even to type 2 diabetes.

One of the fastest growing medical concerns we face in the United States, and around the world, is type 2 diabetes. In 1970 the United States had less than 500,000 type 2 diabetics, yet today there are over 25 million with another 30 to 40 million prediabetics waiting in the wings. In the next 5 to 10 years we could have close to 50 million type 2 diabetics in the United States alone. Ouch! Ten years ago Mexico had very little diabetes, and today Mexico is ranked number two in type 2 diabetes just behind the United States.

The major reason type 2 diabetes is growing so quickly is directly related to the quality and quantity of the foods and beverages we consume. The major villains in the type 2 diabetes epidemic is our overconsumption of trans fats, high fructose corn syrup, and processed foods and beverages. Trans fats, along with high fructose corn syrup and processed foods and beverages, make the cell membrane hard and brittle—making it extremely difficult for insulin to penetrate the cell. *Your first step in getting your cells soft and healthy is to get the trans fats, high-fructose corn syrup, and processed foods and beverages out of your diet and begin to replace them with healthy fats, whole foods, and water.* Healthy fats make the cell membrane soft and receptive to insulin. Regular exercise also improves the health and receptiveness of the cell membrane. Over time you don't need to produce as much insulin because the cell is more receptive and the need for type 2 diabetes medications slowly begins to disappear.

Mitochondria

Another essential part of the cell is the mitochondria. The mitochondria are the power pack of the cell, equivalent to the engine of a car. The mitochondria are directly related to how your body uses energy. The more active the mitochondria, the more calories your body will use for energy. In each cell there are hundreds to thousands of mitochondria, and the number and activity level of each mitochondria is directly related to a healthy lifestyle. Genetics do play a role, but it is small in comparison to a healthier lifestyle!

Many of my seminar attendees along with health and fitness coaching clients tell me that they have a stubborn metabolism. They are exercising more than ever and eating well, but they can't seem to lose weight. When we discuss their food log, I usually see a diet that is low in calories, but missing the essential fats needed to fuel the mitochondria. I tell them they need to feed the mitochondria correctly so the cell becomes more active.

The first step in getting the mitochondria healthy is to drink more water, eat more fruits and vegetables, and most of all, feed the mitochondria the right types of fat. This is another of the many reasons why consuming the right types of fats are essential for optimal health and weight control.

Nucleus of the Cell

Last but not least is the nucleus of the cell. The nucleus is the core and brain center of the cell. The nucleus orchestrates communication throughout the entire human body. Each cell also has a genetic makeup that determines everything from the color of our eyes and hair to the length of our bones. We all have a genetic makeup that we can do little to change, but genetics don't play as big a role on the outcome of our health and how we feel as we once thought.

You can make a huge impact on your health and how you feel every day by improving the quality of the food you eat and what you drink. Can you imagine trying to build a house with poor raw materials? The same can be said with the human mind and body: if you don't feed your cells the right raw materials, how can you produce a healthy outcome within the body?

Most people have been taught that if you eat less and exercise more, weight loss is sure to follow. But there is more than just eating fewer calories and exercising more. Change your beliefs away from how many calories you are consuming. Focus on improving the **quality** of your food and beverage choices. **Focus on getting healthier at the cellular level!** As your cells become healthier, you will begin to have better health, energy, improved sleep, less inflammation, and that stubborn waistline that wasn't getting any smaller will begin to magically shrink. See Figure 6.1.

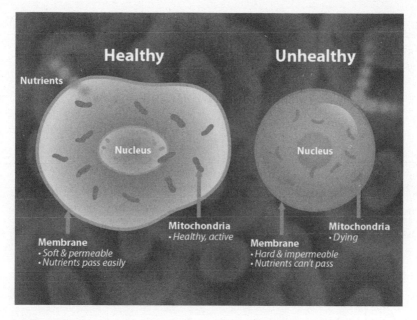

FIGURE 6.1   Your Health Begins at the Cellular Level

THE BOTTOM LINE

1. The human body has over 100 trillion cells, and 3 to 4 trillion of these cells turn over each day.
2. The cell membrane is the outer crust of the cell and acts as the gatekeeper of the cell, controlling what goes in and out of the cell.
3. The mitochondria are the power pack or car engine of the cell, and play a large role in how your body uses energy.
4. The nucleus is the center of the cell and orchestrates communication throughout the entire human body.
5. Focus on getting healthy at the cellular level!

7

pH Balance—The Missing Link to Amazing Health

We cannot direct the wind, but we can adjust the sails.

—Unknown

The second concept I teach in my On Target Living Seminars is centered on balancing your body's pH. Growing up, I had horrible skin for almost 15 years that included psoriasis, dandruff, acne; I was prescribed oral and topical medications, but nothing seemed to work. It was not until I changed what I was eating and drinking that my skin began to improve. Never once did anyone, including my doctors, mention pH balance or anything about what I was eating or drinking. This is one concept I want everyone to understand: why having a balanced pH is so important to your overall health, including having beautiful skin.

Do you remember the old Alka-Seltzer commercial, "Plop, Plop, Fizz, Fizz, Oh what a relief it is"? If you had heartburn (acid reflux) or stomach discomfort, Alka-Seltzer was the popular over-the-counter medication of choice to relieve your discomfort. This commercial was extremely popular around the holiday season, when we all may have overindulged. But what magical ingredient was in Alka-Seltzer that helped decrease your heartburn or stomach discomfort? The magical ingredient in Alka-Seltzer was sodium bicarbonate. So why did they call this medication Alka-Seltzer? Sodium bicarbonate is extremely alkaline, hence the name Alka-Seltzer.

Here comes the chemistry lesson: just stay focused on the concept and hopefully it will all make more sense as we go. Interest in alkaline/acid balance and its role in maintaining optimal health has been growing. Alkalinity and acidity are measured in pH (potential hydrogen).

Every food and drink has an acid or alkaline characteristic and is measured on a pH scale of 0–14, with 0 the most acidic and 14 the most alkaline. The pH of stomach acid is 1, diet soda 2.8, coffee is 4, water is 7 (neutral), venous blood is 7.35, arterial blood is 7.45, sea water is 8.5, and baking soda is 12 (similar to Alka-Seltzer). **Ideally, the human blood pH should be slightly alkaline, between 7.35 and 7.45.** You can monitor your pH on a regular basis by the use of pH strips; these may be purchased online or at most health food stores. The strips measure the pH of your saliva or urine. The pH of your saliva and urine should fall between 6.8 and 7.2. I recommend using pH strips every few months to monitor your pH level. For three consecutive mornings prior to eating or drinking, place the pH strip on your tongue for 10 seconds; use another pH strip to monitor your pH of your urine. Match up the color of your strips to the recommended pH color. If your strips match the recommended colors, your pH is in balance. Having a balanced pH is critical for optimal health, and using a pH strip can help you stay on track.

Foods and beverages are classified as acid-forming or alkalizing depending on the effect they have on the body. An **acid-forming** food or beverage **adds hydrogen** ions to the body, making it more acidic. An **alkalizing** food **removes hydrogen** ions from the body, making it more alkaline. **Whether a food or beverage is classified acid or alkaline is based on the effect they have on the body after digestion, the end product of digestion.** For example, lemons are extremely acidic; however, the end product they produce after digestion is more alkaline, so lemons are alkaline-forming in the body. A simple way to increase the alkalinity in a glass of water is to add a slice of lemon or lime. This is a simple remedy for those who suffer from acid reflux. For the next 30 days, drink a large glass of water first thing in the morning with a half-squeezed lemon or lime and watch the acid reflux improve overnight. One last item before this all comes together: just because a food or beverage is acid-forming does not mean it is unhealthy. Blueberries and walnuts are examples of acid-forming foods, but they also have many wonderful health benefits.

Your body won't allow your pH to become unbalanced; if it did, you would die. **But if your body has to work overtime to maintain a balanced pH this is where the trouble begins!** This is primarily due to our overconsumption of acid-forming foods and beverages and unhealthy stress. We consume considerably more acid-forming than alkaline-forming foods and beverages. We consume too much coffee, caffeine, soda pop, energy drinks, beer, alcohol, processed foods, fried foods, high-fructose corn syrup, sugar, artificial sweeteners, and animal proteins—to name a few. On top of our unhealthy food and beverage choices, we live in a world that keeps speeding up, which may lead to high levels of unhealthy stress.

Health Problems Related to an Acid-Forming Diet and High Levels of Stress

Acid reflux	Osteoporosis
Irritable bowel syndrome (IBS)	Psoriasis
Poor digestive health	Cracked nails
Cancer	Premature aging
Heart disease	Thyroid dysfunction
Cardiovascular damage	Weight gain
Type 2 diabetes	Muscle cramps
High blood pressure	Kidney stones
Hormonal imbalance	Insomnia
Headaches	Fatigue
Constipation	
Diarrhea	

How Does an Acid-Forming Diet and High Levels of Stress Lead to All of these Health Problems?

One thing I find fascinating about the human body is its ability to try to fix itself through endless checks and balances. This is extremely evident with blood pH. If the pH of the blood starts to become unbalanced in either direction by the smallest of margins, the body quickly brings it back into balance through a number of buffering processes. These buffering processes include the lungs, blood, and kidneys, and the use of minerals. As the blood becomes too acidic, less than 7.3, processes kick in to bring blood pH back to 7.4! The rate of breathing will increase to remove carbonic acid by exhaling carbon dioxide, the kidneys increase the acidity of the urine, minerals begin to be leached out of the body, and quickly blood pH is back to normal.

To compensate for an acid-forming diet and high levels of stress, the body uses alkaline-forming minerals such as calcium, magnesium, iodine, potassium, and sodium. As the pH in the body becomes more acid, these alkaline-forming minerals are used to buffer this high acid level. These minerals work in the blood, lymph, and extracellular and intracellular fluids to bind acids, which are then removed through the urine. Over time these minerals may become depleted, leading to a litany of health problems.

It sounds like the body has all the checks and balances in place to maintain a balanced blood pH, so what's the big deal? If we abuse our bodies by poor food and drinks choices, with little or no exercise, and high levels of unhealthy stress, the body can only do so much over time before things start to take its toll.

One of the fastest-growing groups of medications in the United States is medications that relieve digestive problems such as acid reflux. These medications may help to relieve the discomfort, but they are not fixing the problem. You may want to ask yourself, what is acid reflux? Why do I have acid reflux? And most importantly, how can I fix my acid reflux problem, not mask the source by clearing up the symptoms? I have witnessed many who have completely done away with their acid reflux medications by improving the quality of the foods and beverages they consume. Remember how Alka-Seltzer helped to relieve acid reflux? By consuming more alkaline-forming foods and beverages in your diet, acid reflux may quickly disappear!

There are also other health problems that may be linked to an acid-forming diet. In the United States we have one of the highest intakes in calcium in the world, but still have poor bone health when compared with other countries around the world? Doesn't that statement make you stand up and ask why? If we are consuming enough calcium to keep our bones healthy, what seems to be the problem? One of the real culprits when it comes to our poor bone health in the United States is our overconsumption of beverages that are acid-forming in the body, such as soda pop, coffee, energy drinks, alcohol, and cow's milk. To give you an idea of how powerful some of these beverages can be, let's do a simple experiment. You have a little rust on the bumper of your classic car; take a rag, pour some soda pop on the rag, add a little elbow grease, and off comes the rust! The ingredient in the soda pop that takes off the rust is phosphoric acid. Drinking too much soda pop creates an acid environment for the body. As pH slowly begins to shift to the acid side, the body goes to work calling on its buffering systems to bring pH back to normal. Minerals such as calcium play a large role in the buffering process, so over time calcium may be leached from the body causing weak bones. If the soda pop can take the rust off the car bumper, imagine how over time some of these acid-forming beverages can affect your bone health!

Another area of concern in the United States is thyroid problems among our women and now our men. Over 25 percent of all women over the age of 50 in the United States have reported thyroid problems. Many women over the age of 50 report feeling tired or having dry skin, intolerance to cold, muscle aches, depression, and an increase in body fat. One of the main functions of the thyroid gland is to control metabolism. The mineral iodine helps to support the thyroid gland. If your iodine reserves become depleted over time due to unhealthy stress, food and beverage choices, chances are your thyroid gland may also begin to suffer. Remember, your thyroid gland plays a large role in your metabolism. This is one reason diet soft drinks that contain zero calories may indirectly cause a person to gain weight. How can a diet soft drink that contains zero calories cause weight gain?—I missed that. Most soda pops contain phosphoric acid, increasing the acid in the body; over time valuable minerals, including the mineral iodine, are slowly leached out of the body. Remember iodine helps support the thyroid gland. If your body over time depletes your mineral reserves, your thyroid gland along with the overall health of the entire body begins to suffer.

Foods high in iodine include:

1. Agar	13. Kale
2. Artichokes	14. Leafy greens
3. Asparagus	15. Oats
4. Blueberries	16. Onions
5. Brussels sprouts	17. Sea vegetables
6. Carrots	18. Spirulina/chlorella
7. Coconut	19. Strawberries
8. Cucumbers	20. Sweet potatoes/squash
9. Eggplant	21. Tofu
10. Fish	22. Tomatoes
11. Goats' milk	23. Watermelon
12. Green peppers	24. Wheatgrass

I find it interesting that women in Japan have wonderful bone health, only consume 300 to 400 mg of calcium per day, and have virtually no thyroid problems. Their diet is made up of highly alkaline foods such as fish, leafy greens, tofu, spirulina/chlorella, and sea vegetables. Sea vegetables! What are sea vegetables? Sushi nori, arame, dulse, and wakame are all different types of sea vegetables that are extremely high in the mineral iodine. My favorite is sushi nori; I use it as a wrap or crumble it on a salad. Remember, sea water is highly alkaline, so it makes sense that vegetables grown in the sea are highly alkaline and also high in iodine. Now wait a minute, nobody said I had to eat sea vegetables! Sea vegetables can wait for now, but eating more fruits, vegetables, healthy fats, drinking more water, and controlling stress can help move you to the alkaline side.

What Causes Acid and Alkaline to Become Unbalanced?

The first step in your quest to having a balanced pH is awareness. What may be causing your pH to become unbalanced?

High Levels of Stress and Negative Emotions

There is nothing that moves the body to become acidic faster than excessive stress and negative emotions. Stress, fear, and negative emotions trigger the hormones adrenaline and cortisol. Adrenaline and cortisol accelerate acid levels throughout the body, leading to mineral loss.

Eating Too Much Protein

Proteins are acid in nature. Consuming more than 25 percent of your daily calories from protein may cause the body to become acidic. Also, consuming nonorganic animal sources of proteins may increase the acidity level in the body. Thirty years ago we didn't have to worry about consuming nonorganic animal sources of proteins, but now it is a much greater concern: Many animals are raised to grow faster and larger by being fed growth hormones. As the animals begin to grow at abnormally fast rates, the risk of contracting diseases also increases. To shut down disease in these animals, the animals are fed antibiotics. An easy way to improve your pH is to consume more plant-based proteins. Plant-based proteins are more alkaline sources of protein than animal-based proteins!

Consuming foods that contain antibiotics and hormones is not good for the human body. First, consuming foods that contain hormones and antibiotics may upset the natural balance of bacteria in the stomach. Antibiotics can damage the naturally occurring bacteria in the stomach that is essential for proper digestion and absorption of nutrients, which may then lead to digestive problems such as acid reflux and irritable bowel syndrome. Second, antibiotics are highly acidic. So by consuming too much protein along with eating nonorganic animal sources, the body becomes even more acidic. This can result in critical minerals becoming depleted. One of the keys for decreasing inflammation, improving digestion and having greater health, is to move your body to become more alkaline. Life can beat us all up, lack of sleep, little or no exercise, processed foods, and stress, can all cause a swing to the acidic side of the pH table— Figure 7.1.

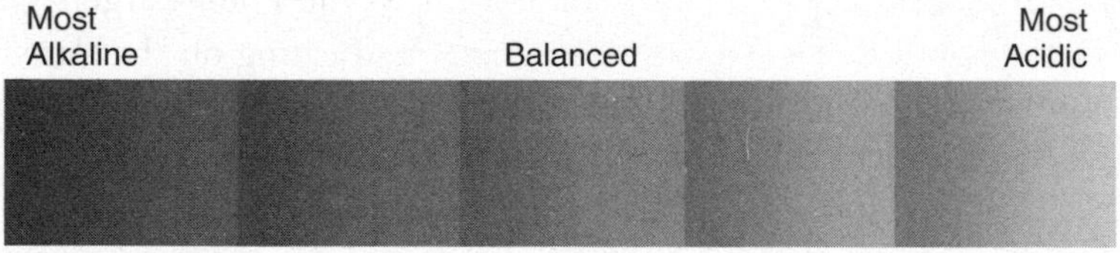

Most Alkaline		Balanced		Most Acidic

FIGURE 7.1 Balancing Acid and Alkaline

High Dietary Intake of Phosphates/Phosphoric Acid

Foods such as processed cheese, ice cream, artificial sweeteners, fried foods, beef, cocoa, sugar, table salt, and cottage cheese create high acid levels. Beverages such as cow's milk, soft drinks, coffee, energy drinks, and alcohol also increase acid levels.

What Can I Do to Balance My Acid and Alkaline Levels?

Your second step is to learn strategies to make your body more alkaline and get your pH back in balance. Remember to start slowly by taking one step at a time; you don't have to do everything overnight!

Consume Foods That Have High Alkaline Levels

Most fruits and vegetables have high alkaline levels and help maintain alkaline-acid balance. Sea vegetables are one of the highest sources of iodine and are extremely alkaline. Oatmeal is one of the highest alkaline whole grains. Most healthy fats such as extra virgin olive oil, cod liver oil, almonds, and flaxseeds are highly alkaline.

I am often asked in my seminars if salt is good or bad. The answer is, *it depends*! It depends on the **quality** of the salt. Are you asking about Celtic Sea Salt, which is highly alkaline or are you asking about table salt, sodium chloride that is highly acidic? Is there really that big of a difference between the types of salt you are consuming? Absolutely! So if you like using salt, Celtic Sea Salt is a much better choice, with Celtic Sea Salt containing over 80 minerals. Throughout this book I will continually stress the quality of food, beverages, and even condiments we are consuming. An easy way to help you choose more alkaline and less acid foods is to use the "Food Target." Eating toward the center of the Food Target—Green Area contains highly alkaline-forming foods and eating on the Outside of the Food Target—Red Area contains highly acid-forming foods! For more information on the Food Target, go to Chapter 17.

Consume Beverages That Have High Alkaline Levels

Coffee is usually acidic, but higher-quality coffee, such as an organic coffee, or moving to a healthier tea choice, such as green tea, can improve the pH of the beverage. Drinking mineral water or adding a slice of lemon to your water is an excellent way to help balance your pH. Plant-based milk options such as almond or coconut milk are alkaline options versus the more acidic cow's milk. Start to slowly improve the quality of your drink sources.

Rest/Recovery

Take time for yourself. Get more sleep. Take regular vacations. Try to get a little downtime each day. Change your breathing patterns. Taking deep, slow breaths for 30 to 60 seconds, spread out a few times over your day, can help to reduce stress. These will all improve your health and the pH balance in your body. To maintain a balance between acid and alkaline, shoot for 65 to 75 percent of all your food and beverage sources coming from the alkaline portion of the pH table.

The pH Table

	Most Alkaline	More Alkaline	Least Alkaline	Least Acidic	Most Acidic
Beverages	Mineral water, lemon water	Green tea, spring water	Ginger tea	Kona coffee, black tea, organic coffee, red wine	Beer, coffee, energy drinks, alcohol, soda pop
Dairy		Human breast milk, almond milk	Ghee, rice milk, goat cheese	Butter, cow's milk, soy milk	Processed cheese, ice cream, cottage cheese
Meat/ Seafood			Fish	Wild game, chicken, turkey, shrimp	Pork, beef, lobster
Beans/ Legumes	Lentils		Tofu, soy	Black-eyed peas, pinto beans, navy beans, lima beans, kidney beans	Tempeh, soybeans, chick peas
Fruits	Lime, lemon, pineapple, watermelon	Apple, kiwi, peach, blackberry	Oranges, bananas, blueberries, raisins	Dry fruit, figs, dates, plums	Prunes, tomatoes, pomegranates, cranberries
Vegetables	Sea vegetables, broccoli, barley grass, wheat grass, asparagus, sweet potatoes	Eggplant, kale, cauliflower, collard greens, bell peppers, sprouts	Squash, lettuce, beets, Brussels sprouts, cucumbers	Spinach, zucchini, string beans	Peas, carrots
Grains/ Cereal			Wild rice, quinoa, oats	Wheat, brown rice, amaranth, millet	White rice, barley, rye, corn
Nuts/Oils	Pumpkin seeds	Almonds, cod liver oil, evening primrose oil	Flaxseed oil, extra-virgin olive oil, organic coconut oil	Sesame oil, safflower oil, canola oil	Pecans, Brazil nuts, palm kernel oil, fried food, lard
Condiments/ Spices	Sea salt, baking soda	Cinnamon, most herbs	Curry	MSG, vanilla	Nutmeg, aspartame, pudding, jam, jelly, table salt
Lifestyle	Sleep, deep breathing,	Optimism, forgiveness,	Willingness, courage, pride	Hate	Guilt, shame, fear, stress, being overworked, having a sedentary lifestyle

THE BOTTOM LINE

1. Alkaline/acid is measured by relative pH in blood. pH can be measured through the blood, urine, or saliva.
2. Lack of exercise, too much stress, and a poor diet may lead to excessive stress on the body's buffering processes.
3. The body balances pH through many buffering processes, including the lungs, blood, kidneys, and alkaline minerals.
4. Many health problems in the United States can be linked to an acid-forming diet and high levels of stress.
5. Try to consume 65 to 75 percent of your foods and beverages from alkaline sources and control unhealthy stress to keep an alkaline/acid balance.

8 Laying the Foundation

The ripest peach is highest on the tree.

—James Whitcomb Riley

I believe most people want to feel good and have good health. As the saying goes "when you don't have your health you don't have anything." This is so true. What does good health and performance look like? It could be as simple as having more energy throughout your day, getting up in the morning with fewer aches and pains, decreasing the amount of medications that you are currently taking, climbing a flight of stairs with less effort, having greater mental focus at work or school, performing better on the athletic field, having more pep in your step, or just plain feeling your best!

Most people want to feel good and perform their best in whatever they do. Wouldn't you like to have this feeling on a more consistent basis? You can create a consistent pattern of feeling your best every day!

Maslow's Hierarchy of Human Needs

Years ago while in graduate school at Michigan State University, I came across Abraham Maslow's Hierarchy of Human Needs (see Figure 8.1). I became fascinated with Maslow's Hierarchy in how it relates to the needs and desires of people. Maslow, a psychologist, noticed while working with monkeys that certain needs take precedence over others. Maslow

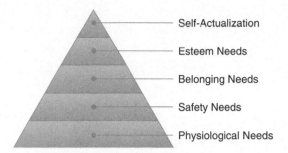

FIGURE 8.1 Maslow's Hierarchy of Needs

discovered that the monkeys would not move up their hierarchy of needs until the needs below were met. For example, if the monkeys were thirsty, drinking would take precedence over eating, and up the hierarchy they would go. Maslow created his Hierarchy of Human Needs based on what he had learned from his studies with monkeys. Maslow then laid out his five layers of human needs: Physiological Needs, Safety Needs, Belonging Needs, Esteem Needs and Self-Actualization Needs.

The first four levels of needs Maslow calls deficit needs, meaning if you don't have enough of something you have a deficit, so you feel the need. The last level of Maslow's Hierarchy of Human Needs is Self-Actualization. This level is where the fun begins. Maslow referred to this level as "growth motivation." These are needs that do not involve balance. These needs get stronger the more attention we give them. They involve the continuous desire to fulfill potentials, to "be all you can be." If you truly want to be self-actualizing then you need to have your lower needs met.

You might be thinking, what does Maslow's Hierarchy of Human Needs have to do with reading a book on health, well-being, and performance? I am always fascinated when I listen to people express their needs, working on a new career, making more money, developing personal relationships, buying a new house, the list goes on. I find it interesting in our society that some of the most basic physiological human needs are so often neglected. For many, taking care of these fundamental needs is not even on their radar screen. It becomes difficult to perform at your best when you don't get enough sleep, eat poorly, and rarely move your body.

The most consistent at following the hierarchy of needs is my dog Dolly. Dolly has the dog hierarchy of needs down to a science! Granted, Dolly does not have a job or many responsibilities, but Dolly does have her rituals in place to take care of her hierarchy of needs. The first thing Dolly does when she gets up in the morning is stretch, one of the traditional yoga stretches, up and down dog stretch. Followed by a strong desire to go outside and do her business. Dolly then comes in the house and gets a drink of water followed by eating her food. Dolly then moves up her hierarchy of needs and wants to play. Building a stronger foundation can be easier than you think. Start slowly, make small changes, and "be all you can be"!

Building "Your" Foundation

The three basic ingredients that form the foundation of Maslow's Hierarchy of Human Needs are **Rest and Rejuvenation, Nutrition, and Exercise (REST/EAT/MOVE)**. (See Figure 8.2.) You can't build a strong house unless you have a solid foundation; the same is true for the human body. The human body requires a few basic principles to stay healthy and perform at the top of our game. Be kind to yourself, take care of the basics, and enjoy life!

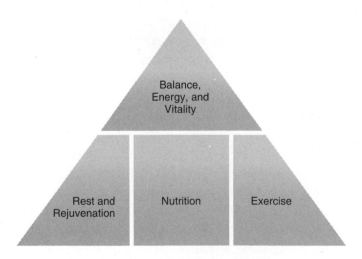

FIGURE 8.2 Balance, Energy, and Vitality Pyramid

Rest and Rejuvenation

When consulting with clients one on one or speaking to large audiences through my seminars, I like to begin with Rest and Rejuvenation as the foundation to being your best. When I first entered the health and fitness industry over 25 years ago, exercise was number one on my list, followed by nutrition; rest and recovery was nothing I planned for—it either happened or it didn't! Today rest and rejuvenation is much higher on my priority list, followed closely by nutrition and then exercise. Don't get me wrong, finding a balance is what we are striving for and exercise is an important part of this balance, but when it comes to hierarchy of needs, rest and rejuvenation needs to be a priority to perform at your best! Getting enough rest is critical for good health and performing at your best! Have you ever taken a vacation and within just a few days your quality of sleep starts to improve, your energy is better, and you start feeling like your old self again? We are a sleep-deprived nation, with a high percentage of our population getting less than six hours of sleep per night on a regular basis. Don't underestimate what rest and rejuvenation can do for you!

Nutrition

Another major piece of the foundational pyramid for better health and performance is high quality nutrition. As a society we underestimate the powerful impact healthy nutrition plays on the human mind and body. This will be discussed in greater detail throughout the rest of this book.

Exercise

The human body is designed to move. If exercise came in a pill form it would be the most prescribed medication on the planet! If there were such a thing as "The Fountain of Youth," regular exercise would be at the top of the list. Moving your body is one of the fastest ways to change your mood. When doing seminars to large audiences and I need to change the energy of the audience, I find ways to get everyone moving. Just by adding movement, such as standing and waving arms, laughter begins, smiles appear, and the energy of the entire room changes (see Figure 8.3). **Motion creates positive emotion!**

FIGURE 8.3 Motion Creates Positive Emotion

THE BOTTOM LINE

1. Abraham Maslow's Hierarchy of Human Needs: Physiological, Safety, Belonging, Esteem, and Self-Actualization.
2. Start slowly building your foundation for optimal health and performance: REST/EAT/MOVE!
3. Bring some planned rest and recovery back into your life.
4. What you feed your body is directly related to how you feel and perform.
5. Regular exercise we all know is good for the body, but how is it good for the brain? Motion creates positive emotion!

Rest and Rejuvenation

9 Life Balance

Work like you don't need money, love like you have never been hurt, and dance like no one's watching.

—Ray Denning

As our world keeps speeding up, it becomes more and more challenging to maintain Life Balance! Work, family, friends, me time, health, sleep, exercise, community service, fun—the list is long, and it is so easy to get out of balance (see Figure 9.1).

I have worked in organizations that believe working long hours, with little sleep, huge demands, and little time for anything other than work was looked upon as a badge of honor! When working at Frito-Lay while going to graduate school, I worked with seven managers in six years! Many times the managers were afraid to go home because their bosses might call in. What kind of message was this sending to the team? I get it that times are tough and everyone is working hard, but my point is, how do you create better performance and have a better life? I don't believe grinding people into dust is the best way to improve performance. How do you become your best is a more interesting question. This is the focus of this book, being your best: being your best at work, being your best at home, and in every aspect of your life.

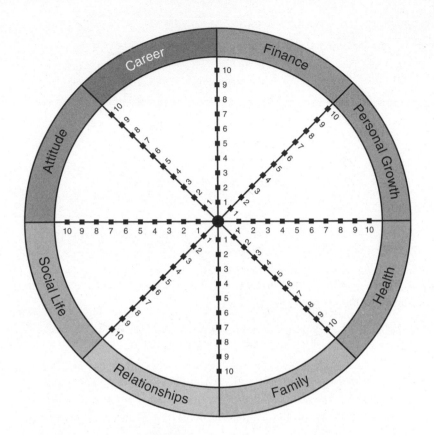

FIGURE 9.1 Circle of Balance

John Carter: Nationwide

In an interview with John Carter, President of Nationwide Financial Distributors, Inc., John shared some of his beliefs and strategies about "Being Your Best"!

Early in John's career, as he came up through the ranks of the financial services industry, he learned that the industry was focused on one thing—the bottom line. John knew there had to be a better and more sustainable way to get the results you were driving for. Working too many hours with little sleep, poor eating habits, no time to exercise, little rest and rejuvenation, and a life with little or no balance, was not the way John envisioned or defined success in his business and in his life.

John believes you can drive results with a different approach.

If you began to look at the whole person and pull together the personal and professional aspects of a person's life, performance would clearly follow. How do you invest in people? How do you tap into what truly drives people? Work, family, outside interests–life is a journey of learning; how do you stimulate and create a culture with this new thinking?

John believes one of the keys for "Being Your Best" is to build a strong foundation centered around health. Many companies look at employee wellness programs as a strategy to improve the health of their employees strictly for reasons to lower employee benefit costs. This is one bottom line strategy, but in John's opinion it is a limiting belief of what is possible! Having a strong mind, body, and spirit enables a person to perform better in difficult times. John believes you need to have tools and strategies for better health and it must be woven into the entire culture.

Begin with a better understanding of how powerful good nutrition can be, why getting a good night's sleep is imperative to better thinking, energy, and performance. It is okay to:

- Take a 90-second stretch break during your work day or lie on a foam roller in the office
- Close your eyes and do belly breathing for one to three minutes or
- Have a healthy snack at meetings

All these simple and acceptable strategies make a difference in how a person feels and how the culture becomes "Their Best" professionally and personally!

For the past six years Nationwide Financial has invested a great deal of their resources in personal development programs that help associates become their best. John also made it clear that support of such programs needs to begin at the top. In the past five years, this organization has greatly improved their engagement scores, lowered turnover, increased profits, and built a culture that delivers results with more life balance. The bigger
(continued)

(continued)
picture is not about losing weight or lowering cholesterol, but developing a stronger mind and body. The bigger picture is that anything is possible.

John believes you need to expect the best from your team, and having a healthy mind, body, and spirit is the cornerstone for "Being Your Best"!

I am fascinated by the word *rejuvenation*! The definition of rejuvenation is to make young again. Picture a gentle morning spring shower; the sun is just coming up, the bright green color of the grass, trees with the moisture on their leaves, birds chirping—that clean refreshing smell of springtime is in the air and the world feels alive! Everything looks and smells new and refreshed—*Rejuvenated!* We all need to have ample rest and recovery to make young again. If you are rested mentally and physically, well hydrated, and well fed, you will perform at a higher level. You will have greater energy and stamina, you will increase your ability to think and solve problems, and most importantly you will just plain feel better and enjoy life more. More and more businesses are beginning to understand the importance of having adequate rest and recovery plugged into daily business practices. Sleep pods are now seen in the corporate world and even on some long distance flights. Many countries around the world have rest and recovery practices as part of their daily routine. Many countries actually shut down for business a few hours every afternoon. It gives workers time to eat, rest, move, and rejuvenate. We all need more down time to rest and recharge our batteries!

When I first entered into the health and fitness world, my main focus was on exercise, as my formal training was as an exercise physiologist. Strength training, cardio, stretching, heart rate, blood pressure, stroke volume, bone density, weight loss—anything that had to do with exercise was number one in my mind. Nutrition was number two followed by rest, but who really needs to teach people how to rest? Boy was I out to lunch with this belief system! I knew having adequate sleep was truly important, but it was nothing I would really take the time to educate people on.

In 1991 when I was developing the personal training program at one of the largest clubs in the world, the Michigan Athletic Club, members and trainers were also focused on exercise. Some were interested in eating better, but learning how to rest was seldom on the radar screen for trainers or clients. Why would anyone pay to learn how to rest? Everyone wanted to burn calories, and exercise was the way to do this and get the results people were looking for. We even had time limits on all the cardio machines because cardio was the way to lose weight, and more time spent doing cardio meant more weight loss. As our training program evolved, I knew something was missing in the way we were training our trainers, or as we call them today health and fitness coaches. At the time I was managing three personal training programs in three different cities throughout Michigan, and I decided to see how our trainers or coaches were training themselves. What daily practices were the trainers doing to stay healthy and fit? I learned many years ago that how you train yourself is usually very similar to how you train your clients. I asked approximately 50 personal trainers to write down everything they were personally doing as part of their daily health and fitness regimen. The three categories for building a solid health and fitness foundation were Nutrition, Rest, and Exercise (Eat/Rest/Move). You should have seen my findings; the list was five miles long under the exercise section, walking, running, swimming, biking, sports, stretching, yoga, Pilates, tai chi, martial arts, exercise classes, strength training, free weights, rubber bands, functional training, the list went on and on! Under the nutrition section were a moderate amount of daily practices, such as eating smaller meals, hydration, serving sizes, avoiding soda pop, processed and fast foods, some healthy fats, fruits, vegetables, and some supplements like a multivitamin or protein smoothies. I was shocked under the rest section: some put down "sleep" and "maybe take a vacation now and then" and that was about it! The list was embarrassingly short! There was absolutely no balance in how the trainers or coaches were living their lives and in most cases how they were training their clients. It was time to create some balance in our training programs.

Today I begin all my training by building the foundation of Rest and Rejuvenation. This is the reason I am beginning your On Target Living Journey with the section on Rest and Rejuvenation.

All three categories (Eat, Rest, Move) are extremely important in your pursuit for being and performing at our best, and all three work together to create amazing results, but there is definitely a hierarchy of needs with rest and rejuvenation being at the foundation.

THE BOTTOM LINE

1. We live in a 24/7 world and life keeps speeding up.
2. Creating a life with greater balance can be extremely challenging!
3. Pyramid of health and fitness needs: Breathing, sleep, hydration, nutrition, posture, and exercise.
4. Rest and rejuvenation is the foundation for being and performing at your best.
5. Could you use more balance in your life?

10 Is Stress Melting You Down?

Joy comes from using your potential.

—Will Schultz

Before jumping right into strategies and techniques to bring more rest and rejuvenation back into your life, I want to address the topic of stress. Stress is one hot topic, not only in the United States but also around the world!

Everywhere you go people are talking about stress! Stress at work, stress at home, financial stress, emotional stress, and physical stress; stressors come in all shapes and sizes and are lurking around every corner. I get that we are all under more stress, but I believe the real threat to our health and performance is not the added volume of stress, **but the lack of recovery**!

I believe having adequate rest and rejuvenation practices is one of the most powerful keys for optimal health and performance. Without adequate rest, the human body breaks down very quickly; it shows up in your daily performance and also in your health. The Centers for Disease Control and Prevention state unequivocally that 80 percent of our medical expenditures are now stress related. Don't let the volume of stress and lack of recovery practices melt you down!

I was once asked by one of my clients to have dinner with one of their up and coming rising stars within their organization to talk about his health. I flew to New York to this fantastic restaurant with little information about the person I was about to meet. I was just told he needed help with his health. He was very friendly as we exchanged introductions, ordered our entrees, and slowly moved into our conversation targeted towards his health. This man was highly educated, had been promoted swiftly to the top, and was making a ton of money, but he had lost his way concerning his health.

At the age of 43, he was approximately 75 pounds overweight, taking medications for cholesterol, blood pressure, sleep, type 2 diabetes, and acid reflux. He was working over 60 hours per week, with high demands, and making a daily commute from his home to the office of more than 90 minutes each way. He would leave for work at 5:30 a.m. each morning and return home by 8:00 p.m. four nights per week. One night a week he would get home around 6:00 p.m. to have dinner with his wife and kids. He did not work on the weekends; this was his "family time." So I begin our conversation with some pretty tough questions, such as how do you define success and do you believe you are successful? Is it possible for you to take a break during the day? Come into work later a few mornings a week? Work fewer hours? We talked a little about getting some exercise, drinking more water, planning meals and snacks for his daily commute and at work, but he already seemed to know all of this lifestyle information and was not really interested in making many changes. What shocked me the most was that he was not curious at all.

His lack of curiosity was a good sign that change was probably not going to happen anytime soon. I asked him to start with just a few baby steps, but he did not really believe he needed to change. He believed he was going down the right path.

Slowly he began to open up and explain his future game plan. He told me he enjoyed his work, but it was not his calling. What he really wanted to do is to continue his work for another 10 to 12 years, then he wanted to teach high school math and coach tennis; he had played tennis in college and wanted to share his love for tennis with others. I asked him how old his kids were, and he said 10 and 12. I said do you realize your kids will probably be gone in 10 years, going to college and moving on in their lives? He had some very powerful WHYs staring him in the face, but for some reason was not recognizing them. He truly believed he was okay and liked his plan! As our dinner ended, I thanked him for dinner and told him if there was anything I could do, to please not hesitate to call. He said he would read my book and give me a call to discuss next steps. I never heard from him again.

All too often people lose their health to make money, and then lose their money to try and get back their health. What many people fail to understand is your health is your greatest asset; don't let an unbalanced life steal your life away!

So What Is Stress?

So what is this thing we call stress? Stress has been defined in popular literature as the "sum of all wear and tear on the body throughout life." Stress is not always damaging. In fact, adaptation and stress are essential for life and growth. The absence of stress would produce impaired growth and development, and eventual death. There is an obvious need for stress control not only in the United States, but also around the world.

For the past 60 years the stress model has not changed. The traditional definition of stress is that "stress is a nonspecific response of the body and mind to any demand made upon it, may it be pain or pleasure." One difficulty in defining stress this way is that the only time the body doesn't have a nonspecific response to stimuli is when you are dead. How helpful is it when everything becomes "stress"? This is how most people think about stress, but equating stress to arousal simply ignores the **difference** in states of arousal. Not all arousal is "stressful," and the experience of challenge is quite different from the experience of too much pressure. For example when you exercise you are placing stress on the mind and body in the hope that you will adapt to the stress made upon you. If your exercise program is too intense, you may get injured or burned out. If your exercise program is too soft or lacking much intensity, you may get little adaptation or benefit. So one of the keys in having an exercise program that works for you is finding the right amount of stress or arousal for optimal benefits.

I always thought of stress as worry, frustration or anxiety, but this is not stress; this may be the response to stress. **Stress is physiological**, meaning your heart rate may increase, your vision may narrow, you may notice your muscles become tense, you may begin to sweat, and your hearing may become more sensitive, all these changes are part of the fight-or-flight syndrome. Most have heard of the fight-or-flight syndrome: when there is a threat or perceived threat the sympathetic nervous system goes into high gear getting the body and mind ready for a fight or flight. All of these bodily responses occur quickly and most of the time without thought. The fight-or-flight reaction is **always** triggered whenever there is a threat. The intensity of the reaction is determined by how intense or big the threat appears to be. Remember, the whole thing is keyed to the individual's perception of a threat being there. Whether or not the threat actually exists is immaterial—it is a matter of perception. So if you don't see the gun pointing at you, you don't react with a fight-or-flight reaction because you don't perceive any threat, but if you think the stick in the person's hand is a gun, you react as if there actually was a threat there even though there isn't any threat at all.

Most stress resources state that the fight-or-flight syndrome is automatic, meaning you have little control over your stress response. That may be true in some cases, like running from a predator or almost getting into a car accident, but how about the fear and anxiety of speaking in front of a large crowd, meeting someone for the first time, or being under the gun with an important deadline—like the writing of this book? Is it possible to control your response to the fear or threat? Most people may believe stress is out of their control, that they have little control over their daily circumstances and stress is just going to hit them smack in the face. Yes some days may feel like no matter what you do, you must be walking under a rain cloud. It is not running from the real danger that is melting us down in our world today, but the small stuff that takes its toll. Deadlines, worry, anxiety, it is the chronic small stuff that beats people up, and we need to learn some basic skills to help control the mind when stressors come calling.

One of my good friends and colleague, Phil Nuernberger, PhD, a leading expert in the world on stress and working with the mind, has truly helped me understand how powerful the mind can be in controlling stress. He believes that stress is neither good nor bad, but how the mind interprets the stress.

Dr. Phil says we confuse stress with arousal—we need challenge in life, we need arousal, but when that arousal is out of balance, then we create some difficulty somewhere in the system. Dr. Phil calls the mind an instrument, and he says we all need the proper skills to control our instrument. I will share some of these simple strategies to help you use your mind in a way to help you cope with your stress later in this section on rest and rejuvenation.

Stress Response: Lions and Tigers and Bears!

When my kids were in middle school, my wife and I took the kids and a few of their friends to the Cedar Point Amusement Park in Sandusky,

Ohio, a mega rollercoaster theme park. From miles away you could see the tallest rollercoaster in the country at the time—the Millennium Force. This rollercoaster was a beast, over 300 feet high—to me it looked taller than the Empire State Building, traveled close to 100 miles an hour in something like five seconds flat! It was safe to say that I was already nervous, and I had not even entered the park yet. My wife and son stated as we walked into the park that they were not going to ride the Millennium Force; they came up with some lame excuse like they were afraid of heights and had no need for speed. On the other hand, my daughter and her girlfriends could not wait to ride this ballistic missile into the clouds! So now I am getting really amped up, it was down to me, it was my turn to play the tough dad, if they only knew what I was feeling. While waiting in line with my daughter and her friends, I was a mess! My hands were sweating, my mind was racing, my mouth was dry, and my stomach was in knots. I thought to myself, "Am I really going to ride this train of terror?" The girls were laughing and so excited to ride this roller coaster; they were treating it like a Merry-Go-Round at the county fair!

As we were about to get onto the train of terror, I could barely breath, my muscles were locked up, and my hands were a puddle of sweat. The anticipation of getting onto this rollercoaster was tearing me up, physically and mentally; the more I thought about it the worse it got, so much so I thought I was going to throw up. At this time I had no training on how to reframe my focus or skills to control my mind or instrument. After our ride on the train of terror, I was completely exhausted, as I had never experienced this type of anxiety and fear before. It left a mark that was hard for me to understand at the time, but helped me to have a better understanding how powerful the stress response can or could be, especially if you do not have the proper training to control your stress.

Even though we rarely need the true fight-or-flight response, it is often triggered whenever we perceive something as threatening to our survival. Our threat could be economic, social, self-esteem, academic, or physical. If you perceive something as a threat, whether it is real or made up in you're mind, your mind and body will respond in the same manner. Today the sheer volume of stress triggers we all face continues to climb in our 24/7 world. Add this to our lack of training to control the mind and how to deal with stress—this is what is melting us down in our world today!

Optimal Stress Level

Have you ever performed at your highest level? I think we all have been in the zone at one time or another. Writing, running, playing a musical instrument, golfing, whatever your passion, being in the zone of excellence can be truly amazing; the hard part is repeating it. How did you get there? What created this peak performance state? A good night of sleep, quality nutrition, positive mind-set, maybe it was a combination of many factors, but the challenge is how to repeat this peak level of performance in the mind and body.

What role does the amount and intensity of stress play in your performance state? Having enough stress to get your attention—arousal. But not too much stress, that could create hyperarousal or damage. Finding the right balance is the key for optimal performance. Remember the story of Goldilocks and the Three Bears? The porridge was too hot, then too cold, and then it was "just right"! You need enough stress to challenge you and make you grow, but not too much that you can't keep up and stress is breaking you down. Finding that "right" balance of stress and gaining the skills necessary to control the mind is critical for your success in business, your personal life, and your health and well-being! Take a look at Figure 10.1.

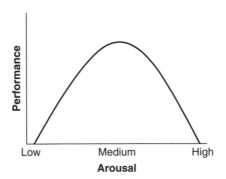

FIGURE 10.1 Optimal Stress Graph

Autonomic Nervous System

Can you imagine if you had to think about your heart beating or taking in a breath of oxygen all day long? What would you do when you were sleeping? The human body is truly amazing in so many ways with all of its checks and balances. One of these powerful checks and balances is the autonomic nervous system (ANS). The autonomic nervous system acts as a stress control center in the body, regulating the heart, digestion, respiratory rate, perspiration, pupil dilation, sexual arousal, many organs, and muscles. The autonomic nervous system is always working and **acts to maintain balance** with our internal systems within the body along with working with the somatic nervous system. Whereas most of the actions of the autonomic nervous system are involuntary, some, such as breathing and heart rate, work in tandem with the conscious mind. Meaning that it is possible to learn how to control many areas of the human body through the conscious mind. With a little practice you can learn how to control many areas of the human body that affect your health and start performing at your best.

The autonomic nervous system is classically divided into two parts, the sympathetic nervous system and the parasympathetic nervous system. The job of the autonomic nervous system is to work with both systems, creating balance and harmony throughout the body.

Sympathetic Nervous System—The Accelerator!

I believe when most people think about stress they envision the sympathetic nervous system. The sympathetic nervous system is the alarm going off at the fire station, all hands on deck and ready to go! Heart rate increases, pupils dilate, blood pressure raises, digestion stops, muscles contract, perspiration increases, the entire body goes into high alert. It does not matter whether the threat is real or perceived, the threat or stressor will trigger the stress response, and action within the brain and body happens very quickly. One of the best known of these threats is the fight-or-flight response as was discussed earlier in this chapter. When a powerful threat is sent out, multiple events take place to get your body ready to act. It starts in the hypothalamus of the brain and sets off many chemical reactions throughout the body.

A great amount of norepinephrine (adrenaline) is pumped into your body, and the entire body becomes on high alert, getting you ready to fight or flee. The pituitary gland then sends a signal to the adrenal glands to release cortisol. Cortisol is an important stress hormone in the body, regulating your energy, blood pressure, immune system, and inflammation. While cortisol is an extremely important and helpful part of the body's response to stress, prolonged levels of cortisol in the bloodstream can lead to many negative side effects.

Don't think of cortisol as a bad thing; think of cortisol as a stress hormone preparing the body for stress. The problem occurs with chronic stress. The definition of **chronic stress is a state of ongoing arousal**. This occurs when the body experiences so many stressors that the autonomic nervous system rarely has a chance to activate the relaxation response. This type of chronic stress response occurs all too frequently in our world today. Too many appointments, heavy traffic, lack of money, pressure at work, unhealthy relationships, working too many hours, no down time, environmental problems, physical issues, poor nutrition, lack of sleep, little exercise, loneliness, final exam, a noisy neighbor, all can keep the body in a state of perceived threat and chronic stress. **The human body is meant to handle acute stress, not chronic stress!**

Without enough rest the adrenal gland becomes over-stimulated, secreting too much of the stress hormone cortisol. High levels of cortisol can break down the body in many ways, leading to problems such as hormonal imbalances, weight gain, low energy, high blood pressure, depression, inflammation, osteoporosis, low thyroid, heart attacks, and decreased immune function—to name just a few.

Many people come to see me because they want to lose weight and improve their health. When I begin explaining the importance of rest and rejuvenation practices such as diaphragmatic breathing, sleep, or planned downtime, they get this quizzical look on their face. Why are you talking about rest and rejuvenation practices when I am here to learn how to eat better, exercise, and lose weight?

I explain to them that having greater balance in their life includes having adequate rest; it is especially and directly related to weight loss and better health. Your digestive system has two hormones that control hunger and appetite: ghrelin and leptin. Ghrelin is secreted by the stomach and sends out a signal that you are hungry. Lack of sleep stimulates the hormone ghrelin, which plays a role in making you want to overeat. Leptin plays the opposite role of ghrelin. Leptin tells the brain that you are satisfied. If you are getting enough restful sleep, your body will secrete leptin, letting your brain know that you are satisfied, having less desire to overeat. Most of the time people want to solely focus on exercise and eating right, when truly the problem many times lies with chronic stress and how it is affecting their health, energy, and vitality.

The Negative Effects of Prolonged Cortisol Production

- Decreased brain function
- Decreased bone density
- Higher blood pressure
- Compromised immune system
- Blood glucose imbalance
- Decrease in muscle
- Suppressed thyroid function
- Increase in belly fat

True Fight or Flight

Very rarely do we have a true fight-or-flight stress response, but thank goodness we do have this hardwired system in place. While in Tuscany years ago, my wife and I went for a hike up into the beautiful countryside. Rolling hills, vineyards, architecture . . . everywhere the eye could see you were surrounded by beauty. As we walked higher and higher up into the countryside, we approached a large group of gorse bushes. From out of nowhere we heard the most threatening, intense deep growl I have ever experienced! I said, "What was that?" What I really said I can't repeat. We both looked at each other and knew this was not good; we had come upon some type of beast and obviously from the tone and power of the growl, we were definitely overmatched. Our hearts were racing, palms were sweating, all hands were on deck! We were in full-blown fight-or-flight response. Should we stay and fight (I had picked up a large rock) or should we run (flight)? This was an easy choice—RUN! When we returned to our hamlet, still all pumped up, I rushed to report our wild beast sighting. The proprietors of the hamlet did not bat an eye and said it must have been a wild boar. I did a little research on wild boars; they grow to over 350 pounds, have large dangerous tusks, and are very mean! It might not have been a problem for the proprietors of our hamlet, but it sure was a big deal to my sympathetic nervous system at the time!

Does your entire day feel like you are running from a wild boar? Does your sympathetic nervous system always seem to be on? There are two major keys for optimal health and performance and dealing with stress. First, learn more about stress, that stress is a physiological response to a stressor and learn to recognize your signs of stress. Second, learn strategies and skills on how to handle the stressors of the world we live in.

Parasympathetic Nervous System— The Brake!

If the sympathetic nervous system is the five-alarm fire, then the parasympathetic division is laying on the beach drinking a piña colada! Think of the sympathetic division as the accelerator and the parasympathetic division as the brake.

Sympathetic and parasympathetic divisions typically function in opposition to each other, but it is better viewed that both systems are working together, trying to create balance and harmony within the body. The **parasympathetic nervous system** generally slows everything down, promoting a **"rest and digest" response**. Heart rate and blood pressure drop, nerves calm, brain waves slow down, muscles relax, dilation of blood vessels, digestion increases, and your pupils constrict. It sounds like we all need more of the parasympathetic nervous system in our lives—and yes we all probably do! But again it comes back to balance: if the parasympathetic division becomes too dominant, we then may move into the "possum response." During the "possum response," everything starts to shut down. We begin to lose muscle tone, depression and withdrawal start to creep in, and many times we feel a level of emotional flatness, with life becoming blah. We begin to sleep too much, we don't feel like getting out of bed, we are tired much of the time, and we feel like we have lost our "juice." One of the best solutions for someone who is parasympathetic-dominant is not more sleep or diaphragmatic breathing, but to get them up and move. To create balance within the autonomic nervous system, you need to stimulate the sympathetic nervous system and speed things up to get balance back into the body!

THE BOTTOM LINE

1. The Centers for Disease Control and Prevention state unequivocally that 80 percent of our medical expenditures are now stress related.
2. Stress is physiological, meaning your heart rate and blood pressure go up, muscles begin to tighten, vision may narrow, and your body begins to sweat.
3. The fight-or-flight response is triggered by a threat. The threat may be perceived or real!
4. Optimal stress level is when your arousal is just right for you to perform at your best.
5. The autonomic nervous system acts as the stress control center and is divided into two categories, the sympathetic (accelerator) and the parasympathetic (brake) nervous system.

11

Hormonal Harmony and Your Health

Those who bring sunshine to the lives of others cannot keep it from themselves.

—James Barrie

Before we move into our rest and rejuvenation strategies, it is critical to understand the impact of stress on our hormones. We are bombarded by so much information on hormones and the problems relating to an imbalance in our hormones. Each night on television you see commercials for hormonal solutions, low testosterone or low T, menopause, hot flashes, increased belly fat, thyroid, bone health, erectile dysfunction . . . the list is long, and somebody must be buying. Again, ask a better question: Why do we have such a problem with our hormones being out of balance?

Let's first begin by understanding a little more about this intricate circuit of hormones. So what is a hormone? Hormones are the chemical messengers that coordinate physiology and behavior, by regulating, integrating, and controlling our bodily functions. Think of your hormonal system as an orchestra playing at Carnegie Hall, all working hard to bring balance and harmony to the body. **Hormones affect almost every system in the human body; here is just a sampling of their work:**

- Stimulate or inhibit growth
- Mood swings
- Increase or decrease the immune system's function
- Regulate metabolism

- Prepare the body for new phases of life such as puberty, parenting, and menopause
- Prepare the body for mating, fighting, or fleeing
- Sexual arousal
- Control reproductive cycle
- Hunger cravings

Hormones, like other systems in the body, are also affected by stress. When most people think of hormones we generally think about sex hormones—steroidal hormones, the hormones that help control metabolism, inflammation, immune function, salt and water balance, sexual characteristics, and the ability to fight off illness and heal the body.

In my business I receive multiple e-mails daily on health and fitness related topics. No longer do I receive just the typical questions concerning exercise, losing weight, injuries, nutrition, or the latest on supplementations, but more and more questions concerning medications and hormones. Recently I received an e-mail from a man asking my opinion on hormonal therapy. His doctor had recommended hormonal replacement due to his low testosterone level. First, I said that I was not his doctor and second, let's begin our conversation with me asking you a few questions. What is the problem? He says he has low energy; his belly fat has increased around his middle, he has little or no sex drive, erectile dysfunction, feels like he is losing muscle and just does not feel good. His doctor tells him his low testosterone level is causing most of these symptoms and his testosterone levels will continue to decline as he ages. He feels like he needs help and is not sure what path to take.

I continue to explain the basics of hormonal balance. Let's begin with rest and rejuvenation: How is your sleep? I explain the power of sleep and how it is during sleep that testosterone is produced. During Stage 4 of your sleep cycle is when your body is in full repair and many of your healthy sex hormones are released, including testosterone. If you are not getting adequate sleep, your sex hormones and your health can easily become imbalanced. He says his sleep has been poor for many years and he has been taking a sleep medication for the past two years. Second question, how would you rate your stress level on a 1 to 10 scale, with 10 meaning you have so much stress you can't function? Do you feel like you are too stressed? He rated himself an 8.5 on the stress scale. This really threw him. "Everyone has stress," he said. I said, "I agree, but do you feel like you have regular strategies to help you recover from your high amounts of stress?" He flat out said no, that he works too much and feels like he is on the hamster wheel that he can't get off. I wanted him to understand the impact that chronic stress has on his hormones, especially cortisol and testosterone. If the stress hormone cortisol is constantly on alert, then your recovery and building of your sex hormones such as testosterone will be compromised, leading again to an imbalance of hormones. Some physicians refer to this as "cortisol steal," meaning if the body is in constant alarm mode then the stress hormones such as cortisol will become the dominant hormones stealing from the healing and building hormones such as estrogen and testosterone (see Figure 11.1).

Hang with me for just a few more questions. "Are you taking acid reflux medications?" He said, "Yes, for over 10 years." I explained that most acid reflux medications leach out valuable trace minerals, including zinc, and that zinc helps in the building of testosterone. Lastly, I asked, "Are you taking a cholesterol lowering medication?" Again the answer was yes, for the past four years. Statin medications block the production of cholesterol, and cholesterol is the backbone of all steroidal hormones along with blocking the production of CoQ10, one of the most powerful antioxidants produced in the human body. So back to your original question, should

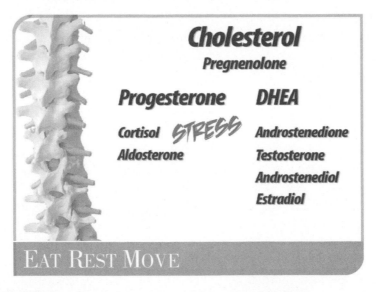

FIGURE 11.1 Cortisol Steal Steroid Hormone Pathway

you be taking a hormone replacement medication? In this case I believe hormonal therapy is not the place to start. Let's begin by getting back to the basics of rest and rejuvenation, quality nutrition, and daily movement! Remember the human body has the amazing ability to heal itself if given the right resources. Start slowly and build a healthy you one step at a time!

THE BOTTOM LINE

1. Hormones are chemical messengers that coordinate physiology and behavior by regulating, integrating, and controlling bodily functions.
2. Hormones affect almost every system in the human body.
3. If your stress levels are high, the stress hormone cortisol is released.
4. Chronic stress may lead to "cortisol steal," hindering the balance of all steroidal hormones.
5. Having daily rest and rejuvenation practices are essential for hormonal balance.

12 Building Your Rest and Rejuvenation Toolbox!

The only people who never fail are those who never try.

—Ilka Chase

Okay, enough about stress and hormones—now is the time to build sustainable rest and rejuvenation strategies that you can build into daily practices. Let's slowly build your rest and rejuvenation toolbox!

Strategy 1: Social Engineering

The logical place to begin with stress control is with the stressor.

If you can identify and weed out many of the unnecessary stressors, you can effectively reduce your stress. One of the most powerful ways you can exert control over your exposure to stressors is social engineering. Social engineering is a coping strategy in which a person begins to rearrange his or her daily behavior to reduce the frequency of encounters with stressors without sacrificing life goals. Social engineering is designed to eliminate unnecessary stressors from life. Can you identify the stressor? Are these stressors predictable? Can the stressor be avoided without sacrificing your goals? Do you have other options or alternatives?

I find that many people don't exercise on a regular basis because they may find it unpleasant or just adds to the pile of stuff they "should be doing" in their day. Can you find a few minutes each day to move your body? Is it possible to reevaluate your current strategy and try another behavior?

When I began writing my first book, I dreaded the thought of writing. I would do almost anything to avoid sitting down and writing. I would read the newspaper, vacuum, do the dishes, look for something to eat; I would do anything but write! One of my goals was to write a book, I wanted to share my thoughts with others, and I knew it would be essential for future career growth, but the process seemed too overwhelming. It seemed like a giant stressor. I was telling my mentor, Al Arens, about this one day during one of our regular meetings. Al said, "You are looking at this all wrong!" "You need to enjoy the process of writing." Al had written multiple textbooks on accounting. I said to Al, "Do you really enjoy the writing process?" He said absolutely! I thought to myself, "How could anyone *enjoy* writing accounting textbooks?" So I began to think of alternative ways to enjoy the writing process. I blocked out uninterrupted time in my schedule, put on the classical music, created a nice environment with a completely different thought process. Today, I truly enjoy the writing process. Social engineering will help you avoid unnecessary stressors, but even more important is learning how to view the stressors in a different light. Taking these small steps can truly make a difference over time and help you achieve your goals without adding to the stressor heap.

Strategy 2: Diaphragmatic Breathing and Breath Awareness

One of the most powerful and effective ways to bring more balance, rest, and rejuvenation back into your life is to learn how to breathe using the diaphragm, or as many people call it *belly breathing*. Think about the basketball player standing at the free throw line with two seconds left on the clock and down by one point. Almost every player tries to slow down, to calm their nerves, and they do this by simply changing the way they breathe.

One of the most important muscles in the human body is the diaphragm, the dome-shaped muscle located at the base of the lungs. Your abdominal muscles help move the diaphragm and give you more power to empty your lungs. There are basically two types of breathing, chest breathing and diaphragmatic or belly breathing. As babies we are all belly breathers, but as we become adults many people slowly become chest breathers. So what is the big deal about diaphragmatic breathing? Diaphragmatic breathing decreases the work load on the heart and lungs by 50 percent, balances the autonomic nervous system, lowers blood pressure, relaxes the mind, improves sleep, and helps keep your pH in balance. If you are a chronic chest breather, you put more stress on the heart and lungs, stay in a chronic fight-or-flight arousal. This increases blood pressure and many times leads to problems with sleep.

The science behind diaphragmatic breathing has to do with balancing the autonomic nervous system (Sympathetic versus Parasympathetic). We have a magical nerve to help us relax and slow everything down called the vagus nerve. The vagus nerve is attached to the base of the diaphragm and travels up into the brain, signaling the parasympathetic nervous system to turn on. When the parasympathetic nervous system is turned on, the sympathetic nervous system is turned off, giving the body and mind a nice relaxation break. Isn't the human body amazing? Whenever you take a slow breath using the diaphragm, the vagus nerve is stimulated, your heart rate slows down, blood pressure drops, digestion improves, energy increases, brain waves slow down, and emotions become balanced. The only time chest breathing is useful is during exercise; the rest of the time should be spent doing diaphragmatic breathing.

How do you know if you are a chest or diaphragmatic breather? If you take more than 12 breaths per minute, you are probably a chest breather. A typical chest breather takes 22,000 to 24,000 breaths per day, as compared to a diaphragmatic breather who takes 9,000 to 13,000 breaths per day. It is pretty simple to see how much more efficient it is and how much less stress diaphragmatic breathing places on the entire body.

Is it possible to learn how to become a diaphragmatic or belly breather? Absolutely, in fact this is one of the first health strategies I teach in my seminars, at our retreats, or during our health and fitness coaching sessions. Here are five tips to follow:

1. Lie on a flat surface, foam roller, or in bed. Bend your knees slightly and place a pillow under your knees. Put one hand on your belly, the other hand on your chest and close your eyes and mouth.
2. Breathe in slowly through your nose so that your belly moves out against your hand. Your chest should not be moving. As you take a deep breath, your belly expands out and as you exhale your belly will come back in.
3. Feel the coolness of the breath through the nose (breath awareness); by focusing on your breath your mind will begin to clear, your body

will relax, and the wonderful benefits of diaphragmatic breathing will appear throughout your body!

4. Practice this exercise everyday for two to five minutes; I personally like to do the belly breathing along with the breath awareness every evening prior to going to sleep. It relaxes my mind and body, and gives me the greatest opportunity to have a restful night's sleep. To increase the intensity of this exercise you can place a heavy book on your belly and watch it rise and fall while paying attention to the breath.

5. If you want to practice diaphragmatic breathing while standing or sitting, follow the same principles along with maintaining good posture (chest up and shoulders down).

Performing diaphragmatic breathing can be therapeutic and with regular practice can become your standard way of breathing!

Strategy 3: The Power of Sleep

One of the most powerful ways to enhance your performance in almost anything you do in life is to get a good night's sleep. I think most people have experienced the feeling of what a good night's sleep feels like and how you performed the following day. I believe we all occasionally have nights when we do not sleep well, especially as we age. Life can be challenging, maybe you had too many demands on your time and did not get in bed early enough or maybe you couldn't shake some of your troubled thoughts; whatever it is, your quality of sleep can suffer now and then. I am not so concerned with the occasional night of poor sleep; what I am seeing in my profession is the chronic sleep issues. We have a serious problem in the United States when it comes to our sleep. Lack of sleep destroys the mind and body. One of the fastest ways to age the human body is lack of sleep. Poor sleep can lead to many health-related problems, such as heart disease, cancer, hormonal imbalances, obesity, headaches, high blood pressure, poor digestion, imbalanced pH, inflammation, joint pain, along with driving accidents and major catastrophes, such as Exxon Valdez and Three Mile Island. Sleep deprivation and sleep disorders cost Americans over $100 billion annually on lost production, medical expenses, sick leave, and environmental damages. On top of these expenses is the cost to our health care system by the dramatic rise in prescription medications for sleep. The answer to our sleep problems is not more prescription medications. The answer lies within you and learning how to improve your lifestyle!

One of my first jobs out of college was driving a bread truck for Butternut Bread. Yes, it is true, I was selling white bread along with Dolly Madison cakes and cupcakes. For an entire year I would wake up at 2:30 a.m. and return home around 6:00 p.m. I was working close to 75 hours a week over a five-day workweek, and I was burned out every way you can imagine. My energy level was extremely low, I had little desire to work out, and I had lost most of my "juice." After leaving Butternut Bread, it took my body almost six months to fully recover, return to my normal sleep cycles, and get my "juice" back. To this day I still have an occasional dream (I call it a nightmare) that I am back working at Butternut Bread; it must have made an impact on my brain and that is why I am sharing it with you.

One of the first questions I ask when inquiring about a person's health and performance is, "how is their sleep?" Most people say their sleep is just okay. Many say they don't get enough sleep, have a hard time getting to sleep, and if they do get to sleep they may wake up multiple times a night and much of the time have difficulty getting back to sleep. I believe most overestimate the amount of sleep they actually get each night. If you are getting less than eight hours per night on a regular basis, or if you fall asleep instantly when your head hits the pillow, you may be one of the millions of people who are chronically sleep-deprived.

So how do we begin our journey toward a better night's sleep? Is it possible to improve the quality and quantity of your sleep? Let's begin by learning more about normal sleep; this may help you recognize what you may be missing in your quest for a better night's sleep.

For an activity we all participate in every 24 hours, most know very little about sleep. There are five stages of sleep that we cycle through approximately every 90 to 110 minutes.

We have all experienced the feeling of falling or twitching while sitting in a meeting, flying on an airplane, or at the movie theater. This is when you are on the edge of sleep—stage 1. Stages 2 and 3 follow very quickly, setting the body up for stage 4, our state of hibernation. Stage 4 is the healing stage for the body and is when your body is in full repair. Your healing hormones like growth hormone, testosterone, and estrogen come out to play and heal the body. Again, this is just one reason when someone has an imbalance with their hormones or is having trouble losing weight;

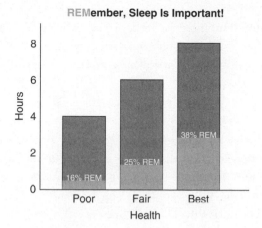

FIGURE 12.1   REM Sleep

the first place to help is by improving their sleep. Stage 5 is when the brain is in healing mode; stage 5 is called Rapid Eye Movement or REM sleep (see Figure 12.1). REM sleep is when we dream; as the night goes on we get into REM sleep quicker. This is one reason it is critical to try and get eight hours of sleep per night due to the amount of time we need to spend in REM sleep. If you are sleeping four to five hours per night, you get very little REM sleep, but if you are sleeping eight hours per night you may double the amount of REM sleep!

So why has getting a good night's sleep become such a challenge? High levels of stress, too much alcohol, energy drinks, coffee, caffeine, soda pop, processed foods, fast food, lack of exercise, health conditions such as heart disease, diabetes, thyroid, COPD, asthma, anxiety, depression, kidney, acid reflux, neurological disorders along with most prescription medications affect the quality of your sleep. I get it that we are not sleeping; now let's focus on the solution.

How Do You Get a Good Night's Sleep?

Step 1: Recognize the Importance of Sleep   Ideally, the human body needs between **seven to eight hours of sleep each night**. The challenge becomes how to get the rest needed to feel your best. Here are a few rest and recovery patterns to start with.

Step one sounds simple, but do you truly recognize how important getting enough sleep plays in your overall health and performance? How a lack of sleep contributes to obesity, poor energy, decreased productivity, poor immune function, increased risk of heart attack, high blood pressure, poor bone health, and hormonal imbalances to name a few? Recognizing the importance of sleep is a major step in your quest for a good night's sleep!

Step 2: Keep a Regular Schedule   When interviewing clients about their sleep habits, I am sometimes amazed how inconsistent their sleep schedules may be. One day they go to bed at 1:00 a.m. and wake up at 9:00 a.m., and two days later they go to bed at 11:00 p.m. and wake up at 5:00 a.m. Keeping a regular sleep schedule is critical in maintaining a synchronized circadian cycle—conditioning the body to expect specific sleep and wake-up times. My general rule is I am in bed almost every night between 10:00 p.m. and 11:00 p.m. (I most likely will turn into a pumpkin if I am not!) and wake up between 6:00 a.m. and 7:00 a.m. Set up a consistent sleep schedule and do the best you can to follow your plan.

Step 3: Sunlight   Getting outside sunlight a few times each day helps the pineal gland, located in the brain, to regulate the production of your sleep hormone, melatonin. During daylight melatonin is low, but as nighttime approaches and darkness sets in, melatonin levels rise. As melatonin levels increase, drowsiness sets in. If you are locked up inside all day long, your pineal gland may have a difficult time recognizing day or night, leading to an imbalance of melatonin production. Just a few minutes of sunlight in the morning and afternoon has a powerful impact on melatonin production.

Step 4: Sleep Environment   One of my keys for getting a good night's sleep when at home or on the road is creating a great sleep environment. Make your room completely dark; if this is a challenge buy some eyeshades. Exposure to excessive light at night, including use of various electronic media, can disrupt sleep or exacerbate sleep disorders, especially in children and adolescence. Any light at night can be disruptive, but in recent years studies have zeroed in on the potent "blue light" emitted abundantly from the energy-efficient screens of our phones and computers as well as many energy-saving florescent bulbs. Because blue light is so prominent in daylight, our bodies associate it with daytime, which is why exposure to blue light can make us more alert. It can also suppress melatonin, our sleep hormone. If there is an illuminated clock in your room, cover it. Don't pick up your phone at night and check your messages. Don't watch television prior to bed if getting a good night sleep is a problem. Any light at all will compromise melatonin levels.

Second, make your sleep environment quiet; for many some type of relaxing sound or white noise can be extremely helpful in drowning out noise. I use a small fan that works the trick for me. One of the most powerful ways to improve your sleep environment is to decrease the temperature in the room to 65 degrees or less. Cool room temperatures play a huge role in stimulating the parasympathetic nervous system, making the body slow down and relax. Also, do you have a good mattress and a form-fitting pillow? Creating an ideal sleep environment can have a great impact on the quality of your sleep.

Step 5: Diaphragmatic Breathing and Breath Awareness Diaphragmatic breathing coupled with breath awareness relaxes the mind and body allowing tremendous benefits in getting to sleep and staying asleep.

Step 6: Hydration Staying properly hydrated has a powerful impact on your overall health and your sleep. Being dehydrated causes the body to become acidic, thus increasing inflammation and constricting blood vessels. Limit caffeine, alcohol, and processed foods and beverages—all of them hinder the quality of sleep.

Step 7: Minerals By now you have a better understanding how important a balanced pH is for overall health. A balanced pH is also important for getting a good night's sleep. If your body is too acidic, the body draws on valuable buffering minerals to maintain this balance. Buffering minerals such as magnesium, which helps to calm the mind and body, may become depleted. Green foods are rich in magnesium, and this is one reason I am such a huge fan of wheatgrass along with spirulina/chlorella, spinach, kale, leafy greens, and broccoli. Cacao (real chocolate), white figs, raisins, and dates also contain magnesium.

Step 8: Healthy Fats Much of our society is deficient in high quality fats. Healthy fats play an important role in brain health, nerve development, and relaxation—along with hormonal balance, all contributing to good night's sleep. Getting enough healthy fats into your daily diet may be your missing link in getting a good night's sleep.

Step 9: Watch Your Stress   Stress can break us down in so many ways, and one of the biggest is how it impacts our sleep. Most of the time it starts slowly, but over time it can be a real killer. If our stress hormones are always on, the adrenal glands get beat up, which may lead to chronic sleep problems. I remember one Saturday morning when I was working at the health club that I was called to the service desk. One of our personal trainers felt like she was having a nervous breakdown. When we met she was crying and could not catch her breath; she was obviously upset, and by looking at her so was I. This was a beautiful person, with amazing passion for health, fitness, and life. She was rundown, highly stressed, not sleeping—not well. We sat privately and slowly she started to calm down. At the time she was raising two young kids, working too many hours trying to make ends meet, along with being a mom and wife. I asked her what was bothering her so much. Personal training can be demanding at times and if you don't get enough recovery time it can burn you out very quickly, and she was definitely burned out. I asked her about her current work schedule; she knew this was a problem, but she did not know how to fix it. She said she had clients each morning at 6:00 a.m., Monday to Friday, and Saturday at 7:00 a.m. She would go to bed around 10:00 p.m., but in the back of her mind she could not relax and stay asleep due to her early morning appointments. I said, what if you started your workday at 8:00 a.m. three mornings a week, and on Saturday you begin at 8:00 a.m., how would you feel? Would you feel more relaxed? Do you think this would help you improve your sleep? I also recommended increasing her coaching fee and cutting out five coaching sessions per week. This would give her similar income along with giving her some needed rest. She slowly began sleeping through the night, had more time to herself, and got her "juice" back!

Step 10: Exercise   Regular exercise has a way of burning up the stress hormones, allowing a calming effect post exercise. Remember the rainy days when you were a kid, stuck inside all day with no place to burn off all of your energy? Go for a walk, take a swim, ride a bike, get moving for a better night's sleep!

Improving your lifestyle and following many of these sleep recommendations can improve the quality of your sleep. Getting a good night's sleep does not have to be a thing of the past!

Strategy 4: Building "White Space" into Your Life

What do I mean by the term "white space"? White space is planned recovery for you. As our lives continue to speed up with work, deadlines, obligations, family, friends, community, we become tugged in so many directions, time feels like it is shrinking, and we sometimes feel we don't have enough time to enjoy life. Everyone tells you, as you get older everything speeds up and the years just fly by. I never understood this when I was in my twenties, but in my mid-fifties I sure do now! If your life schedule is so tight that you have little time for sleep, exercise, eating right, fun, relaxation, you may have to step back and ask "do you like how your life is going?" Is it possible to bring some planned recovery or "white space" into your life? White space can be a simple 90-second stretch or diaphragmatic breathing break during your work day, time to read a book, walk your dog, take a three-day vacation every quarter, turn off your cell phone and computer for 24 hours or maybe have an electronic free weekend. Maybe you're not ready for that just yet, but you get the idea. Time pressures exist for all of us; take time to reflect, step back, and look how you could bring more planned recovery into your day, week, month, and year.

Strategy 5: Meditation

Whenever you hear the word "meditation," what immediately comes to mind? Initially for me it was a 100-year old bearded man, sitting with his legs crossed, high up on a mountaintop searching for the meaning of life. One of my colleagues and mentors in the area of stress and working with the mind, Dr. Phil Nuernberger, changed my thinking on meditation. Meditation is not some hokey type of voodoo medicine, but a simple form of concentration.

Have you ever had some amazing insights while taking a shower, driving down the highway, or going for a long walk? What was it that allowed your mind to open up?

Meditation is a chosen or conscious relaxation exercise, with the goal of clearing the mind, creating peace and serenity, and opening yourself to greater insights. Meditation is a skill that when practiced on a regular basis can help control stress, improve focus, and create a state of calmness and serenity—helping you find the answers to your questions.

Start your meditation journey by paying attention to your breath. Find a quiet place, sit upright with good posture, hands resting on your thighs, close your eyes and mouth, and focus on your breath. Think of nothing, just the coolness of the breath through the nose will quiet the mind and body. Begin your meditation practice with just five minutes per day.

(To learn more about meditation, contact Dr. Phil Nuernberger at www.mindmaster.com.)

Strategy 6: Laugh/Smile/Cry

We all need to spread more love in our world today! I usually am having an amazing day when I can laugh, cry, and smile, all in the same day. How do you feel when you have a good belly laugh, a touching moment that makes you cry or when a stranger gives you a warm smile? The more good you look for in the world, the more you will find. When I am on the road, I try to do three nice things for people, it could be helping someone with their bag on the airplane, opening a door, sharing a smile, or just being kind to someone. I am always looking for opportunities to help people. This may sound a little Pollyanna, but it makes me feel good, and I know it makes others feel good too! For one entire day take this challenge: smile or say hello to everyone you walk by. We all need more love and kindness in our world!

Strategy 7: The Simple Stuff

There are hundreds of simple ways to bring more rest and rejuvenation into your daily life. Here are a few strategies that have helped me:

- Taking a cold shower (even just the last 30 seconds of every shower, boosts your immune system)
- Soft music (Baroque music calms me down)
- Walking barefoot in the grass (I don't do this in the winter in Michigan, but walking barefoot on carpet is the next best thing)
- Take a walk in nature (look and listen to all the beauty around you)
- Massage (I try to schedule a full body massage one to two times per month)
- Foam roller (great for posture and muscle tension)
- Hot tea (try an organic tea, very soothing)
- Stare at the moon or clouds (when I was a kid, we would lay in the grass and look up into the sky—give it a try)

- A 90-second stretch break (changes your focus and feels great)
- Stop and smell the roses!

My goal is to give you a better understanding of stress and strategies to help you deal with stress without turning this topic into a full-blown book. I also want to help you understand how important rest is for you to become your best. There are many wonderful resources on the topic of stress. Start slowly and build some of these rest and rejuvenation practices into your life! (See Figure 12.2.)

Don't underestimate the power that adequate rest and recover can do for you!

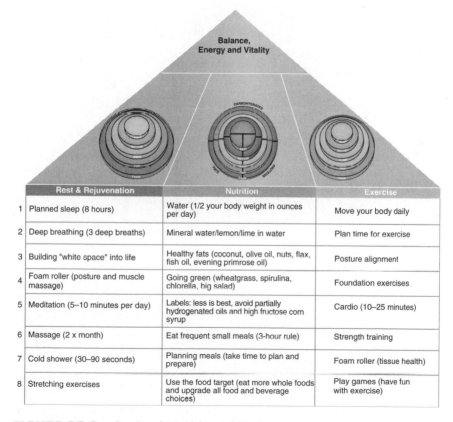

	Rest & Rejuvenation	Nutrition	Exercise
1	Planned sleep (8 hours)	Water (1/2 your body weight in ounces per day)	Move your body daily
2	Deep breathing (3 deep breaths)	Mineral water/lemon/lime in water	Plan time for exercise
3	Building "white space" into life	Healthy fats (coconut, olive oil, nuts, flax, fish oil, evening primrose oil)	Posture alignment
4	Foam roller (posture and muscle massage)	Going green (wheatgrass, spirulina, chlorella, big salad)	Foundation exercises
5	Meditation (5–10 minutes per day)	Labels: less is best, avoid partially hydrogenated oils and high fructose corn syrup	Cardio (10–25 minutes)
6	Massage (2 x month)	Eat frequent small meals (3-hour rule)	Strength training
7	Cold shower (30–90 seconds)	Planning meals (take time to plan and prepare)	Foam roller (tissue health)
8	Stretching exercises	Use the food target (eat more whole foods and upgrade all food and beverage choices)	Play games (have fun with exercise)

FIGURE 12.2 Optimal Health and Performance Pyramid

THE BOTTOM LINE

1. Building rest and rejuvenation practices into your daily life is essential for optimal health and performance.
2. Social engineering is a coping strategy to reduce stressors in your life.
3. Diaphragmatic breathing lowers heart rate, lowers blood pressure, and quiets the brain.
4. Getting a good night's sleep begins with planning your sleep and creating an optimal sleep environment.
5. Planned recovery or "white space" is a key for peak performance.
6. Meditation, laughter, taking a walk in nature, massage, cold shower, foam roller, and listening to soft music are all excellent strategies to bring more rest and rejuvenation into your life!

EAT

13

So What Is Nutrition?

What wisdom can you find that is greater than kindness?

—Jean-Jacques Rousseau

Today more than ever before we are fascinated with the subject of nutrition. Around the world everyone is talking about nutrition.

The Food Network, reality television shows, infomercials, magazines, newspapers, movies, radio, Internet, everywhere you turn, the talk of food has turned into big business. But even more interesting to me is why we know so little about one of the most important sciences of all, nutrition. Growing up in Michigan I learned how to spell, read, write, math, history, but a subject that impacts our energy, welfare, health, and our existence, we know so little about? My first year in college I took "the basics," which included subjects like psychology, geography, creative writing, chemistry, biology, but the subject of nutrition was not included in any of my choices. It was not even an elective class at my university, unless you were going to major in dietetics or another similar discipline. With my graduate degree in Exercise Physiology, we were only required to take two classes on nutrition, and both of these classes had very little if any practical application. Even today most medical schools have little training on the subject of nutrition.

I still don't fully understand why a science that is so amazingly powerful in keeping the human body healthy is not in greater demand with our educational systems. Why is it that over 90 percent of all our cancer research dollars spent in the United States are spent trying to develop medications that help boost the immune system. I believe more of these dollars need to be spent on research learning about the role superfoods and quality nutrition can play in boosting our immune system. We all need to get on board with changing our mind-set towards prevention. We have a wonderful health care system especially when it comes to trauma care, but if you want to stay healthy and prevent most illnesses, our current health care system has no investment and little training in prevention—yet prevention is our future.

Nutrition 101

So what is nutrition? I like to think of nutrition as the process of being nourished. When you eat or drink, the body breaks down the nutrients and uses them for fuel, growth, and repair. Is it possible to be deficient in valuable nutrients with all the food we are currently eating?

There are two types of nutritional deficiencies:

1. A primary nutrient deficiency occurs when the body is lacking a specific nutrient, such as vitamin C, calcium, iodine, or omega-3 fats.
2. A secondary nutrient deficiency occurs when your body fails to absorb or utilize the food or beverages you consumed. You may be eating the necessary foods, but for some reason your body is not absorbing these nutrients.

Nutrition begins with the quality of food and beverages you ingest. Next, how does the body break down these nutrients and absorb them into the body? It is what we ingest and assimilate that fuels the body. This process is called digestion. During digestion the entire body is working not only to break down the foods or beverages you have consumed, but also to help these nutrients to be absorbed into the body. After the digestion process is finished, the body then moves into the elimination phase. Elimination is the process of excreting what is not needed during the digestive process. So what happens if the body is not using the foods or beverages that were ingested along with not being eliminated? These foods become stored, leading to toxicity—and this is where many of our problems begin!

Good Digestion

Upwards of 75 percent of our immune system is based on the health of our gut. If your gut is not healthy, you are not healthy! We have seen an explosion in the amount of digestive health problems, from acid reflux to irritable bowel syndrome, constipation, diarrhea, gluten intolerance, food allergies, bloating and gas, skin problems, asthma, cancer, headaches, inflammation, low energy, type 2 diabetes, poor immune function, along with liver and kidney stress just to name a few. The digestive aisles in most grocery stores and pharmacies continue to expand across our planet. A person who is not digesting food well cannot obtain the optimum amount of nutrients to help build, repair, and regenerate the body. So how do we improve the digestion process so our bodies have the right nourishment it needs? Here are a few steps to follow for improved digestion:

1. **Cut out eating the crap!**

   It all begins with the quality of what you are eating and drinking. If you are overloading the body with a bunch of processed foods and beverages, it will only be so much time before the body says "uncle."

2. **Chew your food!**

   The digestive process begins in the mouth. Your mouth is full of digestive enzymes that help break down and absorb nutrients. This is one reason you should not gulp down beverages: the mouth needs a little time to absorb and activate these powerful enzymes. Also, a major way to improve digestion is to chew your food into liquid. Chewing your food into liquid sounds simple and truly makes a difference. Slow down and chew your food!

3. **Eat more "live" foods!**

   You need valuable digestive enzymes to help break down and absorb nutrients. If you bite into an apple, we all know the apple begins turning brown in just a few minutes. The apple is a live food, full of enzymes, and begins to turn brown after you take a bite as the oxidizing process begins. If you opened a jar of processed applesauce and left it out all day, why doesn't it change color? The enzymes have been compromised in the processing.

   This is big contributor to our digestive health problems in our world today. We are consuming too many dead, processed foods and beverages. Have you ever wondered why some of our foods have a shelf life that goes into the next century? Processed foods have little if any enzymes, making our digestive systems weak and helpless. Consuming "live foods" increases the amount of fiber, anti-oxidants, vitamins, and minerals along with necessary digestive enzymes. You may also buy digestive enzymes at your local health food store, but I suggest starting by eating more live foods first!

4. **Balance your pH!**

    Having a balanced pH in each area of the digestive tract is crucial for optimal digestion and absorption. The stomach needs to be acidic, the small intestine more alkaline, and the large intestine a neutral pH. Balancing pH may take some time if you are currently consuming too many processed, acidic foods and beverages. Consuming more alkaline-based foods and beverages is your first step in balancing your pH, along with daily exercise and controlling your stress.

5. **Control your stress!**

    Have you ever had problems with digestion when you were stressed? I believe we have all felt stressed at one time or another, and our digestion has been compromised. If you are chronically stressed, your digestive workings shut down. This is another way chronic stress can cause disease.

6. **Bring on the "Friendly Bacteria"!**

    In the intestinal tract lies an intestinal flora containing large amounts of friendly bacteria that aids in the digestive and absorption process. When transit time in the intestinal tract slows down, speeds up, or food is not completely digested, our intestinal flora balance can take a hit. Another major reason for a compromised intestinal flora is the widespread use of antibiotics. Antibiotics kill bacteria, including the friendly bacteria, again compromising the digestion process. Adding more friendly or healthy bacteria back into the body may improve digestion.

    Flora-enhancing foods are miso, organic sauerkraut, organic yogurt, organic kefir, and chlorophyll-rich foods such as wheatgrass, spirulina/chlorella, sea vegetables, and most greens. You may also add a high quality probiotic to get more friendly bacteria back into your digestive system. A probiotic supplement may be purchased at most health food stores or from our website.

Five Super Highways of Elimination

A key component in the health of the human body is in its ability to eliminate on a regular basis. The old adage "out with the bad and in with the good" fits when maintaining great health. The human body is designed to eliminate unwanted intruders and toxins. Without regular elimination processes, the body can become toxic and the quality of our health can be drastically impacted. During my seminars I am fascinated by the subject of elimination because for one, most don't truly know how often they should eliminate, and two, this is a subject that is considered private and not to be discussed. Well if your goal is to lose weight, improve energy, decrease disease, and enjoy amazing health, then we need to learn more about elimination. Here are the Five Super Highways of elimination:

1. **Bowel**: How often should you have a bowel movement? This really creates a stir in most of my seminars; most of the time the entire room sits in silence, not knowing for sure the correct answer. Is the correct answer once a day? After every meal? Every other day? What is it? The answer is 1.6 times per day, and your bowel movement should look like a soft banana. The shape of your stool depends on how long it has been in the colon, with 72 hours being ideal. If your dog did not have a bowel movement every day what would you do? Take your dog to the veterinarian? You want to have one to two bowel movements per day, and remember your bowel movement should look like a soft banana. Anything less, you are probably constipated. If you are going more than three times per day and it is still shaped like a soft banana, you are most likely eating too much. Do we really need to know all of these details about poop? Just remember the next time the conversation drags, bring up the subject of bowel movements; you are now an expert.

2. **Urine**: Another way the body eliminates is through the kidneys and urine. Your urine should take on the color of Chardonnay, not too dark and not too light. This is one of the major reasons being hydrated plays such an important role in your health and keeping the body clean. Hydration will be discussed in greater detail in Chapter 16.

3. **Lungs**: You eliminate through your lungs by breathing. This is one reason having good posture and regular exercise is essential for the lungs to help expel toxins.

4. **Skin**: Your skin is the largest organ in the human body and also tells you when digestion is not working correctly. I had skin problems for over 15 years, and it was not until I cleaned up my diet and digestion that my skin improved! Regular exercise, sweating, or using an infrared sauna occasionally helps the body eliminate. What you use on your skin such as lotions, oils, soaps, shampoo, perfume, colognes—even dry cleaning chemicals—can affect the level of toxins the body is exposed to. (This will be discussed in greater detail later in this book.)

5. **Lymph**: The lymphatic system helps in the absorption and assimilation of vital fluids entering the circulatory system. Lymph nodes located under the armpits, in the groin, along the neck and inner thighs play a large role in the elimination of toxins. Lymph fluid penetrates areas too small for blood vessels and functions in the conversion of food to lymph fluid, which then enters the bloodstream. Using deodorants or antiperspirants that contain aluminum chlorhydrate block the lymph under the arm, thus blocking the elimination process of the lymph nodes. Avoid skin products such as creams, lotions, shampoos, soaps, shaving gels, moisturizers, and cosmetics that contain parabens, chemicals used as preservatives, propylene glycol used in anti-freeze or artificial fragrances—all can add toxins to the body along with compromising the elimination process.

THE BOTTOM LINE

1. What is nutrition? Nutrition is the process of being nourished.
2. There are two types of nutritional deficiencies. First, you are deficient in nutrients necessary to keep you healthy, and second, you are not properly digesting and absorbing these nutrients.
3. Seventy-five percent of the immune system is directly related to the health of the gut.
4. To improve digestion, cut out the crap, chew your food, eat more "live" foods, balance your pH, control your stress, and bring on the "friendly bacteria."
5. You have Five Super Highways of Elimination: the Bowel, Urine, Lungs, Skin, and Lymph.

14 Read the Label

All of the significant battles are waged within the self.

—Sheldon Kopp

Ignorance Is Not Bliss!

When we were kids, from time to time we'd find something that looked like it might taste interesting and suddenly Mom or Dad would cry out, "Stop. Do you know what you are putting into your mouth?" The answer, of course, was a shrug of the shoulders and, "No."

We should always know what we are putting into our mouths, and that's precisely why reading food, beverage, or supplement labels should become an essential part of any trip to the market.

For many people, reading a food, beverage, or supplement labels can be so confusing. I love to discuss this topic in my seminars because everyone has their own version of what to look for when reading a label. Food, beverage, and supplement companies may boast loudly about the following attributes: fat free, low carb, cholesterol free, high protein, organic, natural, GMO free, zero trans fats, zero calories, or high in B vitamins. If you looked at a large table of foods, beverages, or supplements, how would you know if one is better than the next?

I truly believe that most people look at calories and taste as the first and second criteria for product selection. I want to move your mindset to *quality* as the number one criteria for product selection. I know taste is important too, but believe it or not, as the quality of the product improves, so does the taste.

Reading labels does not have to be confusing. Here are a few tips that will help you improve your product selections and your health.

Less Is Best!

If you learned one thing about understanding reading labels, this is it: *less is best*. If you picked up a loaf of bread, bag of chips, bottle of salad dressing, box of breakfast cereal, or a frozen pizza and placed them side by side with an identical product, you could quickly determine the better of the two products solely by the number of ingredients listed on the label. For example, a typical loaf of refined white bread may have over 45 ingredients, whereas a loaf of sprouted whole grain bread may have fewer than five ingredients. Generally, the shorter the ingredient list the healthier the food, beverage, or supplement. What do yams, broccoli, almonds, flaxseed, oatmeal, carrots, spinach, natural peanut or almond butter all have in common? They all contain only one ingredient! Less is more—and best.

Avoid Trans Fats

In most traditional grocery stores, there are over 20,000 products that contain trans fats, products such as cookies, cakes, donuts, chips, crackers, bread, refined salad dressings, refined peanut butter, margarine, shortening, microwave popcorn, non-dairy creamers, french fries, and fast food. Trans fats were developed in the 1950's with the hope of lengthening the shelf life to food products; little did the scientists know how trans fats would be so detrimental to our future health! By taking cheap oil such as corn or soybean, adding a metal catalyst and heat through a process called "hydrogenation or partial hydrogenation," the shelf life of the product would last and last and last! The best example of a trans fat is a jar of refined peanut butter, our nation's most popular brand. This jar of refined peanut butter has been traveling with me for over 17 years. It still looks like peanut butter, kind of smells like peanut butter, but what could possibly be in this jar of peanut butter that could preserve it for so long?

Trans fats not only preserve everything they touch but also create havoc on the human body. Trans fats make the cell membrane stiff and rigid, increase inflammation and raise cholesterol. Be aware that "no trans fats" on a label does not always indicate that the product is free of trans fats. According to FDA labeling regulations, a product can claim no trans fats if it contains less than .5 gram per serving. *If you see hydrogenated or partially hydrogenated in the ingredient list, the product contains trans fats.* Today there are so many wonderful options to choose from that are free of trans fats.

Avoid High-Fructose Corn Syrup

Is high-fructose corn syrup (HFCS) something you should avoid? Let's begin with a little history surrounding HFCS. HFCS was first developed in 1957 but it was not viable for mass production. It was not until the late 1970s and early 1980s that HFCS was rapidly introduced to many processed foods and soft drinks. Today HFCS has taken over as the sweetener of choice around the world with the average person in the United States consuming over 60 pounds per year. Think about that: 60 pounds, really? So why has HFCS taken over table sugar as the world's number one sweetener?

- **Price**! It is very inexpensive to produce and corn is also a heavily subsidized crop in the United States.
- **Taste**! It is very sweet and tastes like sugar, containing different combinations of fructose and glucose.
- **Easy to transport**! HFCS comes in a syrup and is transported in tanker trucks, so it is economical and easy to work with.
- **Preservative**! HFCS not only is sweet; it also is used as a preservative.

There is much debate over whether HFCS is worse for you than traditional table sugar. In the 40 plus years since the introduction of HFCS as a cost effective sweetener in the American diet, rates of obesity have skyrocketed. High-fructose corn syrup can't be blamed as the only player contributing to our weight gain and poor health, but HFCS has definitely been major component in our fast growing health concerns.

Reasons to Avoid HFCS

- HFCS does not satisfy your appetite.
- HFCS has an imbalanced ratio between fructose and glucose
- During the manufacturing process of HFCS, fructose molecules are free and unbound, increasing absorption and utilization. Cane or beet

sugar has to go through an extra metabolic step before it can be utilized.

- Most corn grown in the United States is genetically engineered.
- Flat out, we are consuming too much HFCS! HFCS is in everything, from hamburger buns, catsup, yogurt cereal, soft drinks, and everything in between!

If you are eating more whole foods, you have no worries: HFCS lives only in processed foods and beverages!

Say "No" to GMO

Food science is in full swing around the world, especially in the United States. Food scientists are hard at work reengineering thousands of popular foods, beverages, and supplements to contain more nutrients that science and government believe are good, along with getting rid of the bad. With our low-carb, low-fat, high-protein diet phases, food that once contained two to three ingredients on a label, such as peanut butter, bread, or pasta, now has up to 5 to 10 times the amount of ingredients. Why is fat being taken out of peanut butter? How do they take the carbs out of pasta? How do they make bread low in calories? More and more depending on which way the wind blows, food, beverage, and supplement manufacturers are directing their food scientists to come up with ways to reengineer their products to create consumer demand.

Years ago my mom was following a point system program to help her lose weight. She found bread that had very low points and she was so happy, she was convinced this was her ticket to losing weight! The bread she found was Less Bread™. Less Bread™ was a low calorie, processed grain, with almost no fiber; you could pick up a slice and see right through it. No wonder Mom's bread choice had no points; it may have looked like bread, but in my opinion it was air disguised as bread. I helped her understand the concept of food quality versus processed low calories. Mom slowly began to "get it" and today she is leaner, healthier, and in better shape, and if she wants a slice of bread she eats sprouted organic bread. She likes the taste, fiber, and nutrients; it fills her up and contains only a few ingredients.

It is easy to add or delete nutrients with processed foods, beverages, or supplements, but more difficult to change a whole food. Some food science can be good, but when do we stop messing around with Mother Nature?

The Dawning of GMOs

GMOs (genetically modified organisms) are plants or animals created through gene-splicing techniques. This technology combines DNA from different species, creating combinations of plant and animal genes that cannot be found in nature or in traditional crossbreeding. Does this sound like something out of a *Frankenstein* movie? So why were these GMOs developed in the first place? GMOs were developed to offer benefits to the consumer such as increased yield, greater protection from herbicides and drought, along with enhanced nutrition. A growing body of evidence is now showing the claims of many of these consumer benefits are not true, *and* GMOs have been connected with health problems, environmental damage, and violation of farmers and consumers' rights.

Most developed nations do not consider GMOs to be safe. Unfortunately, in the United States, GMOs are in as much as 80 percent of conventionally processed foods and beverages.

Current GMO High-Risk Crops

- Alfalfa (first planting in 2011)
- Canola (90 percent of US crop)
- Corn (88 percent of US crop in 2011)
- Cotton (90 percent of US crop in 2011)
- Soy (94 percent of US crop in 2011)
- Sugar beets (95 percent of US crop in 2011)

Common Ingredients Derived from GMO High-Risk Crops

- Amino acids, aspartame, ascorbic acid, vitamin C, citric acid
- Sodium citrate, ethanol, flavorings, high-fructose corn syrup
- Hydrolyzed vegetable protein, lactic acid, maltodextrins, MSG
- Sucrose, textured vegetable protein, xanthan gum, vitamins, and yeast products

These GMO ingredients are in everything from bread, salad dressings, crackers, frozen pizza, soda pop—almost everywhere you look, GMOs have crept into our food system, and most people have no clue how they got there.

What to do?

To avoid consuming GMO products, eat more organic whole foods, fewer processed foods, beverages, and supplements, and look for the non–GMO product label.

If You Can't Read It, Don't Eat It!

Do you recognize—or can you pronounce—all the words in the ingredient list? The ingredient list starts with the most predominant ingredient by weight and continues in descending order. If you cannot pronounce or recognize ingredients, then this product may be something you don't want to consume on a regular basis.

What *Is* the Serving Size?

When looking at any label, always check the serving size or number of servings in the product. How many times have you reached into a bag of chips and thought nothing of it? After a closer look at the serving size (1 ounce or approximately 7 chips = 140 calories), you may have exceeded the serving size and then some—I know I have. Three or four handfuls of chips, and the next thing I know I have consumed over 400 calories of chips. Be aware that calories can add up quickly if your serving size exceeds the label recommendation.

Also be aware that manufacturers can label products low-fat, light, fat-free or trans fat–free, based on a serving size. If a product has fewer than .5 grams of fat per serving, the Food and Drug Administration (FDA) will allow a product to be labeled fat-free or trans fat–free, even if the product is 100 percent fat. For example, extra virgin olive oil is 100 percent fat, with 14 grams of fat per tablespoon. Compare that to the same brand of extra virgin olive oil no-stick cooking spray, which claims to be free of fat, calories, and cholesterol (food scientists messing around again). This labeling is based on fewer than .5 grams of fat per serving. In this example, a serving size of the no-stick spray is one-third of a second or less. I have tried this many times and have found it impossible to spray the pan for only one-third of a second. So if you use the spray for one-third of a second or less, it is labeled fat-free, but what if you use it for a full three seconds? Read the label and note the serving size.

Supplements—The Good, the Bad, and the Ugly

One of the questions I receive on a regular basis is "Should I take supplements such as vitamin A, vitamin C, Vitamin D, Co-Q10, potassium, iodine, or a multivitamin?" In our busy world it can be difficult to eat as healthy as one would like, and many times people want some sort of security blanket for better health. Most people take vitamins or supplements to replace what's missing in their foods. Now here is the question everyone needs to think about when taking any type of supplement: where is the supplement coming from, the source? There is currently no specific definition for what constitutes a whole food or a synthetic supplement, as far as the Food and Drug Administration is concerned, leaving plenty of room for low quality, inferior supplement options.

When vitamins were discovered, they were discovered in foods, not in isolation, and this is where we began to go in the wrong direction. Most supplements purchased in the United States today are *synthetic*. Synthetic vitamins and supplements are made in a laboratory where chemically reconstructed versions are taken from a food source and then treated with heat, solvents, chemicals, and distillations into isolated vitamins. *Whole food vitamins and supplements*, on the other hand, are found in whole foods and not tampered with in any way that may change their molecules or biomechanical actions. Here is a sample of synthetic vitamins versus whole food vitamins and minerals.

Synthetic Vitamins versus Whole Food Vitamins

Vitamin	Synthetic Vitamins	Whole Food Vitamins and Minerals
Vitamin A	Beta carotene	Carrots/sweet potatoes/spirulina
Vitamin B1	Thiamine mononitrate	Nutritional yeast
Vitamin C	Ascorbic acid	Citrus/oranges/leafy greens
Vitamin D	Ergosterol	Cholecalciferol/cod liver oil
Vitamin E	d-Alpha tocopherol	Wheat germ oil/leafy greens
Calcium	Calcium citrate	Sea vegetables/wheatgrass/almonds
Magnesium	Magnesium oxide	Nuts/spirulina/figs/cacao/sea vegetables, leafy greens
Iodine	Potassium iodine	Kelp/sea vegetables

If the supplement you are looking at does not contain whole foods in the ingredient list, then you are looking at a synthetic supplement that you should avoid. Next time you are looking for a little security to help your diet, choose whole food supplements over the synthetic source.

The supplements I personally focus on come from whole food sources such as wheatgrass, cod liver oil, flax, chia, hemp, spirulina/chlorella, coconut, cacao, nuts, seeds, fruits, and vegetables. More will be said on these Superfoods in Chapter 21.

THE BOTTOM LINE

1. Understanding how to read a label is essential for better health and greater performance.
2. Less is best.
3. Avoid trans fats.
4. Avoid high-fructose corn syrup (HFCS).
5. Say no to GMOs.
6. If you can't read it, don't eat it.
7. Check the serving size.
8. Supplements—choose whole food over synthetic ingredients.

15 Going Organic

Life is an adventure in forgiveness.

—Norman Cousins

What's all the fuss about organic farming? Do we really need to eat more organic foods? Is organic food healthier, more nutritious? Are organic foods always best? What about locally grown foods; do they have to be organic too? Organic foods and beverages are the fastest-growing segment of the U.S. food market, growing at more than 25 percent per year. How foods are grown or raised can impact your health and the environment.

What Does Organic Mean?

The term "organic" refers to the way agriculture products are grown and processed, with specific requirements that must be met and maintained in order for products to be labeled as "organic." In 1990, the U.S. Congress passed the Organic Food Production Act, which ordered the U.S. Department of Agriculture to set certification standards for the production, processing, and certification of organic food. In 2002 the Organic Foods Standards Act finalized these criteria.

Organic food is produced without using pesticides, herbicides, fungicides, antibiotics, and fertilizers made from synthetic ingredients. Organic meat, poultry, eggs, and dairy products come from animals that are not fed or given pesticides, growth hormones, or antibiotics.

103

Benefits of Going Organic

There are multiple benefits by choosing more organic foods and beverages:

- Organic farming is free of pesticides, herbicides, fungicides, and synthetic fertilizers.
- Organic foods taste great.
- Organic farming is better for the environment.
- Organic farming animals are raised without growth hormones and antibiotics.

Eating Locally

For most of my life, I never once thought about where the food I eat comes from. Was last night's dinner of chicken, potatoes, and broccoli grown or raised locally? If not, how many miles away did this food have to travel? 1000 miles? 1500 miles? I think it would be really scary to see where my bologna sandwich, fast food hamburger, or Beefornia came from.

Years ago while traveling in Tuscany, Italy, my wife and I stayed in a hamlet for four days. Every food item on the menu was grown or raised on the property. Our dinner salad, root vegetables, chicken, and lamb, everything that was on our plate came from the farm. The taste and freshness made a huge impact on my wife and me.

There is a wonderful trend toward eating locally. Eating locally represents critical opportunities for all of us. Supporting local food has social, environmental, and economic benefits for everyone. Supporting local farmers markets helps unite communities and is good for the local economy, the environment, and your health. Look for opportunities in your community to support local farming.

How Do You Know It's Organic?

In 2002, the USDA officially divided organic products into four categories, requiring producers and manufacturers to correctly label their products:

100 percent organic: Product states that all of the ingredients are completely organic.

Organic: Product states that at least 95 percent of the contents are organic by weight.

Made with organic ingredients: Product states that at least 70 percent of the contents are organic.

Less than 70 percent of the content is organic: Product may list only those ingredients that are organic on the ingredient panel.

How Much Does It Cost?

Buying more organic foods and beverages does cost more, on average between 10 to 30 percent more. One of the main reasons organic foods are more expensive is that they are *not subsidized*, so consumers are paying more for the cost of growing, processing, shipping, and also preserving the integrity of our land and water sources.

You don't have to move to eating all organic foods overnight. I recommend moving to more *organic animal products first*, due to the growth hormones and antibiotics given to our animals. Choosing local organic eggs and dairy products is a great place to start. You can now buy organic eggs and dairy products in most conventional grocery stores. Buying organic meat sources may be a bit more challenging to find, but there is a large movement to provide more organic animal products at lower prices. Buying more organic fruits, vegetables, and whole grains is important, due to the pesticides and synthetic fertilizers used, but choosing organic animal or fish sources is your first place to start in your organic food journey.

Animal or Fish (buy organic whenever possible)

- Dairy (milk, cottage cheese, cheese, yogurt)
- Poultry
- Game meat
- Beef

If you want to move to more organic fruits and vegetables start with the "Dirty Dozen"! These are fruits and vegetables that have the highest pesticide levels on average, so it's best to buy these foods organically.

Dirty Dozen (high pesticide levels)

- Peaches
- Apples

- Carrots
- Bell peppers
- Celery
- Nectarines
- Strawberries
- Cherries
- Pears
- Grapes
- Spinach
- Lettuce

The "Cleaner Dozen" are fruits and vegetables that have the lowest pesticide levels.

Cleaner Dozen (low pesticide levels)

- Bananas
- Kiwi
- Mangos
- Pineapple
- Asparagus
- Avocado
- Broccoli
- Cauliflower
- Onions
- Peas
- Sweet potatoes
- Tomatoes

Hopefully you are trying to make a few small changes, like drinking more water or eating less fast food, and now the thought of moving to organic food sources seems a bit overwhelming. That's okay. Just keep moving forward with your new changes. As the demand for higher quality food sources continues to climb, more and more farmers markets, health food stores, and conventional grocery stores will offer a variety of organic foods and beverages available to you. Start slowly and enjoy the difference organic foods can make.

THE BOTTOM LINE

1. Organic food is produced without using pesticides, herbicides, fungicides, antibiotics, or fertilizers made from synthetic products.
2. In 2002, the USDA officially divided organic products into four categories: 100 percent organic, 95 percent organic, 70 percent organic, and less than 70 percent of the content is organic.
3. Benefits of eating organic include that it's free of toxins, fresher, tastier, and better for our environment.
4. Eat locally whenever possible to support your local farmers and community.
5. Start slowly and enjoy the difference organic foods can do for you.

16

What Are We Drinking?

Desire creates the power.

—Raymond Holliwell

Over the past 50 years, the variety of foods available, and the consumption of certain foods, has changed dramatically. The same is true of the types and quantity of the beverages we drink. I truly believe the beverages we are currently drinking are causing as many health problems as the foods we are eating.

Soda Pop

Soda pop is the number one beverage in the United States. *Number One!* The average American drinks over 70 gallons of soda pop per year. I am doing the math on this: 300 million plus people × 70 gallons = 3 billion gallons of soda pop per year consumed in the United States. This number continues to grow, especially among our children and teenagers. Mexico has now taken over as the number one consumer of soda pop per person in the world. And now type 2 diabetes is growing so quickly that Mexico now ranks number two in the world just behind the United States in type 2 diabetes, not a stat to be proud of.

In my work and travels, one of the first beverage options I am usually given is soda pop. I was at a gas station not long ago, and this guy comes in to get a refill of his 44-ounce soda pop. Who could possibly need a refill of a 44-ounce soda pop? Is this guy crossing a desert? I try not to be the food police, but how can you not notice a 44-ounce cup? You have to be pretty strong just to hold onto to that monster. Waiting in line at our local movie theater, I was shocked to see there were 72 refill stations for soda pop and energy drinks, but not one was for water. I guess you could refill your water bottle up out of the bathroom facet.

The most negative implication of the upward trend in soda pop consumption is the corresponding increase in sugar, artificial sweeteners, and phosphoric acid. On average, Americans consume over 200 pounds of sugar and over 35 pounds of artificial sweeteners. Too much sugar, artificial sweeteners, and phosphoric acid can lead to a litany of health problems, such as obesity, type 2 diabetes, inflammation, headaches, constipation, acid reflux, poor bone health, and low energy. If you are feeling tired and stressed more than you would like, maybe it's time to cut back or slowly wean yourself off your soda pop altogether. In my seminars I recommend switching over to mineral water with a splash of fruit juice. I like the taste of pomegranate or dark cherry juice. Most people enjoy the naturally occurring carbonation from the mineral water and a little sweetness from the fruit juice. Mineral water is alkaline, curbs your appetite, and is refreshing. If you have an occasional soda pop, not to worry, but if you find yourself drinking multiple servings per day and don't like how you feel, then maybe it's time to make some changes.

Coffee

Americans just love their coffee, over 450 million cups per day! Coffee shops are virtually everywhere and ordering a cup of coffee now has a language all of its own. People enjoy the taste, aroma, warmth, and quick pick-me-up that coffee provides. For many, drinking a cup of coffee is a big part of their morning ritual.

Not long ago, my sister Paula was explaining to me she is going to stop drinking coffee. I said, "Why? You love your coffee." She said "I know, but coffee is not good for me. Coffee is acidic, places stress on the adrenal glands, leaches out valuable minerals, and inhibits the absorption of iron, magnesium, zinc, and B-vitamins." She was giving me an earful of the harmful effects from drinking coffee. I did not ask for a scientific breakdown, but she was giving it to me anyway. "I get all that," I told her, "but the bottom line is you only drink one cup in the morning and you truly love your coffee." She said yes, that she truly loves the taste, the smell, the quick pick-me-up she gets by drinking her coffee. I told her, "Upgrade the quality of your coffee whenever you can and enjoy your one cup each day."

Coffee and tea are crops that use a great deal of pesticides, so if you love your coffee or tea, I would highly recommend choosing organic coffee or tea whenever possible. Organic coffee is pesticide free and less acidic. If you use some form of creamer in your coffee, remember to avoid partially hydrogenated oils; many creamers contain these unhealthy trans fats. There are many healthy creamers to choose from that taste great and are good for you. Also, many of our coaching clients use a variety of plant-based milks such as coconut, almond, or hemp in their coffee.

Tea

Tea is the most widely consumed beverage in the world, second only to water. For years, followers of alternative medicine have touted the health benefits of drinking tea. There are many different types of tea to choose from, such as white tea, oolong tea, black tea, and green tea. All tea is green before it has been aged. Green tea has attracted more and more followers as the word spreads about its health and medicinal benefits. Green tea is high in catechins, antioxidants that block the action of harmful free radicals. The health benefits of green tea include reducing the risk of certain types of cancer, heart disease, boosting the immune system, and aiding digestion by improving the growth of beneficial bacteria in the intestines. Green tea has less caffeine than coffee and is also more alkaline. Remember to choose organic tea whenever possible.

Milk

In the United States, we drink over 25 gallons per person per year. Of the milk we drink, over 90 percent is cow's milk. I personally believe the human body is not meant to consume cow's milk. But what about calcium—if I don't drink milk or consume dairy, where am I going to get my calcium from? In the United States, we drink lots of milk and still have poor bone health. Drinking cow's milk is not a great source of calcium and is highly acidic. Along with being highly acidic, cow's milk has a very large protein molecule and is difficult for the human body to break down, causing digestive challenges, skin rashes, psoriasis, allergies, and asthma.

When my daughter was in middle school she was diagnosed with asthma and put on a bronchial inhaler. I was thinking to myself, why all of a sudden does Kristen have asthma? The doctor never asked Kristen what she was eating or drinking. I knew Kristen was not eating very healthy and with my history of skin rashes, there had to be more to this story. Kristen was a track athlete and her running the 400-meter with asthma really concerned her mom and me. I believed at the time, Kristen was consuming too many dairy products; she was eating too much cheese, yogurt, and milk. I sat Kristen down and said, "Let's cut out all dairy for 60 days and see what happens." She did—and her asthma along with the inhaler went away.

If you are currently drinking cow's milk and are not ready to give it up then move to an organic source of cow's milk. The most consumed milk in the world is goat's milk. Okay, so you may not be ready for goat's milk, but it is a healthy option for those who may be allergic to lactose found in cow's milk. Goat's milk is easier to digest than cow's milk and contains caprylic acid, which is antifungal. Along with goat's milk, there are many wonderful great-tasting milk options available to you. I recommend plant-based milk to everyone. They are easier to digest and are much more alkalizing for the body. My personal favorites are almond, coconut, and hemp milk. Other milk options include hazelnut, oat, multigrain, rice, and soy. If you choose soy milk, make sure you are buying organic soy milk because approximately 90 percent of all soy now grown in the United States is genetically modified. If you have problems with allergies, skin irritations, or respiratory issues, and like drinking milk, it may be time to look at the quality and quantity of the milk you are drinking.

Juice

As our lifestyles speed up, more and more people are looking to juice to get more fruits and vegetables into their diets. Drinking juice makes it easy to get a variety of valuable vitamins, minerals, and antioxidants into your diet. Juicing has become common practice for many health conscious consumers.

Personally I also find it challenging at times to get healthy nutrients into my body. I use a juice extractor once a week, and my favorite juice recipe is a combination of beets, celery, carrots, and apples. It tastes great, is extremely alkalizing, and is an easy way to bring more healthy nutrients into my diet. I make enough for a few days and put it in a glass container to store in the refrigerator. This way I can have the wonderful benefits of juicing last over a few days. You can also freeze the juice in an ice cube tray, which makes easy, great tasting healthy snacks for you and your family. Many people in my seminars ask me about my thoughts on the "Vitamixer." A Vitamixer looks and acts like a blender on steroids. It pulverizes anything you place in it. With the Vitamixer, you get the fiber. With a juice extractor there is no fiber, but the juice is more condensed. They both are wonderful options for making fresh juice and other healthy snacks.

My number one juice is wheatgrass juice. I take wheatgrass juice daily in the form of frozen ice cubes. I suck on it just like an ice cube, or you can mix it with a cup of water. I take three ice cubes first thing in the morning; it is easy, high in vitamins, minerals, antioxidants, and is most alkaline. Believe it or not, it tastes good. Well, I like it. More will be said about wheatgrass in the Super Foods chapter (Chapter 21).

For many of my clients, I also recommend diluting organic cherry, cranberry, or pomegranate juice as a way to keep their bodies alkaline and detoxified on a regular basis. Take eight cups of water to one cup of organic cherry, cranberry, or pomegranate juice, and drink one to two cups per day. There is no substitution for eating whole fruits and vegetables, but drinking high quality juice is the next best thing. When selecting juice, choose only 100 percent high quality juice.

Sports Drinks

One of the fastest growing segments of the beverage industry is that of sports drinks, especially with teenagers and young adults. It seems like everywhere you go, you see sports drinks in the hand of these young people. In the gym, at a sporting event, or just hanging out, these drinks have just exploded onto the beverage scene. Every major beverage manufacturer now has its own line of sports drinks. Many of these sports drinks are disguised as a healthy alternative, but in most cases they are loaded with sugar or high fructose corn syrup and are calorically dense.

If you are engaging in endurance type activities and are looking for a beverage that is high in electrolytes but does not contain a bunch of unhealthy ingredients (including high fructose corn syrup), there are many drinks to choose from. My personal favorites are organic coconut water or alkaline water with a lemon or lime.

Jack-Me-Up Drinks

This is a product line that I have become very passionate about and not in a positive way. If you want to get me jacked up, bring up the subject of energy drinks. Do people truly believe that having an energy shot from a can is a good thing? Okay, Chris, settle down. Let's start with the facts, just the facts.

Today energy drinks have exploded into the fastest growing group of beverages on the planet. The first energy drink introduced in the United States was Red Bull, back in 1997. The energy drink industry has grown into big business with powerful marketing and advertising targeting your kids, teens, young adults, and now anyone with a pulse. We currently have over 100 different energy drink options on the market, and this list will continue to grow. Red Bull, 5-Hour Energy, Monster, Full Throttle, AMP, Cintron, and Rip It; the list is long and ugly. Just the other day I was in our local pharmacy buying some razor blades when on the shelf I spotted 14-Hour Energy! Really, 14 Hours of Energy? I had to buy this rocket fuel to see what it looked and smelled like. It was light blue in color and smelled like the cough syrup I was given as a kid; that smell is etched in my brain for life! Can you imagine trying to get a good night's sleep after drinking this volcanic concoction?

Let's begin with a few crazy questions. Why would a normal, healthy person not be able to get through their day without an injection of a jack-me-up drink? Where do you get energy? Energy comes from the food we eat, proper rest, and movement. Why are so many people looking for more energy? Why are many people so tired? I get that life can beat us up, but do we truly believe getting energy from a can or shot is going to be sustainable? Do we believe there will be no side effects from this liquid TNT?

So what gives us energy from these energy drinks? Most of these high octane, jack-me-up drinks are loaded with thermogenic compounds such as taurine, inositol, choline, ginseng, yerba mate, tyrosine, guarana, and L-carnitine. These thermogenic compounds are purported to produce heat and overstimulate your adrenal glands. Along with the thermogenic compounds, many energy drinks have high levels of caffeine, synthetic B-vitamins, niacin, sugar, and artificial ingredients. Some of the common side effects from energy drinks include dehydration, huge energy swings, mineral depletion, irritability, adrenal fatigue, sleeplessness, increased urination, decreased bone health, acid reflux, poor digestion, increased heart rate and blood pressure, nausea, heart arrhythmia, and even death. If you are chronically fatigued, have lost that pep in your step, energy drinks are not the answer. Avoid all energy drinks and help educate our next generation of the potential hazards energy drinks may bring.

Alcohol

One of the questions I receive on a regular basis is what about alcohol? Is drinking a glass of wine per day good for you? If you wish to drink an alcoholic beverage, is one better than the other?

Calories aside, red wine is your best choice. Many people ask me about resveratrol, the magical fountain of youth antioxidant found in many plants, including the skin of red grapes. But before you run out and buy a case of red wine, you should know that there is very little resveratrol in red wine. You would have to drink over 200 glasses of red wine per day to get even a trace amount of resveratrol. However, red wine is not as acidic and has more antioxidants than other alcoholic beverages, followed by white wine, liquor, and beer. Beer is the most acidic alcoholic beverage. Drink alcohol in moderation.

Water: Your Body's Drink of Choice!

Water is essential for life and keeping the body healthy. The body is 70 to 75 percent water. If you asked me what I pay attention to the most from a nutritional standpoint, my answer would be water, water quality, and the amount of water I am drinking. Drinking enough water is one of my biggest challenges throughout my day. I always try to put water in front of me to remind myself to drink more—in the car, next to my bedstand at night, working out, on the road—wherever I go, I try to make sure I am drinking enough water and staying well hydrated.

So what is the big deal about drinking water? Water is the body's cleansing and waste removal fluid. Water carries nutrients and oxygen, cushions joints, protects organs. Water also aids in digestion and metabolism. A common problem with so many people is fatigue or lack of energy. Not having enough water contributes to fatigue. Water composes over 90 percent of your blood. As the body becomes dehydrated, blood is the first place your body looks for more water. When the body pulls water from the blood, blood volume decreases and your energy also decreases, due to a drop in cardiac output. From a health and performance standpoint, staying hydrated is critical.

Unintentional chronic dehydration may be the root of many serious diseases, including asthma, endocrine and kidney problems, high blood pressure, arthritis, ulcers, pancreatitis, digestive problems, low back pain, and obesity. A mere 2 percent drop in body water may lead to dizziness, short-term memory loss, difficulty focusing, constipation, a drop in muscle contraction strength, muscle cramping, as well as a drop in muscular endurance.

Keeping your body properly hydrated is not just about drinking the right amount of water; it's also important to understand water quality. The quality of the beverages we drink plays a huge role in balancing our body's pH level. Beverages such as alcohol, coffee, soda pop, energy drinks, and many sports drinks are acidic. As the acid levels in the body begin to rise, the body pulls out all of its defenses to bring the pH back into balance. First, the body flushes the acid out of the body, causing greater dehydration. Second, valuable minerals such as calcium, magnesium, potassium, sodium, and iodine are slowly leached out of the body in an effort to buffer higher acid levels. Dehydration and many diseases such as osteoporosis, high blood pressure, kidney stones, and type 2 diabetes are linked to over-acidification of the body.

Is There a Difference in Types of Water?

Okay, so I understand the need to drink more water, but now you are telling me there are differences between the types of water we drink. I thought water was just water? Times have changed, and so has the water we drink. Let's discuss the different types of water and determine the best type of water to drink.

Tap Water

Many sources of tap water may contain chlorine and other toxic ingredients. Chlorinated tap water destroys beneficial bacteria in the body, which can weaken and damage the immune system. High levels of chlorine in drinking water have also been linked to heart disease and cancer. My first recommendation is to get your tap water checked for high levels of chlorine and other toxic ingredients. If you suspect your tap water to be unhealthy, you may want to look into buying an ionized water filtration system. Also to improve the alkalinity of normal tap water, add a slice of lemon or lime.

Ionized Water Filtration System

It seems like every day there's another new miracle pill, cream, exercise tool, or berry that is going to lead us to a life of amazing health. Is there truly a way to make our water healthier? Maintaining a balanced pH is critical for your health; this was discussed in detail back in Chapter 7. Finding a good water source is also critical in your quest for a balanced pH and your overall health. So what is ionized water and is it beneficial?

Ionization simple means the gain or loss of electrons. Water that has been ionized becomes either alkaline or acidic, meaning the pH has been adjusted up or down. Back in the early 1950s, two Russian scientists discovered a way to split a stream of water into two parts, one acidic and one alkaline. The process uses a series of magnets to create an electrolysis process. The result? Negatively charged "ionized" water that is restructured for enhanced absorption, hydration, and is high in antioxidants and minerals. There are three main benefits of consuming ionized water: first, it is a powerful antioxidant; second, it is extremely alkalizing for the body; and third, it is much more hydrating and detoxifying than conventional water.

If you want a great water source in the convenience of your own home, are tired of buying bottled water and concerned about the environment, I would highly recommend buying an ionized water filtration system. I have owned my ionized water filtration system for over 10 years. It attaches easily to most kitchen faucets and costs around $600 to $700. Oh, one more thing: my dog Dolly always chooses the ionized water over the conventional tap water.

For more information on purchasing an ionized water filtration system, go to www.watershed.net.

Mineral Water

One of the easiest ways to improve your health is to drink mineral water on a daily or weekly basis. I personally consume approximately 40 to

50 ounces of mineral water per week. Mineral water is highly alkaline and helps to maintain essential minerals in the body. Choose only mineral water with natural occurring carbonation. Mineral water can also be purchased without carbonation; in Italy they refer to it as "with or without the gas." So if you don't like mineral water due to the carbonation, you can also purchase mineral water that has no carbonation. Add a slice of lemon, lime, orange, or a shot of juice for a refreshing taste.

Bottled Water

Today bottled water is big business with over 700 brands available in the United States. I remember thinking back in the 1970s when bottled water first hit the market: are you kidding me, do they think people are really going to pay for water that they put in a bottle? Yet today bottled water is big business. The important thing to remember when purchasing bottled water is to *choose only natural spring or artesian water*.

Purified or Reverse Osmosis Water

Creating healthy water means removing the harmful ingredients but keeping the beneficial minerals. Purified water sounds healthy, but it is missing some important ingredients, namely minerals. Stripping the water of harmful toxins is good, but removing all the minerals from the water is not good. Drinking purified water over time can leach out valuable minerals from the body. Avoid drinking purified or reverse osmosis water for any length of time.

Distilled Water

More and more people are interested in the detoxification benefits of drinking distilled water. Consumption of distilled water in large quantities washes waste products and toxins from the body due to its acidic nature. So there are some real benefits of drinking distilled water on an occasional basis for detoxifying benefits, *but you do not want to drink distilled water on a regular basis because it draws minerals from the body and causes dehydration*.

Many bodybuilders drink distilled water two to three days prior to a contest in an attempt to rid the body of excess water and create the "ripped" look. A few years ago, one of the contestants I was competing against in a bodybuilding contest was so dehydrated he had to wait over five hours to come up with enough urine to be drug tested. I asked him later what he was doing to cause this excessive dehydration. He said he drank three gallons of distilled water two days in a row and then did not drink an ounce of water for the next two days. The only water he received was from the food he ingested. This may be an extreme case, but remember, distilled water is not to be ingested on a regular basis.

How Much Water Do You Need?

Ideally you should drink half your body weight in ounces of water per day. If you weigh 150 pounds, then you need approximately 75 ounces of water per day. *Your body's need for water increases with exercise.* If you are currently drinking only 20 ounces of water per day, then move to 30 ounces per day. Start slowly and build the habit of drinking high-quality water into your daily plan! Give your body the water it needs: let water be your drink of choice.

THE BOTTOM LINE

1. We are drinking more of our calories than ever before. Limit your calories from beverage sources to 250 calories per day.
2. Beverages such as soda pop, coffee, alcohol, cow's milk, distilled water, and energy drinks have high acidic levels and may lead to dehydration and mineral depletion.
3. Mineral water with a splash of juice or a slice of lemon or lime is a great way to balance your pH, improve digestion, and enhance bone health.
4. Upgrade all the beverages you consume: water, juice, milk, tea, and coffee.
5. Let water be your drink of choice, and drink approximately half your body weight in ounces of water per day.

17

Macronutrients/ Food Target

The Core of On Target Living Nutrition

Slow and steady wins the race.

—Aesop

Many people ask, so what should I eat? I tell them, you should focus on eating macronutrients, or in simpler terms "whole foods." What are macronutrients? Macronutrients are carbohydrates, proteins, and fats. Macronutrients are the fuel source for our bodies and minds:

- Carbohydrates—fuel your body
- Proteins—build your body
- Fats—heal your body

Learning to improve the quality of the foods you eat and beverages you drink is the essence of the On Target Living nutrition program. To help people learn more about the three macronutrients, along with eating in greater balance and improving food quality, I developed a simple, easy-to-use guide, "The Food Target" (see Figure 17.1). The Food Target focuses on a balance of carbohydrates, proteins, and fats while incorporating an assessment of the quality of these nutrients. The Food Target has the lowest nutritional value foods on the outside of the target. These are the foods that contribute the least nutrition to the body and can even be detrimental to your health. In the Food Target, the most beneficial, most nutritious foods—those that make the body stronger—are closer to the center of the target. The idea behind the On Target Living Nutrition program is to

119

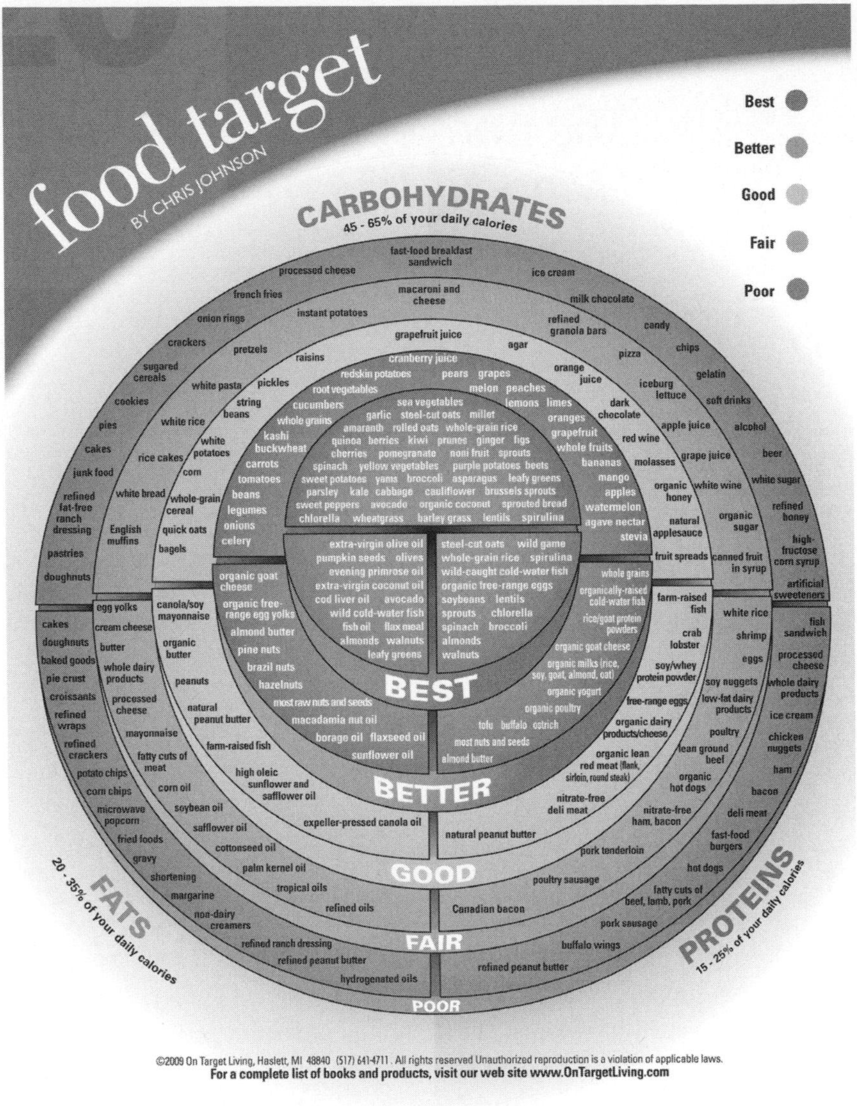

FIGURE 17.1 Food Target

achieve balanced eating around the target and to concentrate your eating as close to the center of the target as possible. You will find foods in their most natural states closer to the center of the target. Most importantly, it allows people to change at their desired pace: you don't have to go from the outer ring to the center all at once. The Food Target is meant to be forgiving. Use the Food Target as a learning tool and a lifelong guide for eating. Throughout the next three chapters, I will help you understand how your waistline, energy, mood, overall day-to-day performance, and your health are affected by the quality and type of macronutrients you consume.

Place the Food Target on your refrigerator and refer to it on a daily basis.

THE BOTTOM LINE

1. Macronutrients are carbohydrates, proteins, and fats.
2. Upgrading the quality of your foods and beverages is the essence of the On Target Living Nutrition Program.
3. The Food Target is a simple, easy-to-use guide to help you improve your food choices.

18

Carbohydrates—
Fuel Your Body!

Life is what happens to you while you're making other plans.
—Napoleon Hill

What is a carbohydrate? Carbohydrates are sugar chains linked together. Generally the shorter the sugar chain, the more processed or refined the carbohydrate. The more refinement or processing that goes into the carbohydrate, the less fiber, vitamins, minerals, phytochemicals, and antioxidants the carbohydrate contains. The longer the sugar chain, the greater the amount of fiber, vitamins, minerals, phytochemicals, and antioxidants; these are the types of carbohydrates that create better health and performance.

Long chain carbohydrates are whole foods with little or no refinement or processing. A doughnut and broccoli are both in the carbohydrate family, but that is where their relationship ends. Doughnuts have short sugar chains, are nutrient deficient, and cause a quick spike in blood glucose. Broccoli, on the other hand, has long sugar chains, is nutrient-dense, and cause little change in blood glucose.

Why do we need carbohydrates? Energy! *Carbohydrates are your body's main energy or fuel source.* Carbohydrates also provide the body with valuable fiber, vitamins, minerals, phytochemicals, and antioxidants for the brain and nervous system.

Are Carbohydrates Good or Bad?

I want to make clear right from the beginning that carbohydrates are necessary for energy, health, and optimal performance. You will be reading

122

a common phrase or question throughout the rest of this book, "*It depends.*" This phrase or question is critical in determining the quality of the foods or beverages you are consuming. So when someone asks, "are carbohydrates good or bad?" Your answer is, it depends! It depends on the quality of the carbohydrate. In our society many people believe the best way to lose weight is to cut back on your carbohydrate intake without fully understanding the role high quality carbohydrates play in keeping the body fit, healthy, and happy. With the growing demand for weight loss diets, many carbohydrates have been lumped together as foods to avoid if you are trying to lose weight.

A few years ago a woman approached me in my hometown grocery store. She asked, "Aren't you that nutrition guy?"

I said, "Yes, I have written books on nutrition and speak around the world about nutrition in my On Target Living seminars."

She asked, "Do you eat bananas?" I had a bunch of bananas in my grocery cart at the time. I said, "Yes, I eat bananas.

She then said, "I am a little surprised that you eat bananas. Did you know that they are high on the Glycemic Index?" "Yes," I said. "I knew that." She said, "Oh, I didn't think you would eat bananas due to their high Glycemic Index." She then started to walk away with a smirk on her face.

Caught off guard, I felt like I had just been scolded, and I think I was. I decided to walk after her. I could not let this go. "Excuse me," I said. "Since when did a banana become an unhealthy carbohydrate choice? A banana is one of nature's perfect foods, beautifully packaged, full of vitamins, minerals, fiber, and tastes great." She was not buying the benefits of eating a banana. In her mind bananas raise your blood glucose quickly and make you fat. Yes, bananas are high on the glycemic index, but due to a banana's high level of vitamins and minerals, bananas fall into the better category on the Food Target. You do not have to go through life being afraid of eating a banana or other fruits that are high in sugar.

In many of the high-protein, low-carbohydrate diet plans, you take fruit out of the diet for the first few weeks, and many fruits are totally forbidden in the diet altogether. Since when does a banana, blueberry, or an orange make you fat? To me this sends a message that fruit makes you fat. Yes, there are many processed carbohydrates that cause poor health and weight gain, but first we need a better understanding of all carbohydrates.

Carbohydrates are our energy foods. Carbohydrates are essential for better health and performance. Along with all the benefits that were mentioned earlier, carbohydrates are necessary to fuel the brain. The human brain needs 400 calories of carbohydrates per day to function properly. And carbohydrates are the only source of energy the brain can use, except during starvation.

Your goal each day is to consume between 45 and 65 percent of your total calories from quality carbohydrates. Examples of carbohydrates include apples, oranges, asparagus, and broccoli, rolled oats, sweet potatoes, lentils, soda pop, and sugar. Some carbohydrates, such as cereals, bagels, and pasta, contain a large amount of carbohydrates. Other foods, such as leafy greens, asparagus, and broccoli, contain a small amount of carbohydrates.

In our fast-paced, convenient, prepackaged food society, carbohydrates fall on a continuum between refined and unrefined carbohydrates. Refined carbohydrates have been processed and stripped of essential nutrients and are lacking in fiber, vitamins, minerals, phytochemicals, and antioxidants. These include refined cereals, white bread, crackers, cookies, potato chips, candy, soda pop, instant potatoes, and sugar, to name a few. Unrefined carbohydrates are foods in their most natural state. These include fruits, vegetables, whole grains, starches, and legumes. Consuming unrefined carbohydrates helps the body stay healthy and perform at its best. Carbohydrates are also our primary source of fiber.

Fiber

Fiber is necessary for optimal health. Fiber helps reduce the risk of certain cancers, lowers cholesterol, stabilizes blood glucose, and promotes regularity. Fiber absorbs water as it moves through the digestive tract and adds bulk to feces. It moves food quickly through the digestive system and enhances fat loss. Fiber also slows down the insulin response; this is one reason that eating whole fruit does not raise your blood glucose as much as drinking fruit juice, which contains little or no fiber.

The National Cancer Institute recommends an intake of 25 to 30 grams of fiber daily. Most Americans eat less than 15 grams per day.

Types of Fiber

Water-Soluble Water-soluble fiber helps reduce cholesterol and slows insulin response. Some water-soluble fiber sources include oats, amaranth, millet, barley, flaxseeds, chia seeds, psyllium, carrots, beans, peas, strawberries, apples, and citrus fruit.

Water-Insoluble   Water insoluble fiber helps supply the bulk that keeps food moving quickly through the digestive tract, acting like a broom sweeping out undigested material, promoting regularity, and reducing the risk of certain kinds of cancers. Leafy greens, whole grains, root vegetables, and skins from fruits and vegetables all contain water-insoluble fiber.

You can easily obtain 25 to 30 grams of fiber per day by eating foods in their most natural state, such as fruits, vegetables, whole grains, nuts, seeds, and beans.

While we are discussing fiber and its benefits, let's discuss the question, "How regular are you?" How often do you have a bowel movement? The answer should be 1.6 times per day, and it should look like a soft banana. If this sounds like a little too much information for you, hang in there: I am almost done with the poop questions.

Are you constipated more than you like? The answer to this question in most cases is directly related to the quality of the food we eat, and the beverages we drink or lack thereof. Some folks are like clockwork: same time, same place, you get the picture. Others are just the opposite; they have no regular pattern, they may go two days in a row, and then they do not have a bowel movement for three days. They have no consistency at all. I have even had coaching clients tell me they have a bowel movement one to two times per week.

Having a consistent bowel movement is one way in keeping your body healthy. If your dog did not have a bowel movement for three days, would you be concerned? "Is my dog sick? Why is my dog constipated? Is my dog not getting enough water? Is my dog eating the wrong type of food?" You may want to ask these same questions of yourself if you are not as regular as you like.

In February of 2000, while playing basketball with my son and a few of his friends, I ruptured the patella tendon in my knee. It was an ugly injury, and I immediately went into surgery to get it repaired. After the surgery, the surgeon explained the surgery, that three screws are holding my knee in place, and that in approximately three to four days I would be in a heap of pain due to the femoral block in my leg wearing off. I had already been taking morphine and now Vicoden was added for pain management, and I was sent home. The surgeon was right, at day three I was in a heap of pain, but it was not due to pain in my leg; it was from being constipated. I had not had a bowel movement in over three days. I had never taken any type of prescription pain medications before, and one of the side effects of these medications is constipation. This was something new to me, and I was becoming desperate in my need to alleviate my discomfort. Due to my injury and surgery, I was highly medicated, dehydrated, and flat on my back, unable to move and out of my normal eating patterns. I was desperate in my need to alleviate my constipation. So I stopped taking my prescription pain medications and went to the old reliable, cod liver oil and ground flaxseeds.

Cod liver oil improves viscosity, and flaxseeds are a powerful fiber source that has been around for hundreds of years. One of the benefits of using ground flaxseeds is that it keeps everything moving, if you catch my drift. I doubled my normal dose of each, taking four tablespoons of cod liver oil and four tablespoons of ground flaxseeds, and placed everything in a large glass with a few ounces of pomegranate juice. Down the hatch, and within two hours I was clean as a whistle. One question that comes up in my seminars occasionally: Can you consume too much healthy omega-3 fat? You now know the answer.

There are many factors that contribute to regularity. Let constipation be a thing of the past by following these seven simple tips:

1. Develop consistent meal patterns.
2. Eat more whole foods and high quality fats.
3. Consume 25 to 30 grams of fiber per day.
4. Stay properly hydrated.
5. Get seven to eight hours of sleep.
6. Watch your stress.
7. Move your body on a daily basis.

Types of Carbohydrates

Fruits: berries, oranges, apples, kiwi, cherries, prunes, figs, lemons, limes, grapefruit, watermelon, peaches, melon, pears, bananas, avocados, mangos, apricot, plums

Vegetables: cauliflower, broccoli, asparagus, sweet peppers, kale, sprouts, cabbage, parsley, leafy greens, wheatgrass, sea vegetables

Whole grains: oat groats, steel cut oats, rolled oatmeal, millet, wheat, rye, amaranth, spelt, barley, quinoa, rice
Starches: root vegetables, sweet potatoes, purple potatoes, red skin potatoes, squash, carrots, rutabagas, parsnips, beets
Legumes: lentils, red beans, soybeans, chickpeas, navy beans, black beans, yellow or green peas

The Carbohydrate Continuum

All sources of carbohydrates fall on a continuum between refined and unrefined (see Figure 18.1). Your goal is to move to more unrefined sources of carbohydrates wherever possible. Consuming unrefined carbohydrates helps the body stay healthy and perform optimally.

Carbohydrate Chemistry

How Carbohydrates Work in the Body

If you disliked chemistry in high school or college, this section may not be for you, but I tried to keep it fairly simple. Digestion breaks down the carbohydrates you consume into glucose. Digestion begins with the saliva in your mouth and continues through the stomach and intestines. As the carbohydrates are broken down, glucose passes into the bloodstream. The

Refined ←		→ Unrefined
White bread	Enriched white bread	100% Whole grain bread
Applesauce	Natural applesauce	Apple
Catsup	Salsa	Tomato
Sugared cereal	Quick oats	100% Rolled oats
Corn syrup	Creamed corn	Whole kernel corn
Orange drink	100% Orange juice	Orange

Fewer Nutrients & Fiber — More Nutrients & Fiber

FIGURE 18.1 Carbohydrate Continuum

pancreas is the organ that controls blood glucose levels by unlocking two opposing hormones: insulin and glucagon.

When you eat, your blood glucose level begins to rise. In response to a rising blood glucose level, insulin is released to allow the cells to be fed. Insulin opens up the cells to allow blood glucose in. The cells then use glucose for energy, or they store it as glycogen (carbohydrate) or fat. The cells call upon these stored nutrients when other nutrients are not available. When energy stores are full, excess blood glucose is stored as fat.

Insulin is the key that opens up your cells for nourishment. Without insulin, your cells would starve to death. Insulin is a fat-storing and hunger hormone. The ideal is to produce a sufficient amount of insulin and have your cells sensitive enough to open up easily. If you produce too much insulin in response to an increase in food intake (like the Sumo wrestlers), your body will store the excess carbohydrates, proteins, and fats as body fat.

Insulin's antagonist is glucagon. Glucagon is the body's safety net in controlling blood glucose. It protects the body by preventing blood glucose from dropping too low. The pancreas releases glucagon as blood glucose drops. Glucagon directs the cells to release stored carbohydrate as glucose to raise your blood glucose level. Glucagon is a carbohydrate- and fat-releasing hormone.

Eating frequent small meals (150 to 400 calories per meal) throughout the day helps keep these hormones in balance. Remember, this is counter to the practice of many dieters, who stimulate their pancreas to overproduce insulin by eating one or two large meals per day.

The Glycemic Index

It can be difficult predicting how certain carbohydrates affect your blood glucose levels. Common sense would lead us to believe most refined, processed carbohydrates cause a rapid rise in blood glucose and unrefined carbohydrates would have a smaller effect on blood glucose levels. In most cases this is all true, but the accuracy of this method of determining how certain carbohydrates affect blood glucose can be greatly improved by using the Glycemic Index.

The Glycemic Index is a numeric tool that determines how individual carbohydrate foods affect blood glucose levels. Foods with a high Glycemic Index cause a large rise in blood glucose levels, and foods with a low Glycemic Index have smaller impact on blood glucose levels. Five factors determine how quickly carbohydrates in a food break down into glucose and enter the bloodstream.

1. **The structure of the carbohydrate**: There are three types of sugar structures: glucose, fructose, and galactose. Glucose is found in grains, breads, pastas, cereals, vegetables, and starches. Fructose is found in fruit. Galactose is found in dairy products. Glucose is the only sugar structure that is released directly into the bloodstream. Fructose and galactose are absorbed first by the liver, which converts them to glucose, slowing down their release into the bloodstream. The sugar in rice cakes, bagels, and pasta enter the bloodstream very fast, while the sugar in apples, pears, ice cream, and yogurt enter relatively slowly.

2. **How much the carbohydrate has been refined or processed**: Refined carbohydrates break down easily into glucose because they are stripped of valuable fiber. Then they quickly and easily enter the bloodstream. White bread has high Glycemic Index as compared to sprouted or whole grain bread in which the fiber is still intact. Grape juice has a much higher Glycemic Index than whole grapes.

3. **The fiber content of the carbohydrate**: Fiber slows down the release of carbohydrates into the bloodstream.

4. **Protein content of the food**: Protein slows the release of carbohydrates into the bloodstream.

5. **Fat content of the food**: Fat slows the release of carbohydrates into the bloodstream.

Glycemic Index

High	Foods rated 70 and above are high glycemic foods.		
	Glucose 100	Pretzels 83	Watermelon 76
	Cornflakes 92	Rice cake 82	Grape juice 75
	Mashed potatoes 92	Sugared cereal 81	Bagel 72
	Carrots 92	White bread 80	Popcorn 72
	White rice 85	Jelly beans 78	Millet 71
	Baked potato 85	Donut 76	Banana 70
Moderate	Foods rated 56–69 are moderate glycemic foods.		
	Angel food cake 67	Raisins 64	Sweet corn 60
	Whole wheat bread 65	Soft drinks 63	White spaghetti 58
	Cantaloupe 65	Bran muffin 60	Peas 57

(continued)

(*continued*)

Low	Foods rated 55 and below are low glycemic foods.		
	Orange juice 52	Yam 37	Avocado 0
	Brown rice 50	Soy milk 36	Leafy greens 0
	Grapes 50	Chickpeas 35	Cucumber 0
	Grapefruit juice 48	Split peas 32	Raw broccoli 0
	Baked beans 48	Lentils 29	Walnuts 0
	Skim milk 46	Yogurt 28	Almonds 0
	Oatmeal 42	Grapefruit 25	Fish 0
	Orange 42	Tomato 19	Egg 0
	Rye bread 41	Soybeans 18	Chicken 0
	Apple 40	Green or red pepper 0	

Notice that the majority of foods at the high end of the Glycemic Index are refined foods, and at the low end most of the foods have little refinement and are in their most natural state. Try to choose foods in their most natural state. Avoid refined carbohydrates that, in addition to being high on the Glycemic Index, may be high in sugar, as well as low in fiber, vitamins, and minerals.

Just a quick note: just because a food has a high glycemic value does not mean the food is a poor choice and should be avoided. Foods such as carrots, baked potatoes, watermelon, and bananas all have a high rating on the Glycemic Index, but they also have many valuable nutrients. Adding some extra virgin olive oil to a baked potato or having a slice of watermelon are wonderful tasting, healthy foods. When was the last time you ate too many carrots or bananas?

Why Do We Crave Carbohydrates?

The Carbohydrate Black Hole

By eating too many of the wrong carbohydrates at one time, blood glucose will rise rapidly, creating an insulin overshoot where the body releases more insulin than is needed. Your blood glucose skyrockets up: you get this great satisfaction for a short period of time before the bottom drops out and your energy plummets, creating a strong desire to raise your blood glucose up again or take a nap. Have you ever over indulged in eating too many of the wrong carbohydrates? Too many chips, crackers, stuffing, processed mashed potatoes, cookies, or ice cream? How did you feel?

A few years ago I found myself in the Carbohydrate Black Hole on Christmas Day by consuming 17, yes, 17 Christmas cookies. My wife, Paula, makes these wonderful tasting date cookies, and I told myself that I would have just one. My first mistake was thinking I was going to eat just one. My second mistake was that I started eating these cookies on an empty stomach. Then one went to three, and by the end of the night I think I consumed 17 cookies. The entire day I felt lethargic, tired, like I had been drugged, and the truth of the matter, I was. I remember some of my relatives asking, "What is wrong with Mr. Positive? He does not seem so positive today." I felt like I was in a food coma for most of the day.

The difficult part occurs once you start down this path of eating these unhealthy carbohydrate sources, it becomes extremely difficult to get out of this black hole. Occasionally we all may enter into the Carbohydrate Black Hole, getting there can be fun, but once we arrive the fun is gone.

As health and fitness coach for many years, I would see this pattern with many of my clients. They would complain of low energy and the need for a quick picker-upper to increase their energy. When I looked at their food logs, I saw too many refined carbohydrates (those foods in the red area of the Food Target), little protein, and virtually no healthy fats. People experience highs and lows as their energy levels rise and fall due to their consumption of refined carbohydrates and the overproduction of insulin that results (see Figure 18.2). Most Americans today try to control their energy with refined carbohydrates, coffee, soda pop, and energy drinks.

Optimal blood glucose levels   Undesirable blood glucose levels

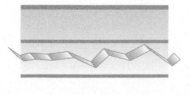
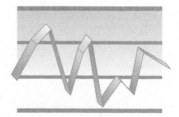

Blood glucose is very stable
throughout the day, leading to
a steady stream of energy.

Blood glucose spikes and dips
throughout the day, leading to
poor energy and poor performance.

FIGURE 18.2 Blood Glucose Levels

Insulin Is a Hunger Hormone

Insulin is a powerful hunger hormone that triggers humans to eat. Once insulin is overproduced by eating too much or the wrong types of carbohydrates (red area on the Food Target), it becomes a powerful hunger trigger.

Thanksgiving gives us a perfect example of how insulin works as a hunger trigger. The average American consumes 2,000 to 4,000 calories at a single meal on Thanksgiving. Within a short time, the nap syndrome kicks in, just like the Sumo wrestlers who promptly go to sleep following their single big meal of the day. Upon waking, your first urge is to eat again. You probably are not craving that leftover broccoli. No, you most likely want a sandwich with lots of bread, mashed potatoes, stuffing, or another piece of pie. This is the effect of the hunger hormone, insulin. As insulin levels rise to extreme heights after a very large meal, blood glucose will drop quickly, creating hunger for more refined carbohydrates.

Carbohydrates as Mood Regulators

When we become stressed or have low mood levels, we instinctively reach for comfort foods, refined starchy carbohydrates. Eating refined starchy carbohydrates, those that lie in the red area of the Food Target, elevates blood glucose too quickly along with increasing the activity of serotonin. Serotonin is a neurotransmitter used by the brain to communicate. Serotonin has a calming effect on the brain. Even though refined carbohydrates increase serotonin activity and you feel good, this good feeling is only temporary due to the spike in blood glucose and the ensuing drop in energy. This is one reason I consume some whole grains such as oat groats, rolled oats, or amaranth in the morning and starchy carbohydrates such as a sweet potatoes or brown rice in the evening. These unrefined carbohydrates, those that lie in the green area of the Food Target, increase serotonin activity, keeping my brain happy and my energy high.

Understanding Your Sweet Tooth

Sugar is a major life force, and our bodies need it as fuel. Sugars in whole foods are balanced with fiber and proper minerals. Have you ever eaten a sweet potato or a fresh piece of fruit? I am always in amazement at how Mother Nature makes it taste just right, with the perfect amount of sweetness. The energy obtained from breaking down and assimilating these sugars is what drives the mind and body.

When natural sugar is refined and concentrated, such as table sugar or high fructose corn syrup, the life force becomes out of balance. Refined sugar passes quickly into the bloodstream—sending shock waves throughout the entire body, creating a drastic rise in blood glucose, forming acid conditions in the body that leach out valuable minerals. Energy goes up quickly and drops quickly leading to further cravings for more sugar.

Approximately 80 percent of the world's sugar comes from sugarcane and the rest from sugar beets. Have you ever seen a sugarcane stalk? The skin of the stalk is tough and difficult to cut through, making it extremely difficult to consume. Imagine how much sugar would you eat if you had to get your sugar fix from a sugarcane stalk?

More and more people are asking whether there are healthier sweeteners available rather than refined sugar or artificial sweeteners. I am going to try and make this section short and sweet! Instead of getting into explaining all the problems with artificial sweeteners (and there is a laundry list of them), or the benefits of using other sugar substitutes, I am going to give you my short list of high quality, healthier alternatives. They include Stevia, raw organic honey, organic molasses, organic maple syrup, and organic cane sugar. Stevia has little effect on blood glucose, whereas organic honey, organic molasses, and organic maple syrup each are quickly absorbed in the body, raising blood glucose quickly.

Stevia

Let's begin with Stevia. Stevia comes from *Stevia Rebaudiana*, a small shrub native to Paraguay in South America. Stevia was first discovered in 1887 by a South American nature scientist named Antonio Bertoni. The herb in its natural form is 10 to 15 times sweeter than sugar. The extracts can range anywhere from 100 to 300 times sweeter than sugar. My favorite is Stevia Plus™. The conversion from Stevia Plus to sugar is $1/4$ teaspoon Stevia Plus™ to 1 teaspoon of sugar. *Best of all, Stevia has little effect on blood glucose, making it an excellent alternative to sugar or artificial sweeteners.*

For over 60 years, Stevia has been used in Japan and today Stevia is being used around the world. The safety record for Stevia usage is truly amazing. With the massive quantities of Stevia and Stevia Extracts that are consumed each year, there have been no known cases of Stevia overdoses or toxicity to humans reported during the past 50 years. Stevia is one sweetener people suffering from yeast-type conditions such as candida can tolerate.

How does Stevia taste? The whole Stevia leaf has a refreshing, sweet taste that most people like. I have had many coaching clients say that they truly like the flavor, but it did take a little getting used to. Stevia is sold as cut herb, in leaf form, as a liquid, or powdered extract and may be added to your favorite beverage, food, or recipe. Stevia does not break down when it is heated, so it can be used in baking or cooking. Stevia can be found in your local natural food stores and is now in many traditional grocery stores and supermarkets. As with many popular foods, be aware of highly processed Stevia imitations.

Raw Organic Honey

Honey has been around for centuries, most likely due to its wonderful texture and taste. Many people believe honey has many health benefits. The truth is honey does contain small amounts of enzymes and minerals that sugar does not have. However, bees are subject to a variety of illnesses, and this is one reason why it is not recommended to give honey to children under the age of two. Honey is also quickly absorbed and will cause a rise in blood glucose. The best source of honey is the honey you can buy from a local source, honey that has not been heated to temperatures over 105 degrees and is slightly cloudy. Too much heat and filtration destroys some of the beneficial properties of honey. Use honey on your cereal, a piece of toast, in your favorite recipe, or in a cup of hot tea and enjoy its wonderful flavor.

Organic Molasses

Organic molasses is thicker than honey and has a strong flavor. Molasses, especially blackstrap molasses, has more minerals than any other sweetener. Blackstrap molasses is rich in iron, calcium, and potassium. Molasses is also the most alkaline of all sweeteners. It is not sensitive to heat, making it an excellent choice for baking. Molasses, like honey, is quickly absorbed in the body, raising blood glucose quickly. Your best choice is organic, dark molasses.

Organic Maple Syrup

The thought of having a hot pancake at Grandma's house with the real deal maple syrup takes me back in time. Maple syrup comes from the sap of the maple tree and is then boiled down into maple syrup. Maple syrup, like honey and molasses, is also quickly absorbed in the body, raising blood glucose quickly. Maple syrup contains a small amount of trace minerals such as zinc and manganese.

Organic Cane Sugar

Most of the white sugar that is so common in the United States is genetically modified and highly refined by chemical processes from sugarcane, sugar beets, or corn. So if you want to consume, sugar make sure you are purchasing organic cane sugar. It looks like sugar and tastes like sugar, but without the GMOs. Organic cane sugar is quickly absorbed in the body and does raise your blood glucose level. Organic cane sugar can be found in many traditional grocery stores and most natural food stores.

Beware that more and more sweeteners are coming into the market daily with claims for their health benefits. Any food that is highly processed and taken out of its whole food environment will have compromised fiber, minerals, vitamins, and enzymes, leaving you with nutrient-deficient product. Use sweeteners only in moderation.

How Many Carbohydrates Should You Consume Each Day?

Carbohydrates are essential for optimal health and well-being. Choose carbohydrates in their most natural state, those carbohydrates that lie in the green areas of the Food Target. Your goal should be to get approximately 45 to 65 percent of your calories from high quality unrefined carbohydrates.

THE BOTTOM LINE

1. Carbohydrates are the main energy source to drive the human body!
2. Your brain needs 400 calories per day to function properly.
3. Carbohydrates are sugar chains linked together. Some, like soda pop and candy, are short (red area of the Food Target), while others, including oat groats or broccoli, have long sugar chains (green area of the Food Target).
4. The National Cancer Institute recommends 25 to 30 grams of fiber per day.
5. Carbohydrates include vegetables, fruits, whole grains, beans, and legumes.

19 Proteins—Build Your Body!

You create your own universe as you go along.

—Winston Churchill

The word "protein" comes from the Greek word *proteins*, which means of prime importance. Protein is essential to life. Protein plays a role in every cell of the body, with all the tissues in the body built and repaired with protein. Proteins create hormones, maintain the immune system, build muscle, transport vitamins, and maintain our blood, skin, and connective tissue. We all need to consider the *quality, quantity*, and the *frequency* in which we eat protein.

What Is Protein?

Our bodies break down protein into smaller nitrogen-containing units called *amino acids*. There are 22 amino acids: 9 essential amino acids, and 13 nonessential amino acids. The body cannot manufacture essential amino acids, so we must get them through the foods we eat. If one or more of the essential amino acids are missing from our diet, a protein deficiency will develop.

Complete and Incomplete Proteins

Complete proteins contain all nine essential amino acids. Sources of complete protein include eggs, meat, dairy products, poultry, fish, soy, and most nuts and seeds.

Incomplete proteins include some, but not all, of the essential amino acids. Foods that contain incomplete proteins include grains, rice, vegetables, and beans. It is relatively easy to get all of your essential amino acids from incomplete protein sources if you are eating a variety of *whole food sources*.

Benefits of Protein

In addition to keeping the body strong and healthy, there are further benefits to eating high quality protein.

Cell development: Protein ensures that your body receives appropriate amounts of the essential amino acids for cell development. This includes connective tissue, skeletal muscle, skin, hair, and nails.

Increased energy: Protein increases your energy level almost overnight. Having a stable blood glucose level is the name of the game in maintaining a high energy level throughout your day. Protein helps to stabilize your blood glucose level. If your blood glucose is stable, insulin will not be overproduced, leaving you with greater energy. It is as easy as adding a piece of salmon on your favorite salad for lunch or adding a few nuts to your cereal in the morning; this will help stabilize your blood glucose and help maintain that much needed energy required to feel your best.

Reduced cravings for refined carbohydrates: By adding protein to your daily diet, your cravings for carbohydrates, especially the refined carbohydrates, those in the "red area" of the food target, will diminish.

Glucagon stimulation: Glucagon is insulin's opposing hormone. Insulin is a fat and carbohydrate-storing hormone. Glucagon is a releasing hormone that aids in stabilizing blood glucose and boosting metabolism. Protein helps to stimulate glucagon.

Improved brainpower: Adequate amounts of protein can improve cognitive skills, memory, focus, and alertness. The first brain function to suffer the effects of age is memory. Memory begins to decline at about age 30, and loss of memory accelerates after age 40. To prevent this decline in memory and improve cognitive skills, focus, and alertness, all nine essential amino acids must be consumed daily in adequate amounts.

What Kinds of Protein Should You Eat?

If you asked most people in the United States what is the first thing that comes to their mind when they hear the word protein, I believe the answer would be meat, eggs, or dairy—proteins that come from animal sources. For years we have focused our attention on animal sources of protein to reach our protein requirements. We need to understand a great deal of our daily protein can and should come from plant sources.

During one of my seminars, a member of the audience asked me what I ate for breakfast. I said a typical breakfast for me consisted of organic rolled oats, some type of nut such as slivered almonds, walnut, or pecans, organic raisins, dried cherries or some type of frozen berries, almond or coconut milk, and a dash of cinnamon. I mix all the ingredients together and let it sit in the refrigerator overnight, no cooking required. I call this oatmeal on the run. I love the taste; it is quick and easy, well-balanced, high in quality, and gives me great energy to start my day. The member of the audience asked, "Where is your protein? Your breakfast seems low in protein." So I said let's take a closer look and see if this breakfast is low in protein.

CJ's Breakfast

2/3 cup organic rolled oats: 8 grams of protein
Slivered almonds, macadamia nuts, walnuts, or pecans:
    5 grams of protein
Organic almond or coconut milk: 2 grams of protein
Organic raisins, dried cherries, or frozen berries: 1 gram of
    protein
Total grams of proteins: 16 grams

I think many people were surprised by the amount of protein. This breakfast is just one example of getting high-quality protein from plant-based sources.

The Protein Debate

There is a growing debate over the best type of protein for the human body—animal or plant sources of protein. From an environmental standpoint, eating plant-based protein is a great deal more efficient for our environment. It takes over 50 grams of grain to make one gram of protein from beef, let alone the waste material from our animals. I want you to know that I am not a vegetarian; I enjoy many sources of animal protein, but I want you to realize that plant sources of protein are not only good for our environment; they are also good for the human body. The real question is how can you improve the *quality* of your protein sources, whether it comes from an animal or plant?

If you choose to consume animal-based protein sources, try to move to more organic sources. Why? The quality of our animal proteins is not what it used to be. In this age of growth hormones, antibiotics, pesticides, and synthetic fertilizers, the quality of our animal proteins has changed. Organic animal sources of protein look and taste better, and are healthier for the human body. For example, when comparing eggs from an organically raised chicken to a non-organically raised chicken, the organically raised chicken wins hands down. The eggshell is harder, the egg yolk is brighter in color, and the egg is much more flavorful.

Choose pesticide, growth hormone, and antibiotic free organic animal sources of protein whenever possible.

Eggs

When most people think of eggs, their first thought is that eggs are high in cholesterol and that eating eggs may cause heart disease. Yes, the egg yolk does contain 200 mg of cholesterol. A high intake of cholesterol for some people directly affects the amount of cholesterol in the bloodstream. But let's clear up a few misconceptions about eggs. First, the egg white itself is free of fat. Each egg white contains six grams of complete protein. The egg yolk is low in saturated fat and contains many other nutrients that are good for you, such as vitamins E and B, folate, choline (needed for proper brain functioning), and lecithin. Lecithin acts as cholesterol-lowering agent and a natural emulsifier, helping prevent plaque buildup from blocking arteries. Eggs are also inexpensive and easy to prepare.

When buying eggs, choose organic free-range or cage-free eggs as your first choice. Organic free-range eggs come from chickens that are raised in healthier environments, creating a healthier egg in return. Eggs can fit nicely into a diet for people who enjoy them; I like to eat eggs once per week. I use one tablespoon of organic extra virgin coconut oil and scramble four to five eggs including the yolk, with a few vegetables, and in just four to five minutes I have an easy, balanced, great-tasting meal!

Fish

Fish is a high protein food that provides a range of health benefits. White-fleshed fish are lower in fat than any other source of animal protein, and fish high in oils contain substantial quantities of healthy omega-3 fats. Though generally a good source of protein, *not all fish are created equal.* Just as the quality of our animal proteins is changing, the same can be said with the harvesting of the fish we eat. Most of the fish we consume in the United States today is farm raised. Ninety-five percent of all salmon consumed today in the United States is farm raised. Is farm-raised fish good for you? My answer is *it depends!* It depends on the environment and what the fish are being fed; these two factors determine how good the fish is for you. Our rivers, lakes, and oceans are slowly becoming more polluted and the fish living in these environments are becoming more toxic. Women who are pregnant should avoid consuming fish, such as blue fin tuna, grouper, swordfish, marlin, orange roughy, and Chilean sea bass due to their high mercury content.

Your best fish choices are always fish that are caught in the wild, such as wild caught Alaskan salmon. Wild caught Alaskan salmon that is fresh can be difficult to find, but the canned version is always available although it is also going to be more expensive. I look at it this way: If I can have a great meal of fresh or frozen wild caught Alaskan salmon for $15 to $20 per pound, add a nice salad, some asparagus, and a few fingerling potatoes for $12 to $13 per person, I can't beat the price. What about farm-raised fish; is this good to eat? Farm-raised fish is slowly becoming the future of our fish industry whether we like it or not. We are starting to see a greater separation in the quality of farm-raising fish practices similar to the methods being used today in raising organic animals. If you have an opportunity to eat wild Alaskan salmon or rainbow trout caught from a stream in the mountains of Colorado, thank your lucky stars and enjoy the great taste and wonderful health benefits. If you don't have access to fish grown in the wild, then farm-raised fish may be a good source of protein, especially if purchased from a high quality fish farm. The wonderful benefits of fish oils will be discussed in greater detail in the next chapter.

Best Seafood Choices

- Anchovies
- Catfish
- Clam
- Crab
- Crawfish
- Flounder
- Haddock
- Herring
- Mackerel
- Oysters
- Perch
- Salmon
- Sardine
- Scallop
- Shrimp
- Sole
- Squid
- Tilapia
- Trout
- Tuna (albacore or canned light)
- Whitefish

Poultry

Chicken: As when choosing eggs, your best choice is organic, free-range chicken.

Turkey: Turkey is much lower in saturated fat than most red meat. Like red meat, it is available in many forms—whole, or in parts, for roasting or baking, sliced for grilling, or ground as a delicious, healthy substitute for hamburger in soups, stews, pasta sauce, casseroles, and your other favorite recipes. Choose organic, free-range turkey whenever possible.

Ostrich: Ostrich is becoming a popular alternative to both red meat and other forms of poultry. It is low in saturated fat, high in protein, and is typically served as ostrich steaks, burgers, or in soups. Ostrich is great for grilling and has excellent flavor.

Lean Red Meat

Most red meat contains high levels of saturated fat, which may lead to many health problems. However, the occasional serving of lean red meat can be part of a healthy, balanced diet and is a good source of iron. When choosing red meat, look only for lean cuts such as flank steak, top sirloin, round steak, or beef tenderloin.

Most game meats are lean options when compared to traditional meat choices. Buffalo, lamb, and venison are examples of excellent meats popular with health-conscious consumers who want high quality meat protein sources that taste good.

Throw a few buffalo burgers on the grill along with some grilled vegetables and a few sweet potatoes or cook a buffalo roast in a crockpot with a bunch of root vegetables on a cool autumn day. Yum!

Dairy Products

If you enjoy dairy products coming from a cow, such as cow's milk, cottage cheese, yogurt, cheese, or butter, choose 100 percent organic sources whenever possible.

When my daughter Kristen was in middle school, she was on the track team, running the 400-meter, and she was having a difficult time breathing during track practice and in meets. Kristen went to the doctor and was told she had a low grade of asthma, was prescribed an inhaler and sent home. Asthma is nothing to take lightly, but I was not convinced my daughter truly had asthma. Kristen was in middle school, and her diet was anything but perfect. Kristen was eating too many processed foods along with too many dairy products, including cow's milk and processed cheese. Kristen and I sat down and discussed her diet, especially her dairy consumption. I said, "Kristen let's clean up your diet and see what happens." Kristen was ready to make a change; she did not like the feeling of having trouble breathing, she wanted to continue to run faster, and the 400-meter race is a very challenging event. She switched over to almond milk and cut all the cheese and dairy out of her diet. Within weeks, her breathing improved and her inhaler was history.

Personally I don't recommend cow's milk to anyone due to the size of the protein molecule and difficult challenges our digestive system has in breaking down and absorbing cow's milk. Cutting back on dairy is one of the first steps in helping improve digestion, skin, allergies, and asthma. Many people are or may be allergic to lactose found in cow's milk and are looking for alternatives. Another option to traditional cow's milk is goat's milk. Goat's milk is the most widely consumed dairy beverage in the world. Sixty-five percent of the world's population consumes goat's milk. Those who have digestion problems may truly benefit. Goat's milk is generally easy to digest and absorb due to the small size of its protein molecule, whereas cow's milk requires up to two to three hours of digestion and absorption, goat's milk requires only 20 to 30 minutes.

Okay, I may have lost you with the recommendation of goat's milk. There are many milk options other than goat's milk that taste great, are plant based, more alkaline, and lactose free. These include almond, coconut, hemp, oat, and rice, just to name a few. I personally use almond, coconut, or hemp milk on my oatmeal most mornings. They taste great, are alkaline, and easy to digest.

Plant-Based Proteins

I think many people are confused over plant-based proteins. I have had numerous questions about the Food Target as to whether a food is a carbohydrate, protein, or a fat. I have to explain that most foods have a mixture of the three macronutrients. For example, broccoli, which is a vegetable and is also part of the carbohydrate family, also contains protein. In fact, one cup of broccoli contains 4 grams of protein, containing over

40 percent of its calories by weight. Here are a few other examples of plant-based proteins:

Plant-Based Proteins

Steel-cut oats (1/2 cup): 12 grams of protein
Hempseeds (1 tablespoon): 11 grams of protein
Rolled oats (1/2 cup): 6 grams of protein
Kidney beans (1/2 cup): 7 grams of protein
Soybeans (1/2 cup): 10 grams of protein
Sprouted whole grain bread (1 slice): 6 grams of protein
Quinoa (1/3 cup): 6 grams of protein
Almonds (1 ounce): 6 grams of protein
Natural peanut butter (1 tablespoon): 5 grams of protein
Peas (1/2 cup): 5 grams of protein
Broccoli (1 cup): 4 grams of protein
Walnuts (1 ounce): 4 grams of protein
Sweet potato (1): 4 grams of protein
Spirulina/chlorella (20 tablets): 3 grams of protein
Banana: 1 gram of protein

So the next time you are looking for high quality protein sources, don't forget your plant-based protein sources.

Protein Supplements

If you are following a vegetarian diet or just plain busy, protein supplements can be a beneficial, quick, and easy addition to help balance your diet. There are many types of protein supplements to choose from: hemp, alfalfa, pea, rice, goat, or whey. Most protein supplements come in a powder form. There has been some debate over which protein supplements are best.

Hemp: Hemp contains all essential amino acids, is highly alkaline, high in fiber, chlorophyll, magnesium, zinc, and iron, and is easy to digest. Hempseed is one of nature's superfoods!

Organic sprouted grains: Organic sprouted grains such as brown rice, amaranth, quinoa, millet, and buckwheat are all excellent sources of plant-based protein, are inexpensive, absorbs easily, mix well, and have a mild flavor.

Alfalfa: Alfalfa is another plant-based protein that is high in trace minerals, vitamins, fiber, and protein. Alfalfa mixes easily, is easy to digest, and tastes great when mixed with your favorite fruits or vegetable juice.

Organic peas, nuts, and seeds: Organic peas, nuts, and seeds such as peas, beans, lentils, flaxseeds, sunflower seeds, pumpkin seeds, chia seeds, and sesame seeds are all excellent sources of plant based proteins that now come in powder form.

Goatein: Goatein is my first choice when choosing an animal-based protein supplement. Goatein is made from goat's milk, is easily digestible, mixes well, and inhibits candida, a fungus that inhabits the intestinal tract and mucous membranes of every living person. If the immune system is compromised when friendly bacteria in the gut are killed by taking antibiotics, a candida infection may quickly follow. Goatein is an excellent source of protein for those who may be allergic or have problems digesting other sources of protein supplements. Goatein has strong flavor, but that can be easily masked by adding your favorite fruit in a smoothie beverage.

Whey: Whey is derived from cow's milk; one reason I don't recommend whey protein powder. Whey is low in lactose, easy to mix, and has a mild flavor. If you wish to use whey protein powder, choose an organic brand whenever possible.

How to Use Protein Supplements

One complaint I get from seminar attendees or coaching clients is that it is challenging to eat frequently and that getting protein throughout the day can be difficult. It can be challenging to find time to eat and especially to get a balance of protein throughout the day. This is where a smoothie drink containing a balance of high quality proteins, fats, and carbohydrates may come in. Instead of reaching for a prepackaged meal-replacement drink, a candy bar, a bag of chips from the vending machine, or a quick trip to the fast food drive through, make your own high-quality, healthy, balanced smoothie.

Make up the smoothie the night before, using a variety of ingredients such as frozen berries, banana, spinach or kale, water, carrot juice, flaxseed meal, cacao, almond or natural peanut butter, shredded organic coconut, and a protein powder of your choice. This allows you to eat frequently, keep your energy high throughout the day, and get the balance of carbohydrates, proteins, and fats you need to keep your body strong and healthy. Oh, I almost forgot: experiment with the ingredients to find a recipe that works for you and tastes great.

A few years back one of my coaching clients was complaining of having low energy late in the afternoon. I recommended he needed to eat some sort of balanced snack in the afternoon to maintain his energy level. At the age of 75, full of juice, and the CEO of his company, he thought this was a great idea, but felt it might be difficult to eat a balanced snack due to his meeting schedule. So I suggested making up a balanced smoothie the night before and using this as his afternoon snack. "Great," he said. "I will start this tomorrow." The following week we met again and he had this weird look on his face. I said, "How are you doing? Did the balanced smoothie improve your energy?" He said, "No!" and then proceeded to tell me that it was the nastiest drink he ever tried. I said, "Your smoothie did not taste good?" He said, "It was awful; nobody should ever have to drink something that bad." "Okay," I said, "tell me exactly how you made your smoothie." He said, "I did exactly what you told me, 1 banana, 16 ounces of frozen berries, 1 cup of greens, 3 cups of water, 2 tablespoons of flaxseed meal, and 3 cups of protein powder." I said, "You added 3 cups of protein powder?" I said, "It was supposed to be 3 ounces of protein powder, not 3 cups." He said, "It was like trying to drink mud." I said, "It was mud." We had a great laugh over this. He tried the real recipe, and his energy improved greatly. He also liked the taste. The moral to this story: your food and beverage choices do not have to taste bad to be good for you. Experiment with your food and beverage choices. If they are not exactly what you are looking for, keep trying.

Protein/Energy Bars

Today there are hundreds of protein, energy, or snack bars available. I believe the quality of many of the new bars coming onto the market has greatly improved, but there are still too many bars that are heavily marketed as healthy, but are not. Many bar manufacturers are now using high quality, whole food, organic ingredients in their bars along with having good taste. Like the smoothies, protein/energy/snack bars can be beneficial as a quick and easy snack when traveling or if you simply have a busy schedule and need some nourishment on the run. I caution my seminar attendees and coaching clients against using these bars as meal replacements on a regular basis. Don't get caught up in the idea that they can or should replace quality whole foods every day.

Recently while walking out of our health club, one of the members asked, "What is that greenish thing you are eating?" I replied, "It is an organic Raw Revolution Bar." He said, "That looks awful!" I said, "It may not look so good, but it actually tastes great." I don't have much credibility when it comes to my opinion on something tasting good. Then I explained how healthy it is, how it has high-quality ingredients, contains healthy fats, and is balanced. You name it: I was trying to sell him on why I was eating it. I don't think he was buying any of it. I don't think he could get out of his mind how anyone could eat something that looked that bad. So I said to him, "Try a piece and see what you think." He actually ate a piece after much begging on my part. It was like Mikey on that old Life Cereal commercial: he liked it. Two days later I saw him eating one of those bars as he was walking out of the club.

When choosing a protein/energy/snack bar, many people make the mistake of first looking at the total number of calories in the bar. Second, they look at the number of protein grams in relationship to the carbohydrate and fat grams. They believe, back to the belief systems, if the bar is high in protein and low in carbohydrates and fat, it must be a good choice! Remember getting adequate, high quality protein in your diet is important, but high quality carbohydrates and fats are also important. When choosing a protein/energy bar or snack, be sure to read the label and pay close attention to four considerations:

1. **Number of ingredients:** A good rule of thumb, the fewer ingredients the better.
2. **Quality of ingredients:** Choose bars with the highest quality ingredients. If you cannot pronounce a word in the ingredient list, then

you probably don't want to put it in your body. Many bars now contain organic, high-quality ingredients. Avoid bars with fractionated or hydrogenated oils, synthetic vitamins and minerals, GMOs, and those that contain high-fructose corn syrup.

3. **Balance:** Choose a bar that is balanced with high-quality carbohydrates, proteins, and fats.
4. **Taste:** You can have your cake and eat it too when it comes to taste. Just because a protein/energy/snack bar is good for you does not mean it has to taste yucky. There are many bars that fit into the category of good for you along with great taste.

For a list of healthy bar options print "Brand Favorites" off of the On Target Living website, www.ontargetliving.com. One of the keys for having steady energy throughout the day is to have a stable blood glucose level. By eating frequent small meals with adequate protein with each meal will help you maintain the energy you desire. Figure 19.1 is a comparison of blood glucose levels with and without adequate protein.

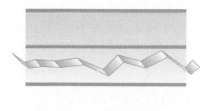 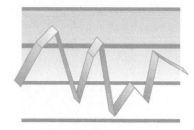

With adequate protein blood glucose more stable throughout the day (steady energy throughout the day)

Without adequate protein blood glucose goes up and down (energy levels fluctuate like these peaks and valleys)

FIGURE 19.1 Daily Blood Glucose Levels

The Protein Continuum

All sources of protein fall on a continuum between refined and unrefined. Your goal is to move to more unrefined sources of protein whenever possible. Consuming unrefined proteins helps the body stay healthy and perform optimally.

How Much Protein Is Enough?

Protein has tremendous nutritional benefits when balanced correctly in your diet. Your goal should be to get 15 to 25 percent of your daily calories from high quality protein sources, spread evenly throughout the day. The more physically active you are, the higher amount of protein your body will need. Rarely does one need more than 25 percent of their daily calories from high quality proteins. Upgrading your protein choices can be simple and can make big difference in your health and performance (Figure 19.2). Start slowly and build new upgrading habits!

Another easy method is to take your body weight, cut it in half, and that number is the amount of protein in grams you need per day. So if you weigh 150 pounds, then you would need approximately 75 grams of protein per day. If you are eating more **whole foods** throughout the day, getting enough high quality protein should not be a problem.

What happens if I eat too much protein? Getting more than 25 percent of you daily calories from protein may cause the body to become too acidic (refer to Chapter 7 for more information on pH balance). When proteins are broken down, they must be neutralized by buffering minerals, namely calcium, magnesium, and iodine, to offset the high acid levels in the body. If your protein intake is too high, these buffering minerals may become depleted over time, which may lead to a poor bone health, low thyroid function, as well as digestion and absorption problems in the stomach and digestive tract.

Eating too much protein also places stress on the liver and kidneys, which have to work harder to rid the body of the by-products of excess

Refined	The Protein Continuum	Unrefined
← Fewer Nutrients and Fiber		More Nutrients and Fiber →
Whole milk	Skim milk	Organic low-fat milk
Sweetened refined cereal	Quick oats	Steel-cut oats
Soy chicken	soy burgers	Soybeans
Eggs	Free-range/cage-free eggs	Organic free-range eggs
Hamburger	Lean ground beef	Organic ground buffalo
Chicken nuggets	Chicken	Organic chicken
Fish sandwich	Farm-raised salmon	Wild Alaskan salmon
White bread	Whole-wheat bread	Organic whole-grain sprouted bread
Partially hydrogenated peanut butter	Natural peanut butter	Organic peanut butter

FIGURE 19.2 Protein Continuum

protein metabolism. Remember, your first challenge is to look at the *quality* of proteins that you are using. Second, start to pay attention to the *quantity* of protein you are consuming.

Protein Chart

Recommended Protein Consumption Based on Daily Calorie Intake

Total Calories	Grams of Protein	Number of Protein Calories
1,200	45–75	180–300
1,500	56–94	225–375
1,800	68–113	270–450
2,000	75–125	300–500
2,500	94–156	375–625
3,000	113–188	450–750

THE BOTTOM LINE

1. Proteins are important to the health and performance of the human body in many ways. Proteins are necessary for cell development, increased energy, reduced cravings of refined carbohydrates—*and* they improve brain power!
2. The protein debate: Animal- versus plant-based proteins, which is the best type of protein?
3. Organic animal-protein sources: If you choose to consume animal-based proteins, try to choose organic sources whenever possible.
4. Consume 15 to 25 percent of your daily calories from high quality protein sources. An easy method to figure your daily protein intake is to take your bodyweight in pounds and cut it in half; this will give you grams of protein to consume per day.

20 Fats—Heal Your Body!

A candle loses none of its light by lighting another candle.

—Unknown

We are a nation obsessed with a fear of fat. Sixty percent of Americans rank cutting fat as their number one nutritional concern. You cannot walk through the grocery store aisles without seeing "fat free" plastered on every type of food imaginable. We have been led to believe that if a food has little or no fat, it must be okay to eat, and that foods containing fats should be avoided at all costs. This is flawed thinking. By the end of this chapter, I want you to understand that consuming healthy fats is one of the best things you can do to keep your mind and body healthy, improve your energy, and perform at your best. View healthy fats as *your body's healing nutrients*.

In my On Target Living seminars, I spend a great deal of time explaining the benefits of eating high quality fats and giving directions on how much fat to consume daily. Nonetheless, it never fails that immediately following the discussion of high quality fats, a participant will approach me to lament that extra virgin olive oil or cod liver oil—which I just recommended–has 12 to 14 grams of fat per tablespoon. I ask them if they had the same thought process when we were discussing carbohydrates (a half-cup of oatmeal has 27 grams of carbohydrate) or proteins (one chicken breast has 20 grams of protein). Until convinced about the importance of incorporating quality fats into the diet, many people just look at the labels, see the amount of fat, and wonder how I could possibly recommend that much fat be added to their diets.

I see the same mind-set with some of my coaching clients. A coaching client may seek my services with the goal of increasing energy, decreasing medications, balancing hormones, improving sleep or blood pressure, controlling diabetes, decreasing inflammation, or simply losing weight. I spend a considerable amount of time explaining cellular health, balancing pH, and the benefits of eating the right kinds of fats; I cite research, share testimonials, and share my own experience with—and passion for—eating healthy fats. Clients with this information sometimes still reject the idea of adding any type of fat to their diet; their response is "how could I ever use those extra calories?"

We have been led to believe that most fats are unhealthy and will cause us to gain weight and become fat—the old you-are-what-you-eat way of thinking. True, fats do contain over twice the calories per gram (nine calories) as carbohydrates and proteins (four calories). However, consuming healthy fats keeps the cell membrane soft and permeable, creates satiety, decreases the desire to overeat, balances hormones, decreases inflammation, and increases metabolic rate by fueling the power pack of our cells, the mitochondria.

One conclusion that can be drawn from recent medical research is that you don't have to give up fat to lose weight or enjoy better health. In fact, the opposite is true. Eating healthy fats is essential for better health, energy, and weight control.

So let me get this straight: by eating healthy fats I will improve my health, increase my energy, and be able to control my weight? Absolutely! One of the primary goals of On Target Living Nutrition is to help you distinguish between healthy and unhealthy fats.

Medical Research Supporting Healthy Fats

The most definitive study showing the benefits of consuming good fats is the Seven Countries Study, a 15-year study that began in the 1950s. Pioneering nutrition researcher Ancel Keys and his colleagues looked at the eating patterns of 16 populations in seven countries. Keys and his colleagues studied over 12,000 men from Greece, Italy, Netherlands,

Finland, Japan, Yugoslavia, and the United States. This study concluded that the people of the Greek island of Crete (eating a diet virtually unchanged since 4,000 BCE) had the lowest death rates from cancer and heart disease. Crete had half the death rate from cancer and one-twentieth the death rate from heart disease of the United States. So what is unique about the Cretan diet?

First, the overall fat intake is high—35 percent of their total calories come from fat. Second, the types of fat consumed are much different than the types of fat consumed in the United States. The Cretan diet is low in trans-fatty acids (such as french fries, refined peanut butter, and margarine), refined saturated fats (such as whole dairy products, processed cheese, and fatty cuts of meat), and refined omega-6 fatty acids (such as corn, soy, and cottonseed oil), all unhealthy forms of fat. The Cretan diet is high in whole fruits, vegetables, leafy greens, raw nuts and seeds, extra virgin olive oil, fish, and flaxseed. The Cretan diet is loaded with a variety of healthy fats!

How did the United States compare? We continue to increase our intake of trans-fatty acids and saturated fats from processed snacks, fast food, and animal products. Americans are also consuming too many refined omega-6 fats and not enough omega-3 fats. As a result of our poor eating habits, we have seen a dramatic rise in numerous health problems:

- Obesity
- Type 2 diabetes
- Inflammation
- Arthritis
- High blood pressure
- Heart disease
- Cancer
- Depression
- Dementia
- MS
- Autoimmune diseases

Our poor eating habits also result in a dramatic rise in our use of prescription medications.

Where Have We Gone Wrong?

Since the early 1950s, we have slowly decreased the quality of the fat we are consuming. The more refining or processing that goes into producing food, the more quality (healthy fat) is stripped away. We are a nation of convenience eaters, and unfortunately many countries around the world are following in our unhealthy footsteps! In return, we get unhealthy, refined, convenient food sources. Our entire food supply has been affected by our demand for convenience and packaged foods.

In his book *Fast Food Nation* (published by Houghton Mifflin in 2001), Eric Schlosser says, "Americans spend more on fast food than we spend on higher education, personal computers, new cars, movies, books, magazines, newspapers, videos, and recorded music combined."

Why do food manufacturers and the fast food industry use poor-quality fat in packaging and preparing food? There are two reasons:

1. **Money:** The two most consumed oils in the United States are refined soybean and corn oil. Refined soybean and corn oil are extremely abundant and inexpensive to produce, and are used in thousands of food products to increase shelf life and enhance taste. The next time you are at the grocery store, pick up a packaged food product and see if one of the evil twins is in the ingredient list. If they are, avoid these highly refined oils. Refined omega-6 oils are inexpensive and are used in thousands of food products to enhance taste. Refined omega-6 fats are not healthy and lie in the orange area of the Food Target.
2. **Shelf life:** Manufacturers in the food industry understand that the longer a product can stay on the shelf without becoming stale or spoiling, the greater profitability of that product. Manufacturers start with refined soybean or corn oil and take them through hydrogenation. Hydrogenation is a process in which these refined oils are subject to extreme heat and then a metal catalyst is added, turning these refined oils into trans-fatty acids. Trans fats are extremely unhealthy and lie on the outer ring, the red area of the Food Target.

My first experience with hydrogenated food products started with one of my first jobs out of college. I took a job with Frito-Lay, a large snack food company as a route salesperson, delivering potato chips and other snack food items to large grocery stores. While working at Frito-Lay there was a shelf life of approximately 5 weeks on most potato and tortilla chips. After my second year, Frito-Lay rolled out a new line of soft cookies. The soft cookies had a shelf life of over 3 years! For almost seven years, eight hours a day, I lived in the grocery stores, stocking shelves, putting up displays, and trying to acquire more shelf space to increase sales. I observed shoppers in every shape and size and their buying practices. The experience and knowledge I gathered truly helped me understand the power of the food industry along with how many people truly do not understand what they are putting into their grocery carts and then into their precious bodies.

In my On Target seminars, I try to make the point that once partially hydrogenated oils are used in a food product, the shelf life of that product lasts a long, long time. I have a jar of a well-known brand of refined peanut butter that I display for this very purpose. It has been in my garage for over 17 years! If trans-fatty acids can preserve a bag of cookies for more than three years and a jar of refined peanut butter for more than 17 years, think about the effect they have on your body once they are consumed.

These are just two examples of how unhealthy fats make their way into our cupboards and onto our dinner tables. In our society, we have to search for healthy fats while working overtime to avoid unhealthy fats.

Why Is Eating Healthy Fats So Essential for Good Health and Improved Performance?

The human body is made up of over 100 trillion cells. Each cell has a specific job to do and is in a constant state of change. On the most basic level, fats help form the membrane that surrounds each of our cells. The cell membrane, as mentioned earlier, controls the nutrients that enter and exit the cell. This is one of the major functions of the body that is threatened by eating trans-fatty acids (unhealthy fats). Trans-fatty acids interfere with normal fat metabolism by crowding or pushing out essential fatty acids from cell membranes. This makes the cells less fluid, less permeable, and reduces the number and sensitivity of the insulin receptors.

When working with a client that has type 2 diabetes or for that matter anyone who wants to become healthier, one of my first goals is to get their cells healthier, and this includes getting the cell membranes soft and permeable. A stiff and insensitive cell membrane is a major factor in type 2 diabetes. When insulin approaches the cell and tries to open it up to allow nutrients to enter, it has a tougher time doing its job if trans-fatty acids have made the outer membrane of the cell rock solid like an M&M candy shell, hard on the outside, soft on the inside. Over time the cells become insulin-resistant and type 2 diabetes may be soon to follow.

Replacing your unhealthy fats with healthy fats is the first step to cellular health and having softer cell membranes that are more permeable and sensitive to insulin. Eating healthy fats also satisfies your hunger due to the release of two hormones that help control appetite: leptin and cholecystokinin (CCK). Without sufficient fat, you are more likely to overeat. Fats also slow down the digestion of carbohydrates and proteins so that there is a more sustained release of nutrients into the blood, resulting in a stable energy level. If your goal is to lose weight, improve your cholesterol, blood pressure and blood glucose, decrease inflammation, or you just want to feel great, start replacing your unhealthy fats with healthy fats.

Categories of Fats

Learning to distinguish between a healthy and an unhealthy fat is critical for good health and better performance. There are four categories of fat to learn more about and understand:

1. Trans-fatty acids
2. Saturated fats
3. Monounsaturated fats
4. Polyunsaturated fats (omega-3 and omega-6 essential fatty acids)

Trans-Fatty Acids

These are the worst of the bad fats. Hydrogenating, or hardening, vegetable oils create trans-fatty acids, also known as hydrogenated or partially hydrogenated fats. As noted earlier, the food industry widely uses trans fats because they are inexpensive, improve taste, and increase shelf life.

Trans-fatty acids are difficult for the body to break down, and they impair the normal use of healthy fats by hardening the cell membrane. Trans-fatty acids raise LDL cholesterol and lower HDL cholesterol, creating an imbalanced cholesterol profile along with increasing the risk of type 2 diabetes and many other health related problems. Today, the average American consumes over 20 percent of their calories from trans-fatty acids. Studies show that there is *no acceptable level* of trans fats.

Unless we are vigilant, it is easy to consume trans-fatty acids because they are hidden in almost all processed foods. Trans-fatty acids are found in most fast food, margarine, shortening, doughnuts, french fries, pound cake, crackers, potato chips, packaged soft cookies, baked goods, microwave popcorn, non-dairy creamers, and refined peanut butter, to name a few.

Today the Food and Drug Administration (FDA) requires all food and beverages to list trans fats on the label. So this is good news, right? Yes and no. I believe it will create more awareness on the detrimental effects that trans fats have on the body, but the buyer needs to understand what to look for to avoid these unhealthy fats. So now you may be thinking, I don't have to worry about trans fats being in the food that I buy; I can just look at the label and it will tell me if the product has trans fats or not. Not so fast. There is a little loophole that you need to know about the labeling of fats.

The FDA allows food manufacturers to label a product fat or trans-fat free if it contains less than a half a gram of fat per serving. Manufacturers then manipulate the serving sizes to such small levels so they can make these claims on their products. So what you are telling me is that a product may contain trans fats, but the label can say it has zero trans fats? Unfortunately, yes. The only way to truly know if a product contains trans fats is to look at the ingredient list first. Any time the words "hydrogenated or partially hydrogenated" appear in the ingredient list, the product contains trans-fatty acids, regardless if it says zero trans fats.

Saturated Fats

Can saturated fats be good for you? It depends on the quality of the saturated fat. We as consumers have been told for years that saturated fats are unhealthy and are responsible for heart disease, cancer, obesity, and a host of other degenerative diseases.

Do you really need saturated fats in your nutritional plan for better health and performance? The answer is yes! Healthy saturated fats give structural integrity to the cell. Just as you need a variety of fruits and vegetables to fill many of your nutrient requirements for fiber, vitamins, minerals, and antioxidants, the same is true when consuming healthy fats.

Ideally you want a variety of healthy fats in your eating plan to achieve the nutrient requirements your body needs.

How do you know if a saturated fat is healthy or unhealthy? Your best bet is to look for saturated fats in their most natural state (whole foods), just as you would with your selection of carbohydrates and proteins. Most saturated fats are solid at room temperature. Animal products such as meat, eggs and dairy, as well as most seeds and nuts, all contain some saturated fat. The quality and amount of saturated fat in food depends on the quality of food the animals were eating and the environment in which they were raised. The best quality saturated fats come from animals raised under the most natural conditions (walking around grazing on grass, insects, and seeds). Most nuts and seeds are excellent sources of saturated fat, protein, and fiber.

One of the healthiest fats for the body just happens to also be a saturated fat. Can you guess what this wonderful fat could be? If you answered organic coconut or extra-virgin coconut oil, you were right! For years we as consumers have been told that coconut is high in saturated fat and we should avoid it at all costs. I ask this question in my seminars—are saturated fats healthy or unhealthy? The correct answer, *it depends!* It depends on the quality of the fat. Is the coconut that I am discussing found in a refined candy bar, or out of a package that you sprinkle on a German chocolate cake? If you were on a tropical island and a coconut fell to the ground, do you think the coconut would be something healthy to eat or drink? The fact is, coconuts have nourished humans for thousands of years. From skin problems to an upset stomach, coconut was your remedy of choice.

What makes organic coconut or extra-virgin coconut oil so special? It is rich in lauric, capric, and caprylic acids, which are loaded with antiviral and antifungal properties. Lauric acid is also present in mother's breast milk.

Some of the wonderful health benefits of organic coconut or extra-virgin coconut oil include:

- Aids digestive disorders (such as acid reflux, irritable bowel syndrome)
- Aids weight loss
- Improves thyroid function
- Protects against heart disease
- Promotes beautiful looking skin
- Is high in antioxidants

Organic coconut or extra-virgin coconut oil has a wonderful flavor and can be used as a butter replacement. It is also excellent for cooking and in recipes due to its wide temperature ranges. I add one tablespoon of shredded organic coconut on my oatmeal most mornings, sprinkle it on frozen cherries as an evening snack, or use extra-virgin coconut oil on a cracker, a piece of toast, in scrambled eggs, or in a smoothie drink. It makes me feel satisfied and helps curb food cravings. Oh I almost forgot: I also give a little bit to my dog Dolly. She loves the taste, and it keeps her coat and tummy healthy.

Store your organic shredded coconut in the refrigerator, but keep your extra-virgin coconut oil in the cupboard at room temperature. It will melt easily if the temperature exceeds 76 degrees. Organic shredded coconut or extra-virgin coconut oil can be found in most health food stores. **Recommended serving: one to two tablespoons per day.**

Monounsaturated Fats (Omega-9 Fats)

Monounsaturated fats (also know as omega-9 fats) play an important role in a balanced diet. Monounsaturated fats contain the fatty acid known as *oleic acid.*

Health Benefits of Monounsaturated Fats

Monounsaturated fats protect the arteries from cholesterol buildup, reduce the risk of breast cancer, accentuate the effect of omega-3 fatty acids in the blood, and help in the formation and development of all cell membranes, which is important for cell, tissue, and organ health. One of the main reasons monounsaturated fats are so protective against heart disease is that they lower LDL cholesterol while they maintain or even raise HDL cholesterol, creating a balanced lipid profile, good for the heart and also beneficial for your sex hormones. *No other fat has this effect.*

Monounsaturated fats are preferred over polyunsaturated fats for cooking because they have a single double-bond between their carbon atoms, making them stable at high temperatures, not easily oxidized, and great tasting. Anytime a recipe calls for oil, your best choices are monounsaturated fats and organic extra-virgin coconut oil.

Where Do You Find Monounsaturated Fats?

Monounsaturated fats are found in olives, extra-virgin olive oil, avocados, avocado oil, almonds, almond oil, almond butter, peanuts, natural peanut butter, macadamia nuts, macadamia oil, pistachio nuts, pecans, cashews, hazelnuts and pine nuts.

What to Look for When Buying Oils Made from Monounsaturated Fats

The process of refining destroys many of the wonderful health benefits of oils and other products made from monounsaturated fats. Food producers use refining techniques to improve profits without regard for the negative effect that refining has on the products and the consumer. For example, olive oil is refined oil. Virgin olive oil is a better choice because it is less refined. Extra-virgin olive oil is even better. To be classified as extra-virgin olive oil, the oil must be from the first pressing, the highest quality, and extracted under strict adherence to specific guidelines.

If olives are damaged or bruised, they begin to spoil. The oil pressed from these olives is of such poor quality that it must be refined, degummed, bleached, and deodorized, resulting in poor quality olive oil. The processes used in mass-produced oils remove and strip many of the essential nutrients that provide critical health benefits. When selecting monounsaturated fats (oils, nuts, or seeds), choose only high quality, unrefined sources whenever possible. Store all your monounsaturated fats at room temperature in a dark container or in the cupboard.

How Much Monounsaturated Fat Should You Eat?

Approximately 10 to 15 percent of your daily calories should come from monounsaturated fats. If you consume approximately 2,000 calories per day, roughly 200 to 300 calories (20 to 30 grams, two to three tablespoons) should come from monounsaturated fats.

What does 300 calories of monounsaturated fats look like?

- One large tablespoon of slivered almonds or macadamia nuts added to your cereal for breakfast
- One-half avocado added to your salad for lunch
- One tablespoon of extra-virgin olive oil added to a sweet potato for dinner

Polyunsaturated Fatty Acids—Essential Fatty Acids

Polyunsaturated fats include essential fatty acids. This means we must obtain them from the foods we eat, and they are *necessary* for proper function of our bodies. At the microscopic level, polyunsaturated fatty acids have two or more double-bonds in their carbon chains, and the more double-bonds on the carbon chain, the more unsaturated the oil. Flaxseed, chia seed, and fish oil are the most unsaturated of all oils, and this is one reason why you never want to heat or cook these polyunsaturated oils. All polyunsaturated oils are liquid at room temperature and remain liquid when refrigerated.

In the past, we believed that any type of polyunsaturated fat was healthy, with little distinction between types of polyunsaturated fatty acids. We now understand that polyunsaturated fats fall into two distinct groups: *omega-3 and omega-6 essential fatty acids*, each aiding specific functions in the body. The type and refinement or processing is important with regard to the *quality* and benefit of these fats.

With all the refinement of our foods today, approximately 92 percent of U.S. adults and children are deficient in these essential fatty acids. When working with coaching clients one on one, I have them turn in a two- to three-day food log to get a better understanding of how they fuel their body. I rarely see essential fatty acids in their nutritional plan. Most don't know what an essential fatty acid is, and most importantly where to find them. In the past, our entire food chain—greens, eggs, meat, nuts, seeds and fish—contained these wonderful essential fatty acids. We were all eating more whole foods that delivered these wonderful essential fatty acids to our bodies. Unfortunately this is not the case today; we have to search for these wonderful fats.

Omega-3 Essential Fatty Acids

Omega-3 fats are the superstars of the healthy fats and make the body strong and healthy. The primary fatty acid in the omega-3 family is alpha-linolenic acid (ALA). ALA is found in green leafy vegetables, flaxseeds, chia seeds, walnuts, Brazil nuts, and pumpkin seeds. Flaxseeds and chia seeds are the richest sources of ALA.

There are several levels of omega-3 breakdowns, or conversions, in the body. ALA converts to one of two other types of fatty acids, depending upon its breakdown pathway. ALA is converted into eicosapentaenoic acid (EPA) and then into docosahexaenoic acid (DHA). Scientists became aware of the wonderful health benefits of EPA and DHA when Danish physicians observed that Greenland Eskimos had exceptionally low incidence of heart disease and arthritis, despite the fact that they consumed a high-fat diet. They found that the *type* of fat the Greenland Eskimos were consuming was high in EPA and DHA, found in cold-water fish such as salmon, trout, tuna, mackerel, herring and in cod liver and fish oils.

People attending my On Target Living seminars often ask, "If I eat omega-3 fats, such as flaxseeds or chia seeds, which are high in ALA, do I also need to consume wild cold-water fish, cod liver, or fish oils?" Ideally, yes! The conversion from ALA to EPA and then into DHA is not efficient in most adults and especially in seniors and children. I recommend one serving of flaxseeds or chia seeds along with cod liver oil on a daily basis to fill all of your omega-3 essential fatty acid needs. If you are just trying to make a few changes to begin with, don't worry about doing everything day one. Get comfortable with your new changes and then down the road you may want to do both (flaxseeds or chia and cod liver oil).

Benefits of Consuming Omega-3 Fats

Boost weight loss with omega-3 fats: Many people are surprised to hear that consuming fats, especially the right types of fats, can actually help you to lose weight. They are concerned that if they add more calories to their own food plan, weight gain will most certainly follow. I recently had a young woman at one of my seminars ask, "So let me get this straight—you are recommending to this entire audience that we consume approximately 400 to 800 calories per day of good fats?" Everyone was waiting for the answer because many were thinking the same thing. My answer was a most definite yes. **First**, going back to the cell, remember the cell membrane and the mitochondria? When you start eating the healthy fats, the cell membrane becomes healthier and the mitochondria get more metabolically active. **Second**, healthy fats make you feel satisfied, help control appetite, food cravings, and most importantly your blood glucose level. **Third**, with greater energy you want to move your body more.

Balance hormones with omega-3 fats: Polyunsaturated fatty acids are important for creating hormonal balance in the body. Both the omega-3 and omega-6 fats work by forming short-lived, hormone-like substances called *prostaglandins*. Prostaglandins regulate metabolic processes throughout the body at the cellular level. They control cellular communication and are essential in regulating the immune, reproductive, central nervous, and cardiovascular systems. Omega-3, along with omega-6 fats, is also one of the raw materials necessary in building your sex hormones such as DHEA, testosterone, and estrogen.

Improve heart health with omega-3 fats: Prostaglandins formed from omega-3 fats aid in the cardiovascular system by reducing constriction of blood vessels and decreasing the stickiness of the blood, making it less likely to clot. Eating too much unhealthy fat (trans-fatty acids, refined saturated and omega-6 fats) and not eating enough of the omega-3 fats will likely create a prostaglandin or hormonal imbalance throughout the body. Omega-3 fats help to maintain elasticity of artery walls, prevent blood clotting, reduce blood pressure, and stabilize heart rhythm.

Having high or unbalanced cholesterol is a growing concern in the United States and throughout the world. Cholesterol-lowering statin medications today are as common as taking a baby aspirin. Is there a better way? Absolutely, positively, yes!

Start by getting your cells healthy. Get the trans fats out of your diet, drink more water, eat more whole foods, add one to two tablespoons of ground flaxseeds or chia seeds to a glass of juice, in a smoothie, or on a salad, add one to two tablespoons of cod liver oil, and work closely with your physician.

Over the past decade, I have received hundreds of e-mails, letters, phone calls, and in-person testimonials, all wanting to share their personal stories on the drastic improvements to their health and cholesterol levels. Yes, you do have options!

Enhance cellular health for diabetics with omega-3 fats: Anytime I have an opportunity to work with someone who has diabetes, I get very excited to share with him or her the power of eating the "healthy fats." Whether they have type 1 diabetes (their body is no longer producing insulin) or type 2 diabetes (their body is still producing insulin, but the cell is not receptive to the insulin that is produced), consuming omega-3 fats will improve cellular health. Again back to the cell! Step number one: get the cell membrane soft and receptive to insulin. As the cell membrane becomes softer and more sensitive, the demand for insulin decreases. Regular exercise, drinking water, eating whole foods, and consuming healthy fats goes a long way in making the cell membrane more sensitive. It sounds pretty simple: exchange the unhealthy fats with the healthy fats, especially the omega-3 fats. Remember, your body is always trying to heal itself! If you have type 1 or type 2 diabetes, work with your health care professional and start getting the healthy fats in your nutritional plan.

Reduce inflammation with omega-3 fats: We all know what inflammation is. A bee stings you and your arm swells up. Or you sprain your ankle and it swells up. But what about the chronic inflammation that affects millions of people on a daily basis? Have you ever wondered why some people have more inflammation than others? Do you ever feel like you have been in a train wreck when you get out of bed in the morning? Would you like to have fewer aches and pains? Most people don't link inflammation to their diets. Could it be connected to what we are eating or not eating? Most people don't realize that *omega-3 fats have natural anti-inflammatory benefits*. The right foods and beverages are powerful ingredients to decrease inflammation. Instead of purchasing the over-the-counter or prescription anti-inflammatory, begin using omega-3 fats as your anti-inflammatory of choice.

Consume omega-3 fats for a healthy brain: Our brain needs the omega-3 fats eicosapentaenoic acid (EPA) and docosahexaenoic (DHA) for brain development and sustainable brain health. DHA is the building block of human brain tissue and is abundant in the grey matter of the brain and the retina of the eye. Low levels of DHA have recently been associated with depression, memory loss, dementia, and visual problems. DHA is particularly important for fetal and infant development. The DHA content of an infant's brain triples during the first three months of life. Optimal levels of DHA are, therefore, crucial for pregnant and lactating mothers. Unfortunately, the average DHA content in breast milk in the US is the lowest in the world, most likely due to our failure to consume enough omega-3 fats.

Dr. Barbara Levine, Professor of Nutrition in Medicine at Cornell University, sounds the alarm concerning the inadequate intake of DHA by most Americans. Dr. Levine believes that common health problems in the United States such as postpartum depression, attention deficit hyperactivity disorder (ADHD), and low IQs are linked to low DHA intake. Dr. Levine also points out that low DHA levels have been linked to low serotonin levels. Serotonin is the "feel-good" neurotransmitter that is boosted by consuming omega-3 fats containing DHA. Moms, get busy consuming the proper omega-3 fats to keep mom and baby or babies happy and healthy!

Low levels of EPA and DHA have also been linked to an epidemic rise in many brain problems such as dementia, Parkinson's, Alzheimer's, and MS. We are now learning that many of these brain problems may be linked to a breakdown of the myelin sheath—the protective coating or insulator that wraps around every nerve fiber in the human body. (See Figure 20.1.) Nerve fibers control every thought, emotion, and movement throughout the human body and with any breakdown of the myelin sheath; brain problems are not far away!

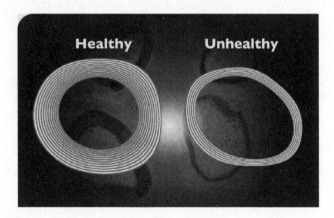

FIGURE 20.1 Myelin Sheath

So what may be causing the breakdown of the myelin sheath?

- Inflammation—high levels of inflammation caused by a highly acidic diet
- Cholesterol-lowering statin medications—break down the myelin sheath
- Lack of the raw materials—deficient omega-3 fats to help build and repair the myelin sheath

Personally, I have been consuming flaxseeds along with cod liver oil for years. Sometimes I have to laugh at myself when I can't remember where I parked my car, or how to spell the word "the," or am feeling a little blue. Where would I be if not for my omega-3 fats? It is just like the bald guy who is trying to keep his hair by using hair growth lotion; if asked, "Does that stuff really work?" he responds, "I don't really know, but I can't afford to stop using it!"

Omega-3 fats are worth making the effort to incorporate into your diet every day. Like I ask my coaching clients, do you brush your teeth everyday? They all say the same thing, "of course I do." Then create a similar ritual for taking your omega-3 fats. They are truly magical!

Where Do You Find Omega-3 Fats?

It is a challenge to get enough omega-3 fats unless you know where to look. I tell my clients, "You must search for omega-3 fats." Why is that? Omega-3 fats are extremely unstable and spoil quickly. Most products that are sitting in the grocery store most likely do not contain omega-3 fats. There are, however, excellent sources of omega-3 fats available.

Flaxseeds: Flaxseeds have been around for thousands of years, making them one of mankind's earliest food supplies. In the eighth century, Charlemagne considered flax so essential for health that he passed laws requiring its use!

Flaxseeds are tiny, hard seeds, either gold or brown, that are loaded with omega-3 fatty acids. The seeds themselves are not digestible, so to reap the wonderful health benefits of the omega-3 fatty acids, the seeds must be ground into flax meal or pressed into flaxseed oil. Flaxseeds are inexpensive and are an excellent dietary source of fiber; this is one of the main reasons I prefer the ground flax meal to the flaxseed oil. Flaxseed oil is much more expensive than the ground flax meal. Flaxseeds contain *lignans*, which have antiviral, antifungal, antibacterial, and anticancer properties. Lignans are found in the seedcoat and only a small amount of lignans end up in the oil. If you want the benefits of lignans, use fresh ground seeds (flax meal). Flaxseeds may be used on salads, cereals, or in baking. Whole flaxseeds are high in fiber and help curb appetite.

> *Wherever flaxseeds become a regular food item among the people, there will be better health.*
>
> Mahatma Gandhi

Flax meal: Flax meal is ground flaxseeds. Flax meal is sold in health food stores, but I recommend that you purchase flaxseeds and grind your own to ensure freshness and maximum nutritional value. Buy a cheap coffee grinder specifically to grind your flaxseeds. Once a week I grind two cups of flaxseeds and place them in a container and store in the refrigerator. This takes only a few minutes and lasts me the entire week. The flax meal is fresh and costs only pennies per day. Flax meal may be added to a variety of foods or beverages such as a glass of juice, smoothie, cereal, salads, or yogurt and adds a nutty flavor. The recommended daily serving of flax meal is one to two tablespoons per 100 pounds of body weight.

Chia seeds: Chia seeds like flaxseeds are also high in omega-3 fat (ALA). Chia seeds are dark in color, easy to digest, help with food cravings, decrease inflammation, and are extremely heart-healthy. Chia seeds do not need to be ground and can be eaten raw, soaked in juice, and added to your favorite salad or smoothie recipe. Chia seeds are also excellent for baking. Serving size:, one to two tablespoons per day. Do you need to consume both flax meal and chia seeds in the same day? The answer is no. I try to get both in my diet each week by rotating back and forth between ground flaxseeds and chia seeds.

There are many other sources of omega-3 fatty acids (ALA), such as walnuts, walnut oil, butternuts, Brazil nuts, filberts, pumpkin seeds, pumpkin seed oil, hemp seeds, hemp oil, and soybeans. Many of these nuts and oils contain omega-3, omega-6, and omega-9 fats. Leafy greens also contain small amounts of ALA.

Wonderful Fish Oils

We as a nation have a major omega-3 deficiency, especially EPA and DHA. Eicosapentaenoic (EPA) and docosahexaenoic (DHA) can be manufactured in small amounts by healthy cells from alpha-linolenic acid (ALA), which is found in great quantities in ground flaxseeds and chia seeds. However, the conversion from ALA to EPA and DHA is small and can be impaired by degenerative conditions such as diabetes. To get EPA and DHA directly into your body, take advantage of the wonderful benefits of fish oil. The richest sources of EPA and DHA are cod liver, anchovies, sardines, herring, mackerel, and wild Alaskan salmon. Unfortunately today much of the fish we consume in the United States and around the world is not what it used to be. Most of the salmon we buy today is farm raised, and many other sources of fish contain levels of mercury, PCB's, and pesticides. Personally I try to eat fresh fish on a regular basis. I love the taste of wild Alaskan salmon, but it can be expensive. I also buy canned wild Alaskan salmon or canned light tuna and use on my salad two to three times per week.

To get the health benefits that fish oil provides, I recommend to almost all my clients to take cod liver oil daily. Did I read this right, cod liver oil? Daily? Hold on, this is not the nasty-tasting cod liver oil many of us had to take as a kid or when we got into trouble. Well, here is the skinny on cod liver oil and fish oil. Norwegian Arctic cod is the most complete omega-3 source Mother Nature has to offer, has an excellent price point when compared to Krill or other fish oils, has stringent environmental protection, and the stock of Norwegian Arctic cod is increasing—creating a fully sustainable, environmentally healthy source of EPA and DHA. Cod liver oil also has more vitamin D3 than fish oil, so unless you live around the equator, I recommend cod liver oil over the fish oil to get more vitamin D3 into your diet.

What do you look for when choosing cod liver oil? Look for a brand of cod liver oil that has been tested by an independent laboratory for freshness, potency, and purity because not all cod liver oil is created the same. I recommend you buy cod liver oil from our website www.ontargetliving.com or from your local health food store.

How much cod liver should you take per day? This is where most people are falling short. I will ask my audience participants during my On Target Living seminars if they are taking some form of fish oil daily. Many in the audience raise their hands. Then I explain the serving sizes and how much cod liver oil or fish oil we truly need. The newest research is now showing most adults need approximately 1,000 to 3,000 mg of EPA and DHA per day. Most cod liver or fish oil soft gels contain approximately 100 mg of EPA and DHA per capsule. So if you are consuming two to three soft gels per day, you are getting approximately 200 to 300 mg of EPA and DHA per day, not nearly enough EPA and DHA per day! An easier, more efficient method for consuming cod liver oil is to take it in the oil form. One tablespoon of cod liver oil equals 1500 mg of EPA and DHA per day. So for most adults taking one to two tablespoons of a high quality brand of cod liver oil, they are getting the necessary amount of EPA and DHA per day. What about our kids? Should they be taking cod liver oil too? Absolutely, our kids are also deficient in omega-3 fats, especially EPA and DHA. EPA and DHA are essential for brain development, cognitive awareness, energy, growth, and overall health. Cut the cod liver dosage in half for kids and keep your cod liver oil refrigerated after opening. Oh, I almost forgot, the taste? Buy the fruit-flavored cod liver oil; our family likes the lemon-flavored cod liver oil. It tastes like a lemon drop.

Recommended adult daily serving size of cod liver oil is one to two tablespoons per day. Recommended kids' daily serving size is one to two teaspoons per day.

How Much Omega-3 Fats Should You Eat?

The question is, do you need both, flaxseed or chia *and* cod liver oil to reach all your daily requirements of your omega-3 fatty acids? Ideally, yes. If you are just starting to use flax or chia and that has been a major change for you, then leave it at that. As your habits begin to change, you may want to add the cod liver oil to your plan.

Flax, chia, and cod liver oil are truly magical in the health benefits they bring to the body. Whether you have high cholesterol or triglycerides, hormonal imbalance, diabetes, inflammation, ADHD, depression, poor energy, or are struggling with your weight, these wonderful omega-3 fats can truly make a difference!

Omega-6 Essential Fatty Acids

The second type of polyunsaturated fat is comprised of omega-6 fatty acids. The primary fatty acid in the omega-6 family is *linoleic acid* (LA). Vegetable oils such as corn, soybean, cottonseed, safflower, sunflower, pumpkin seed, and sesame seed all contain linoleic acid. It is also found in many nuts, seeds, and leafy greens. Animal sources of omega-6 fatty acids include lean meats, organ meats, and mother's breast milk.

Like the omega-3 fatty acid family, which converts ALA to EPA and DHA, the primary omega-6 fatty acid LA converts into two fatty acids, gamma-linolenic acid (GLA) and arachidonic acid (AA).

Like the omega-3 family, the omega-6 family contains essential fatty acids. The body cannot produce these essential fatty acids, so they must come from the food we eat.

Health Benefits of Omega-6 Essential Fatty Acids

As with omega-3 fats, omega-6 fats are essential for optimal health. Omega-6 fats are necessary for production of *prostaglandins*, the short-lived, hormone-like substances that regulate most of the body's life-sustaining systems. The body produces prostaglandins from the essential fatty acids we consume each day.

How Is Your Brown Fat Working?

Our bodies have two types of fat cells, white fat and brown fat. White fat is the fat under your skin that insulates the body and is used for energy. This is the fat most of us are trying to lose.

Brown fat is the substance surrounding your organs and differs from white fat in many ways. Brown fat acts as a thermostat and helps the body acclimate to hot and cold temperatures. It aids in weight loss by helping the body convert calories into heat via thermogenesis. Brown fat helps burn 25 percent of all fat calories. In this regard, *brown fat is an important element in metabolism.*

As we age, brown fat begins to lose its burning capability. Think about the difference between senior citizens, who are often sensitive to the cold and gain weight in their late years, and youngsters, who are height-weight proportionate and tolerate cold temperatures easily. Most young children have metabolically active brown fat. I remember going to my grandparents as a kid, and the heat would be cranked way up. It felt like a sauna. I never understood why they always felt cold; this was especially true in the winter months. As kids, we all remember being told "put on your coat so you would not catch a cold!" I remember putting my coat on to please my mom, but as soon as I was out of her sight, off came the coat.

So how do you increase your brown fat? Gamma-linolenic acid (GLA), like its twins from the omega-3 family (EPA and DHA), helps fight heart disease, cancer, diabetes, inflammation, arthritis, and also promotes weight loss. GLA in your daily diet is the raw material needed by the prostaglandins to stimulate brown fat. Dietary deficiencies and disease may block or slow the conversion of LA into GLA. This is one reason it may be necessary to find a direct source that contains GLA. The highest sources of GLA are borage oil, evening primrose oil, and black currant oil.

Where Do You Find Omega-6 Fatty Acids?

Just as you must search for omega-3 fatty acids, you must also search for high quality omega-6 fatty acids. The best sources of omega-6 fatty acids are hemp seeds, soybeans, pumpkin seeds, pumpkin seed oil, sunflower seeds, sunflower seed oil, sesame seeds, sesame seed oil, evening primrose oil, borage oil, black current oil, and leafy greens. Most raw nuts also contain omega-6 fatty acids. To get adequate amounts of GLA into your diet, use unrefined borage, evening primrose, or black currant oil. You must protect omega-6 fatty acids, just like omega-3 fatty acids, by buying them fresh and storing them safely in the refrigerator or freezer. Do not heat or cook with omega-3 or omega-6 fats. Heat destroys the benefits of these fats. Use only saturated fats such as extra virgin coconut oil and most monounsaturated fats for cooking. Do not use refined omega-6 oils such as corn, soybean, cottonseed, and safflower oils.

Arachidonic Acid Overload

Unlike omega-3 fatty acids, which are universally healthy fats, there are great differences in the quality and health benefits of omega-6 fats. *Arachidonic acid* (AA) is the end product of omega-6 fatty acid conversions (LA-GLA-AA). The body needs some arachidonic acid to function optimally, but too much can promote poor health. Refined oils, such as corn or soybean oil, along with too much animal protein, especially red meat, can lead to arachidonic overload. To correct this, try to consume more unrefined oils and limit your consumption of red meat, refined oils, and processed foods.

Omega-3 fats also help by blocking out the conversion to arachidonic acid, keeping your essential fats in balance.

How Much Omega-6 Fat Should You Eat?

Make an effort to get one or two servings (one to two tablespoons) of unrefined, high quality omega-6 fats in your diet each day. Use unrefined oils, raw nuts, seeds, or leafy greens in your daily diet.

Omega-3 and Omega-6 Fats in Balance

Your body functions best when your diet contains a balanced ratio of omega-3 and omega-6 fatty acids. The World Health Organization recommends a two-to-one ratio of essential fatty acids: two omega-6 fats to one omega-3 fat. In the United States, we generally eat an unbalanced ration of omega-3 and omega-6 fatty acids. We have a 16-to-1 (or greater) omega-6 to omega-3 ratio. Ouch!

This imbalance may lead to heart disease, diabetes, cancer, obesity, arthritis, inflammation, Alzheimer's disease, and a host of other autoimmune diseases. A large percentage of the American population over the age of 45 is regularly taking self-prescribed or over-the-counter anti-inflammatories such as aspirin and ibuprofen. These anti-inflammatories may address the symptoms but not the underlying causes, which may be due to an acidic diet along with an imbalance in the consumption of omega-3 and omega-6 fats. Consequently, bringing these fatty acids back into balance can relieve many modern-day health problems.

Since the 1960s, the U.S. consumption of omega-6 oils has doubled. One of the reasons the U.S. population is overeating omega-6 fats is that they are in almost every refined or processed food we consume. With technological improvements in oil extraction over the past 60 years, oil manufacturers can use inexpensive raw materials, such as corn and soybeans, and deliver a tremendous amount of this low-grade oil that is then used in thousands of products delivered to our grocery stores and fast food restaurants. The next time you are in the grocery store, don't be shocked if you see these refined oils everywhere.

Improving the Quality of Fat in Your Diet

Don't become overwhelmed by trying to balance out your omega-3 and omega-6 fats. Start by removing all the refined oils such as corn, soy, cottonseed, safflower, and canola oils that are in your cupboard or refrigerator. Replace all your old cooking oils with high quality saturated and monounsaturated oils. Then move to the high quality omega-3 and omega-6 fats, such as flaxseeds, chia seeds, hemp seeds, cod liver oil, borage, evening primrose or black current oil, seeds, nuts, and leafy greens. Most of high quality omega-3 fats also contain some omega-6 fats.

I have outlined a sample day of consuming healthy fats. Your goal is to improve the quality along with getting a greater variety of healthy fats in your diet. Start slowly and experiment how you are taking these healthy fats.

Sample Day of Fats

Beginning

1. Cut the trans-fatty acids out of your diet. Improve the quality of your peanut butter, crackers, chips, and pizza, anything that may contain trans fats.
2. Add one to two tablespoons of flax meal or chia seeds. You can put this in your cereal, on a salad, in a smoothie drink, or in a glass of juice.

Moderate

1. Add one to two tablespoons of raw nuts or seeds. Add a few almonds, walnuts, macadamia nuts, pecans, pine nuts, organic shredded coconut, sesame, pumpkin, sunflower, or hempseeds to your favorite cereal, salad, or eat a handful as a snack.
2. Add one to two tablespoons of extra virgin olive oil or an avocado. Add a tablespoon of extra virgin olive oil or a slice of avocado to your favorite salad.
3. Add one to two tablespoons of flax meal or chia seeds. You can put this in your cereal, on a salad, in a cup of yogurt or cottage cheese, in a smoothie drink, or in a glass of juice.

Advanced

1. Add one to two tablespoons of raw nuts or seeds (as above).
2. Add one tablespoon of organic shredded or extra virgin coconut oil. Organic coconut oil is excellent for cooking at high temperatures, tastes great on a cracker or a piece of toast, or melted over popped popcorn.
3. Add one to two tablespoons of extra virgin olive oil or avocado (as above).
4. Add one to two tablespoons of flax meal or chia seeds (as above).
5. Add one to two tablespoons of cod liver oil.
6. Add one two soft gels borage, evening primrose oil, or black current oil.

There is no other nutrient available that can heal the body and keep it healthy from infancy to old age like healthy fats.

THE BOTTOM LINE

1. Good fats are the body's healing nutrient.
2. Good fats make you satisfied, improve your energy, and create hormonal balance.
3. Your goal is to eat a variety of high quality, saturated, monounsaturated, omega-3 and omega-6 fats on a daily basis.
4. Avoid trans fats, refined saturated fats, and omega-6 fats.
5. Your goal is to consume four to eight tablespoons of good fats per day.

21

Superfoods—Eat Like a Super Hero!

The price of greatness is responsibility.

—Winston Churchill

Imagine a food, not a typical food that gives you a few vitamins, minerals, and energy, but a potent superfood. A food—not a drug—powerful enough to balance your cholesterol; lower your blood pressure; decrease your risk of heart disease, cancer, and type 2 diabetes; improve digestion; improve hormonal balance and brain health; decrease inflammation; and help you feel great! Sign me up!

So what is a superfood? Superfoods are nutrient-dense, whole foods that offer many amazing health benefits packed into a small amount of food. One of the main reasons I am so passionate about superfoods is they can cover so much ground with just one or two of them. Also, superfoods are easy to find, easy to implement into your daily diet, and most superfoods are not expensive. Just like Superman—superfoods are very powerful!

One frustration I hear on a daily basis is how challenging it can be to know what foods, supplements, or herbs someone should use in their quest for better health, energy, and vitality. I find many people want to target their specific needs or problems with a specific food, supplement, or herb. Want to decrease the risk of catching a cold? Take vitamin C. Want to improve digestion? Take a probiotic. Lower cholesterol? Take niacin or a statin medication. Want to decrease inflammation? Take an aspirin, ibuprofen, or bromelin. Have hot flashes? Take evening primrose oil, borage oil, or black currant seed oil. Want to increase energy? Consume the latest energy drink. Want to improve bone health? Take calcium, magnesium, and vitamin D.

We have to get away from the mind-set of taking foods, supplements, herbs, or medications for isolated needs. It is not the most effective approach to begin with. One key for sustainable success is to build a solid health foundation first. Your health foundation needs to include proper rest and rejuvenation, daily movement, and quality nutrition. Adding one or two superfoods is a great way to begin building your health foundation. Once the nutritional basics are in place, then specific foods, spices, or herbs can be added to target individual needs. A healthy diet incorporating a variety of superfoods will make your cells healthy, balance your pH, maintain your weight, boost your immune system, improve your energy, and help you be your best!

There are so many superfoods to choose from; in fact, just about every brightly colored vegetable or fruit along with most nuts, seeds, beans, herbs, and spices could be classified as superfoods. Here is my top 10 list of superfoods to pick from. You don't have to do all the superfoods overnight. In fact, I recommend beginning with just one or two superfoods. Build a habit, and then if you wish, add another superfood. Start slowly and experience the amazing benefits superfoods can bring to your life.

Cereal Grasses

Grasses are the foundational food for most land-based life. Cereal grasses such as wheat, oat, rye, spelt, or barley grass are extremely high in *chlorophyll* and loaded with over *90 minerals*, making cereal grasses one of the most therapeutic foods in the world. Nutritionally, all the cereal grasses are virtually identical and the juices can be used interchangeably. My favorite is wheatgrass. Wheatgrass is a powerful superfood in keeping the human body healthy and performing at your best. Ann Wigmore was the pioneer for wheatgrass; she started juicing wheatgrass in the 1950s. She later formed the Hippocrates Health Institute in Boston, working with thousands of people over the years.

Wheatgrass juice is a powerful raw, living food. The grass itself comes from the common wheat plant when it is young, vibrant, and full of rich green chlorophyll. Wheatgrass is then harvested when the grass reaches its nutritional peak, just before the jointing stage, when the plant is between 7 and 11 inches tall. When wheatgrass is juiced, it is immediately flash frozen to maintain the life force without compromise. Wheatgrass grown outdoors has more benefits due to the natural air, rain, sun, and soil, but it can also be grown indoors.

You can buy wheatgrass in an ice cube (flash frozen) or in tablet form. I personally prefer the frozen wheatgrass ice cubes: I take four ice cubes each morning and just suck on the ice cubes. I like the taste. Most people prefer to place the ice cubes in a small cup of water and let them melt. How does it taste? It tastes like grass—and has a clean refreshing taste. I know you are excited now! I did not start out thinking wheatgrass ice cubes were going to taste like a chocolate milkshake, but I wanted the amazing benefits they provide, and in just a few days I was hooked. Wheatgrass is best taken first thing in the morning on an empty stomach for optimal absorption.

Benefits of Cereal Grasses

- High in minerals and chlorophyll
- Extremely alkaline, helps balance pH
- Boosts the immune system
- Detoxifies the body and aids digestion
- Reduces inflammation
- More energy and better sleep
- Increases mental clarity
- Improves overall health

Recommended Serving

- 2 to 6 wheatgrass ice cubes per day
- 7 to 10 wheatgrass tablets per day

People with allergies to wheat or other cereals are almost never allergic to them in their grass stage.

Cod Liver Oil

Cod liver oil is high in omega-3 essential fatty acids (EPA and DHA). The liver of the Norwegian cod fish has a naturally high concentration of vitamin D, along with a moderate amount of vitamin A. (For more information on cod liver oil, see Chapter 20.) I take 2 tablespoons of the lemon-flavored cod liver oil every morning. Keep cod liver oil in the refrigerator after opening.

Benefits of Cod Liver Oil

- Improves cellular function
- Boosts cardiovascular health
- Provides hormonal balance
- Aids weight loss
- Improves brain and nerve function
- Supports healthy vision
- Boosts the immune system
- Improves bone and joint health
- Decreases inflammation

Recommended Serving

- 1 to 2 tablespoons (1,500 to 3,000 mg of EPA/DHA per day) or soft gels equivalent for adults
- 1 to 2 teaspoons (500 to 1,000 mg EPA/DHA) or soft gels equivalent for children

Spirulina/Chlorella

Spirulina and chlorella are micro-algae cultivated in fresh water ponds. These amazing superfoods are high in protein, nucleic acid (RNA/DNA), GLA, vitamins, minerals, and fiber, are extremely detoxifying and excellent for improving digestion along with boosting the immune system. Spirulina and chlorella have a grass-like smell due to their high amounts of chlorophyll. Due to the potency of spirulina and chlorella, they are both known as survival foods. Spirulina and chlorella are available in tablets or powder form. I take 30 to 40 tablets of the spirulina/chlorella 50/50 blend throughout my day. I find the tablets easy to take and great for travel.

Benefits of Spirulina/Chlorella

- Great source of plant protein
- Extremely detoxifying
- Balances pH

- Provides rich source of minerals like calcium, magnesium, and iron
- High in nucleic acid and GLA
- Supports heart health
- Boosts weight loss
- Improves energy and overall health
- Low expense

Recommended serving: Start slowly to allow your body to acclimate to the detoxifying benefits of spirulina/chlorella, 10 tablets in the first 30 days.

- 10 to 40 tablets or 2.5 to 10 grams per day for adults
- 5 to 10 tablets or 1 to 2.5 grams per day for children

Note that 1 gram = 4 tablets.

Super Seeds (Flaxseeds, Chia Seeds, or Hemp Seeds)

Flaxseeds are tiny, hard seeds, golden or brown; chia seeds are granular and dark in color; and hemp seeds are soft and light in color. Flaxseeds and chia seeds are high in omega-3 essential fatty acids (ALA). Hemp seeds are high in omega-6 essential fatty acids (LA and GLA), along with being high in protein. Flaxseeds are not digestible, so to reap the wonderful health benefits, the seeds must be ground into flax meal. Use a coffee grinder and grind up a week's worth and store in the refrigerator. Do not buy flax meal already ground as it oxidizes quickly and loses its potency. Chia and hemp seeds do not have to be ground.

Along with being high in omega-3 fats, flax and chia seeds are high in fiber, antifungal, antibacterial, and can be added to a small glass of juice, your favorite smoothie, salad, or cereal. Hemp seeds have a nutty flavor, taste great, and can be taken by the spoonful or added to your favorite salad.

Benefits of Super Seeds

- High in omega-3 fats
- High fiber source
- Supports heart health
- Boosts cellular health

- Decreases inflammation
- Aids weight loss
- Reduces food craving
- Lowers risk of diabetes
- Low expense

Recommended Serving

- 1 to 3 tablespoons per day for adults
- 1 tablespoon per day for children

Sea Vegetables

The powers of sea vegetables or seaweeds are truly amazing and have been used for hundreds of years in creating better health. Why would anyone want to eat seaweed? Scientists are now learning more and more about the powerful health benefits associated with sea vegetables. Sea vegetables contain more than 10 times more calcium than milk, along with high levels of natural iodine, which is necessary to support the thyroid gland. Sea vegetables help neutralize an acidic diet by balancing blood pH and also is a powerful blood purifier. Sea vegetables are one of the oldest food sources along with being one of the most nutritionally dense plants on the planet. There are many sea vegetable options to choose from: wakame, kelp, nori, kombu, arame, and dulse; my favorite is sushi nori. Sushi nori comes in square dried strips that I sprinkle on a salad or use as a wrap with vegetables. You can find many sea vegetable options at your local health food store or traditional grocery stores.

Benefits of Sea Vegetables

- Excellent source of calcium, iodine, B vitamins, and iron
- Balances pH
- Blood cleanser
- Cancer protection
- Healthy thyroid function
- Bone health
- Healthy heart
- Stress relief
- Greater energy
- Improved overall health

Recommended Serving

- Try to get some sea vegetables into your diet on a weekly basis.

Coconut

How did a food that is 92 percent saturated fat make it into the top 10 superfood list? I am not recommending the coconut found in a processed candy bar or the processed coconut that we used to sprinkle on a German Chocolate Cake; no, I am talking about the real, whole coconut. What makes coconut so special? Coconut is a healthy saturated fat that is rich in lauric, capric, and caprylic acids, which are loaded with antiviral, and antifungal properties. More than just a sustainable food crop, every part of the coconut tree is useful to mankind, including the roots, trunks, leaves, husks, fiber, fruit, water, sap, milk, and meat, making coconut as "The Tree of Life!" I use some form of coconut every day. Extra virgin coconut oil is great for cooking and baking due to its high heat point, and you can also spread it on a piece of toast or cracker. Coconut water is high in potassium and magnesium, has a refreshing taste, and is an excellent way to stay hydrated after a workout. I also use shredded coconut and coconut milk on a regular basis, sprinkling shredded coconut on my oatmeal or on frozen berries as an evening snack. I sometimes like to add the coconut milk on my cereal or in a smoothie for breakfast; it makes the smoothie rich and thick. Experience what coconut can do for you!

Benefits of Coconut
- Aids digestion and nutrient absorption
- Promotes brain health
- Reduces risk of Alzheimer's
- Boosts weight loss
- Promotes beautiful skin
- Improves thyroid function
- Supports heart health
- Reduces risk of type 2 diabetes
- High in antioxidants
- Promotes cellular health

Recommended Serving
- 1 to 2 tablespoons per day for adults
- $1/2$ to 1 tablespoon per day for children

Cacao

So what is cacao? Cacao is chocolate, dark chocolate with very little sugar content. Cacao has been a staple with many cultures for centuries and has been labeled *food of the gods* due to its amazing health benefits. I use the cacao nibs; they look like small pieces of dark chocolate and have a bittersweet chocolate flavor. I add cacao nibs to cereal, a smoothie, or in trail mix. I love the chocolate flavor and all the amazing health benefits cacao has to offer.

Benefits of Cacao

- Promotes brain health
- Enhances mood
- Supports heart health
- High in magnesium, manganese, zinc, and iron
- Reduces PMS
- Boosts weight loss
- Improves energy

Recommended Serving

- 1 tablespoon of the cacao nibs or cacao powder per day for adults
- 1 to 2 teaspoons of cacao nibs or cacao powder per day for children

Berries

It is almost impossible to pick up any type of nutritional resource without hearing about the wonderful health benefits associated with eating berries. Strawberries, blueberries, blackberries, raspberries, cranberries, acai berries, goji berries—berries, berries, and more berries! If you want to eat a food that is extremely high in vitamins, minerals, antioxidants, low in calories, and tastes awesome, you can't go wrong with berries. I add a variety of berries to my oatmeal most mornings and my go-to snack in the evening is a cup of frozen berries with a little organic shredded coconut on top, yum!

Benefits of Berries

- High in fiber
- High in antioxidants

- High in phytochemicals
- High in vitamins and minerals
- Improves memory
- Supports heart health
- Decreases inflammation
- Extremely alkaline
- Fights cancer
- Low in calories and tastes great

Recommended Serving

- 1 to 2 cups per day

Leafy Greens

I think most of us have been told to eat our greens from childhood. Green leafy vegetables are so easy to find and highly nutritious, but like many, we are just not eating enough. Try adding more fresh green leafy vegetables like spinach, kale, lettuce, dandelion greens, parsley, chicory, endive, and broccoli sprouts to your daily diet. I try to eat a large salad every day at lunch or dinner.

Benefits of Leafy Greens

- High in fiber
- High in chlorophyll
- High in vitamins and minerals
- Improves brain health
- Supports bone health
- High in omega-3 fats
- Low in calories

Recommended Serving

- 1 to 3 cups of leafy greens per day

Nuts and Seeds

Bring on the nuts and seeds! Nuts and seeds are two of nature's perfect superfoods—packed with fiber, vitamins, minerals, healthy fats, and protein. Try to get a variety of nuts and seeds into your daily diet, including almonds, walnuts, Brazil nuts, pecans, pistachio nuts, hazelnuts, cashews, and one of my favorites, macadamia nuts, as well as pumpkin and sunflower seeds. Throw a few nuts or seeds on cereal or salad, in a smoothie, or just take a handful as a snack.

Benefits of Nuts and Seeds

- Supports heart health
- Decreases inflammation
- Strengthens arteries
- Boosts weight loss
- Improves brain function and memory
- Fights cancer
- Aids digestion
- Promotes bone health

Recommended Serving

- 1 to 3 tablespoons per day

Super Whole Foods

There are so many amazing foods that could fall into the superfood category. Here are a few more: avocados, garlic, alfalfa, ginger, oat groats or rolled oats, millet, amaranth, quinoa, figs, sweet potatoes, beets, onions, cabbage, parsley, bell peppers, kiwi, asparagus, pumpkin, broccoli, carrots, celery, apples, oranges, pomegranate, sprouts, prunes, lemons or limes, cherries, Brussels sprouts, olives, bee pollen, royal jelly, and maca—to name a few.

Visit www.ontargetliving.com to order your superfoods or go to your local health food store.

Start Slowly

I recommend starting out with only one or two superfoods, develop a habit, and when you are ready add another. My first superfood was flaxseeds almost 30 years ago. Just like many of you, I started slowly and over time added a few more superfoods. Today they are part of my daily habits.

Sample Superfood Plan

Here is a snapshot of my daily superfood plan.

Remember to start slowly and add just one or two superfoods until you are ready for more.

6:30 a.m.: Water with lemon, three to four frozen wheatgrass or oatgrass ice cubes, and one to two tablespoons of lemon-flavored cod liver oil

7:00 a.m.: Oat groats ($2/3$ cup), raspberries, pecans, shredded coconut, and unsweetened almond milk

10:00 a.m.: Flaxseed meal or chia seeds (2 tablespoons) with two ounces of organic pomegranate juice, spirulina/chlorella (10 tablets) with water

12:30 p.m.: Big salad with romaine lettuce, sushi nori, beets, carrots, walnuts, can of wild caught Alaskan salmon, extra virgin olive oil, and apple cider vinegar

3:30 p.m.: Macadamia nuts (5), cacao nibs (1 tablespoon) raisins or goji berries (2 tablespoons), and spirulina/chlorella (15 tablets) with water

7:00 p.m.: Tuna steak, avocado, broccoli, sweet potato, and extra virgin olive oil

8:00 p.m.: Frozen organic cherries (10), dried white fig (1), shredded coconut (1 tablespoon)

8:30 p.m.: Mineral water with lemon (16 oz.)

Start slowly by adding a few superfoods into your daily nutrition plan and feel like a superhero!

THE BOTTOM LINE

1. Superfoods are nutrient-dense whole foods that offer amazing health benefits packed into a small amount of food.
2. There are multiple superfoods to choose from, such as cereal grasses, cod liver oil, super seeds, coconut, cacao, spirulina/chlorella, sea vegetables, berries, leafy greens, nuts and seeds, and super whole foods.
3. Start slowly—pick one or two superfoods and build them into a daily habit.

22

The Art and Science of Dieting

All glory comes from daring to begin.

—Eugene F. Ware

With the obesity epidemic in full swing, more and more people in the United States are looking for ways to lose weight. You could say the American population is obsessed with dieting and weight loss, spending over *$50 billion* a year on weight loss related products and services. There are over 45,000 nutrition and diet books on the market today and virtually hundreds of diet programs to choose from, with more new diet programs being introduced each year.

On top of all the old and new diet options available to consumers, weight loss surgery is now one of the fastest growing options to weight loss. Bariatric surgery (weight loss surgery) reduces the size of the stomach, but it is a very serious surgery, with multiple complications and side effects attached.

With all our weight loss options at our fingertips, why is the success rate of losing weight and keeping it off so poor? Is it possible to lose weight and keep if off for a lifetime? How do you increase your odds of becoming successful at losing weight? Let's begin with the Art and Science of Dieting.

The Science of Dieting

There are multiple weight loss programs available that compromise cellular health, pH balance, and in the end, your health. How do you know if a weight loss program is healthy or unhealthy? Let's begin with a little common sense. If a weight loss program guarantees you can lose a pound a day, for 30 days, eat only 500 calories per day and not be hungry, with no exercise required, do you truly believe this plan is healthy, sustainable, and can work for you? On this plan, do you believe your body is getting the necessary nutrients to be healthy from 500 calories? On this diet, your body becomes acidic extremely fast, leaching out valuable minerals. And stress, what about stress to the body? What do you think your stress and sex hormones are doing on this plan? Nothing good! What new habits have you developed on this plan? What have you learned? When the 30 days is up, then what?

This is one of the problems I have when people are on a high-protein, low-carbohydrate diet. The first few weeks you stop eating fruit, increase protein (amino acids), your body becomes acidic, pH becomes out of balance, minerals are depleted, hair starts to fall out, skin becomes dry, energy drops, your stress hormones are on full alert, sleep gets out of whack, you're constipated, and you have bad breath (ketosis), but hey, look at me, I look great!

To fully understand dieting, let's begin with the science of dieting and some basic concepts about how the human body works. Believe it or not, we all function in a similar fashion: our hearts pump blood, our lungs deliver oxygen, our liver cleans and filters toxins, and our muscles move our bones. We eat food for energy, and energy can be measured in calories.

Cellular health is the first science concept I teach in my seminars and to all my coaching clients. Everything begins at the cellular level. If you are feeding your cells processed, low calorie foods, how do you think your cells will respond? As you improve the quality of the nutrients you are feeding your body (your cells), your body becomes more efficient and effective. Your skin, hair, nails, digestion, blood work, hormonal balance, energy, and weight control all become more in balance. Treat your body like your partner, your companion, as you nurture your body by eating and drinking higher quality nutrients, and your body begins to work with you not against you. If your goal is to lose weight and keep it off, improving cellular health is your first key for success!

pH Balance is the second science concept that is critical for overall health and weight control. For a healthy body, you need a balanced pH. As your body becomes too acidic (consuming processed foods and beverages, too much protein, stress, lack of sleep), your body looks for minerals to balance your pH (buffering minerals). In many diet plans, the goal is to quickly move the body into an acid state in its quest to speed up metabolism, dehydrate the body, and lose weight. As the body becomes acidic, heart rate increases, blood pressure rises, water is released from the body, fat-burning increases, and weight loss is accelerated. Sounds great, but wait! Does it make sense to increase inflammation, deplete minerals, activate stress hormones, and upset sleep patterns, along with increasing hair loss, dry skin, cracked nails, constipation, and bad breath? You don't have to sacrifice your health to lose weight.

Hormonal balance is one area that is not talked about enough when it comes to losing weight. Hormonal balance is critical for optimal health and weight control. If you are highly stressed, lack sleep, and have little or no "white space" in your life, weight loss will be an uphill battle. (Go to Chapter 11 to learn more about hormonal balance, stress, and rest and rejuvenation strategies.)

Meal patterning or frequency of eating is an important science component for sustainable energy and weight control. A favorite trick of practiced dieters is to skip meals to lose weight. Many dieters starve themselves much of the day and eat only one to two meals. Let's look at the value of this technique by acquainting ourselves with Sumo wrestlers, who are experts at gaining weight. The Sumos have learned that it's not just what you eat that makes you gain weight, but also how, when, and what you do after eating. To gain weight, the Sumos are gorgers. They eat one or two meals of 3,500 to 4,500 calories each day. Immediately after eating, they take a two- to three-hour nap.

As an example, one budding Sumo wrestler initially weighed in at 350 pounds, and ate 6,000 calories a day spread over three meals. His typical calorie intake was 2,000 calories at breakfast, 2,500 at lunch, and 1,500 calories at dinner.

To gain more weight, he decided to change his approach to eating or the patterns of his meals. At the end of 18 months, he had gained almost 230 pounds while cutting his caloric intake by 2,000 calories a day. How did he do it? He simply adopted the life of established Sumo wrestlers. He decreased his frequency of eating and changed from eating three daily meals to one. He increased the quantity of food, eating 4,000 calories at his single meal, and he went to sleep immediately after eating.

$$4,000 \, \text{calories} \times 1 \, \text{meal/day} + \text{nap} = \text{230-pound weight gain in 18 months}$$

How is it possible to reduce the total calories consumed and the frequency of meals and still gain weight? It *is* possible because of two processes the body uses to protect itself from starvation.

Your body protects itself from skipped meals. A key protector is *lipoprotein lipase*. Lipoprotein lipase is the key enzyme that stores fat to protect the body from starvation. When you decrease the frequency of meals or snacks, your lipoprotein lipase enzymes become more sensitive to storing calories. As the frequency of your meals decreases, your lipoprotein lipase enzymes begin to work overtime in an effort to store extra calories, in the form of fat throughout your body.

After eating, the body's blood glucose level rises, initiating a release of the hormone insulin. Insulin opens cells to use nutrients. Once the needs of the cells are met, the rest of the nutrients are stored as body fat. The increase in insulin levels leads to an increase in body fat stores as well as greater insulin resistance.

By the way, many Sumo wrestlers develop type 2 diabetes by the age of 30 and many die in their late 40s.

By increasing your frequency of eating to four to five smaller meals per day, you will increase your metabolic rate, maintain a steadier blood glucose level, and reduce your chances of overeating at a given meal. Plus, you will not be as hungry during the day. Other benefits to spacing out your meals will be improved mental focus all day (avoiding the typical 2:30 p.m. slump that often leads to binge eating at dinner) and a balanced sense of well-being and energy throughout the day and evening. Bottom line: you will just plain feel better and have a smaller waistline.

Calories? Does a calorie = a calorie? One belief I find hard for many people to change is their belief that a calorie equals a calorie. Do you believe 100 calories of a processed bag of cookies or a doughnut equals 100 calories of broccoli or an apple? Do you think your cell membrane and mitochondria in each of your cells would be affected by these foods in the same manner? Do you believe the impact on your pH would be the same? Does the amount of sleep and stress make a difference in how many calories you consume each day?

When people talk about calories in food or beverages, what do they mean? A calorie is a unit of measurement—but it doesn't measure weight or length. A calorie is a unit or measurement of energy. Food and beverages contain calories, and calories give us energy. So it is easy to understand why many people believe if you just limit your calories and move your body more, losing weight is just going to happen. In fact, many people believe it does not really matter what you eat as long as you are not eating too many calories. This type of thinking is not going to get you far, and the results will be short term. *Calories are important, but the quality of the foods and beverages you consume comes first.*

A common weight loss approach is to determine the number of calories required to maintain your current weight and reduce the number of calories consumed. For example: if your body needs 2,000 calories per day to maintain your current weight, the theory is that by cutting back to 1,500 calories per day, you should lose one pound per week (7 days × 500-calorie deficit per day = 3,500 calories = 1 pound of fat loss). Adding exercise to the plan is a bonus, and calories burned through exercise should contribute to further weight loss. This approach seems pretty simple. Eat less, exercise more, and watch the weight fall off. The truth is, it's not that simple.

The number of calories each person needs each day depends on many variables. The variables include activity level, frequency of meals, food quality, the quantity of food at each meal, lean muscle tissue, food combinations, genetic factors, stress, and hormonal balance. It is possible to cut calories and still gain body fat.

With On Target Living, you will learn that calories are important, but the quality of food you eat, the combination of fat, protein and carbohydrate, frequency of eating, cellular health, pH balance, quality of your sleep, planned down time, and quality exercise all play an important role in weight loss and great health. So the next time you hear, "Does a calorie = a calorie?"—you can answer, absolutely, positively, no.

> Imagine purchasing a $6 million racehorse and then feeding it low-quality, low-calorie, processed foods and beverages. Would you feed your racehorse a cup of coffee or a diet soda and a low-calorie breakfast bar or free muffin for breakfast? Add inadequate rest, not enough water, and lots of stress. How do you think your racehorse would perform?

The Art of Dieting

Where most people fail in their quest for sustainable weight loss is the Art of Dieting. What do I mean by the Art of Dieting? Successful weight loss is as much about knowing what to eat, when to eat, and how to eat (the Science of Dieting) as it is learning how to use your mind, changing beliefs, maintaining focus, and slowly building new habits (the Art of Dieting). One request On Target Living Health and Fitness Coaches and I receive on a regular basis is, "Can you just give me a specific eating and exercise plan to lose weight?" I can, but there are many more components than just following a prescriptive, structured dieting plan. I believe having a plan of action to give you structure and guidance is necessary, especially in the beginning, but true success comes from learning how to tweak your plan to fit your specific needs.

It's Go Time!

Step one in your weight loss journey is to recognize that it is your time to get busy. Maybe you can no longer button your favorite jeans. You get out of breath climbing a flight of stairs. You see a picture or video of yourself from a family gathering and do not like what you see. Or your health is rapidly declining. You go to your doctor, and they want to put you on another medication. You feel embarrassed in a bathing suit or do not feel comfortable in your own skin. You used to be athletic and want to get back into the game. Perhaps you stepped on the scale and have gained fifty pounds. You stopped doing activities you used to love. Whatever your reason, you know it's your time to get busy and get started on a new plan. It's Go Time!

What Do You Want and Why?

Step two is to understand what you want and why. People go on diets for many reasons, but the main reason is most are not satisfied with their current nutritional plan. Whatever the reason, a good portion of our society, right now, is on some type of diet to lose weight. So ask yourself, what do I want and why? This is the fun part for me when working with a coaching client: trying to figure out what people truly want and why. I want my clients to visualize what they want, how they will feel, and the deeper we go, the more successful they will become. Your weight loss journey always begins in your mind. Is it possible to lose weight, improve your health, and find a plan that is right for you? Once you discover what you want, what is behind your *why*, then put a timeline to your plan and write it down. Put your wants and why's in writing! This exercise might take some time, but this is a very important and powerful exercise for your success.

How Did You Get Here?

Step three is to go back in time and examine your past practices or habits. Be honest with yourself: How did you get here? How did you gain your weight? Was it a slow process, gaining three to four pounds a year, or maybe your weight gain came quickly? What does your current lifestyle look like? Do you skip breakfast? Eat one or two big meals per day? Eat out too much and make unhealthy choices? Eat too many foods in the red area of the Food Target? Drink too much soda pop or alcohol? Have limited knowledge of what types of foods to eat? Have little or no "white space"? What are some of your challenges or roadblocks? What strategies have you tried in the past to lose weight? What worked? What did not? Step three is to go back and evaluate your past successes and past failures. This exercise will give you a better understanding of how to move forward and not repeat past failures.

You Can Do It

Step number four is believing you can do it. People ask me on a weekly basis if it is possible to lose weight and keep it off. I always say the same thing—Absolutely! If you knew in your heart that your plan worked 100 percent of the time, how excited would you be to start and follow your new plan? I have competed in over 10 physique contests dating back to 1985—you know, the guys who get up on stage in their little bikini shorts and flex their muscles. Occasionally I turn into one of those guys! It gives me a goal, amps up my focus, and I like the journey of getting into peak physical shape. Every time my plan works like clockwork, but more importantly, I believe 100 percent that my plan is going to work; I know it is going to work! My diet plan is 13 weeks in length, consists of eating only in the green area of the Food Target, along with my superfoods, eat every three to four hours, pay attention to proper rest, and my exercise program stays virtually the same, just with more focus and greater intensity.

The reason I am telling you this is this: the most important ingredient for successful weight loss is believing your plan is going to work. Many people start down their weight loss path knowing they are going to fail before they begin. They don't truly believe they can sustain this type of lifestyle for more than a few weeks. Many are defeated before their first carrot stick, exercise class, or weight loss shake. When people fail to lose weight, they begin to lose confidence in their plan, evident by the hundreds of weight loss programs available, but more importantly they lose confidence in themselves—and unfortunately they begin to lose hope. When people lose hope, they can become desperate, evident with the huge increase in bariatric surgeries performed in the United States and now around the world. Hope has arrived: you can lose weight and keep it off. Now is the time, it is your time to shine.

The 80/20 Plan

Next time you are thinking about going on a diet ask the question, is this program something that makes sense? Can I really live on 1,000 to 1,200 calories per day? No fruit? Little fat? Only raw foods? Most of us at one time or another have tried some type of diet, only to abandon the mission after a specified period of time or specific result. Then we usually go back to our old way of eating. A better option is to follow what I call the "80/20 plan."

The 80/20 plan is a healthy eating plan that you can follow most of the time. Eighty percent of the time you eat in a healthy way. Or if you feel like you are not ready to move this quickly, then think about doing a 70/30 or 60/40 plan; no matter where you are, the key is to find a plan that is right for you. In following the 80/20 plan, most of your food choices fall in the green areas of the Food Target. The other 20 percent of the time, you allow yourself to enjoy foods and beverages that may be outside the green area. When you vow to give up a certain food or beverage you like, you end up focusing on that food or beverage anew. You feel deprived.

One of my coaching clients, Stephanie, came to see me about improving her cholesterol and blood chemistry numbers, but she also had a goal of losing weight. After eight weeks of following the On Target Living Plan, Stephanie was feeling frustrated that she had not lost weight. She explained that she was eating many high quality foods from the center of the Food Target, had added a few superfoods, but the scale was not budging. I asked Stephanie how many days in each month she ate in a healthy way. She thought about it for a few minutes, and I think her answer surprised her. She said she ate healthy approximately 15 days per month. As soon as she said 15 days per month, she knew what the problem was. She was following the 50/50 plan! Her curiosity was piqued and she asked what it would take for her to lose weight. I told her to do exactly what she had been doing on her better days, but do it more frequently. In a one-month period, she would eat healthy (only green areas of the Food Target) for 24 days and treat herself only to 6 days of the month. Three months later, Stephanie had lost 25 pounds and her blood chemistry had greatly improved without medications. Stephanie says she feels fantastic and has found a plan that she can live with the rest of her life.

Many clients come to me as their last chance. They've tried countless diets, supplements, drinks, pills, and elixirs. Most diets don't work. Thousands of my coaching clients and seminar participants have proven this to me. Not only do most diets set up a destructive cycle of deprivation and indulgence, but they also have one fundamental flaw. Following a restrictive diet is a short-term fix. Without an understanding of how the body works and how food works in your body, once the diet is over, the dieter can't manage situations that don't exactly fit the diet. They get bored. Counting and computing calories becomes tedious and unrealistic, so people stop doing it. And sooner or later—often sooner—they end up right back where they started. Only it's worse because they feel as though they've failed; they feel hopeless. But there is hope. And it's easier than you think.

Your goal is to make small changes and slowly develop an eating plan that you enjoy and can sustain.

Monitoring Your Success

Step number five is setting up a monitoring system. How are you going to measure your success? What tools are you going to use to see if your plan is working? Make it simple. Here are a few ways to measure your success on a daily, weekly, and monthly basis:

- Body weight
- Mirror
- Belt
- Pants
- Resting heart rate
- Resting blood pressure

- Sleep
- Energy
- Skin, hair, nails
- Blood work

When it comes to monitoring my weight, the tools I rely on the most are the scale and a belt. I weigh myself two to three times per week and try to keep my weight within three to five pounds all year long (except sometimes over the holidays, I can get a little reckless), along with my belt (fourth notch). If my weight begins to creep up or my belt starts getting a little tight, I know it is time to get my focus back and dial it up a notch. I can sustain my diet plan all year long, and I feel great. When competing in a physique show, I follow the same basic On Target Living Nutrition principles, but eat only in the center of the Food Target for 13 weeks, along with not eating as much. I can follow this plan for 13 weeks, but long term is too strict for me.

There are multiple ways to monitor your plan. You may also want to use a food, exercise, and rest log. Writing down what you eat, drink, sleep, rest, and exercise can be a powerful tool. Make it simple and don't get frustrated if the scale is not moving as fast as you like. Remember to focus on your plan and the results will follow.

The Plan

Step number six is finding a weight loss plan that is right for you. I believe most people fall off the wagon now and then when trying to follow a healthy lifestyle, especially what we eat and drink. Maybe you had a tough weekend, a tough six months, or maybe it's been a lifetime of unhealthy food and beverage choices. Having a plan brings focus and structure back into your life. My goal is to teach you the On Target Living principles so you can tweak any nutritional plan and make it work for you.

One of my longtime friends and health and fitness clients, Bob Cornwell, and I were discussing the Art and Science of Dieting. Bob is a professional pianist and teacher, but those lucky students who get to study and work with Bob know Bob is also a teacher of life. Bob teaches and inspires his students to become better human beings; I believe this is Bob's true gift. A few years ago I was invited for dinner at Bob's house. He gave us a tour of his piano studio with three pianos and lights; it was a beautiful sanctuary of learning! I have always wanted to play the piano, but music is not high on my skill set. Bob asked me to sit down at the piano; he then placed colored tape on specific keys. Bob sat down at another piano and instructed me to follow his tempo and hit specific colors on his command. After just a few minutes, we started to jell and music was coming from my fingertips! I was shocked at the sound and how much fun it was to play the piano. After my short stint at Carnegie Hall, it dawned on me that I had learned how to play a song on the piano, but I still didn't know how to play the piano.

Following a prescriptive diet is very similar to learning how to play a song versus learning how to play the piano. Once the diet ends or you get into situations outside your diet plan, then what? If Bob took the tape off the keys, I was sunk: I had no idea what to do then. Having a structured plan is helpful, but your real success comes when you learn how to develop a nutritional plan that you can sustain for a lifetime. Following is a Big Picture outline for eight weeks.

Personal Action Plan

Week 1—Write Out Your Plan and Keep It Where You Can See It!

- What do you want? Discover your Why? Describe what "healthy" means to you. What are your goals on this journey (lose weight, get off your medications, improve your health, increase your energy, walk/run in a race)?

Week 2—Planning and Accountability

- Start a food, rest, and exercise journal.
- Drink more water.
- Plan your meals. Where can you upgrade?
- Start eating more whole foods and superfoods (not all at once; start slowly!).

Week 3—Setting Up Your Environment for Success

- Now is the time to set up an environment to support your plan.

- Clean out the cupboards—bring in the new!
- Build a support team (friends, family).
- Set up your home, car, and work environments for success. Buy a cooler for your car. Prepare snacks for travel. Create healthy environments for success!

Week 4—Move Your Body

- Start moving your body. If you do not exercise, start with a 10-minute walk.
- If you are currently exercising, how can you improve the quality of your workout? How can you make your workouts more fun?
- Set a training goal: run or walk a 5K, train for a triathlon, lose 20 pounds.

Week 5—Rest and Rejuvenation

- Are you getting enough rest? How can you improve your sleep? Add some White Space into your day?
- Practice diaphragmatic breathing throughout the day.
- Take foam roller and stretch breaks during the day (two to three minutes each).
- Control your stress.

Week 6—Time to Reevaluate

- Evaluate what is working and what is not.
- What are your roadblocks?
- What tools are you using to monitor your success?
- What do you need to change? Continue to do?

Week 7—Step It Up

- What do you need to add or delete?
- Are you ready for another superfood? Learn a new recipe?

(continued)

(continued)

- Can you make your exercise program more consistent? Increase the intensity? Try a new sport or take an exercise class?
- Hire a health and fitness coach.

Week 8—Building Your Foundation

- Habits take time to build, so be patient!
- What changes have you noticed?
- Stay focused on what you want and why.
- Beliefs are powerful.
- You can do it!

Here are a few plans to choose from.

Go Green 10-Day Detox

Eat strictly within the center of the Food Target for 10 days. This 10-day detox program is a great way to jump-start your body and get healthier at the cellular level in no time at all. The body has an amazing ability to repair and heal itself from the impurities and damage of everyday life. A "detox" can speed this process along by cleaning your body with pure, wholesome foods.

Be nice to your body and it will be nice to you!

Kristen's 21-Day Challenge

Eat strictly within the two inner circles of the Food Target for 21 days. This 21-day program gets you in a routine of eating healthy for life. It takes time to build healthy habits and for 21 days you are starting to build routines, break old habits, and build new habits. Use the Food Target to plan your meals and snacks, and learn what foods make up a healthy menu plan.

Challenge yourself and the returns will be amazing!

On Target Living 13-Week Action Plan

This is a big-picture view of what I eat and drink prior to competition. This plan will give you incredible results in 13 weeks!

Pre-Breakfast

- Wheatgrass ice cubes (2 to 4 ice cubes)
- Cod Liver Oil (1 to 2 tablespoons)
- Large glass of water with lemon

Breakfast

- Oatmeal, oat groats, steel cut oats, amaranth, or millet with nuts, fruit, shredded coconut, cinnamon almond milk, hemp, or coconut milk
- Or egg white omelet with vegetables and extra-virgin coconut oil or olive oil

Snacks

- Small salad
- Apple, celery, carrots
- Small piece of chicken or fish and 1/2 sweet potato
- Smoothie with frozen berries, carrot juice, banana, greens, rice or hemp protein powder, and water
- Juice: Beets, celery, apples, carrots
- Tuna salad with lettuce wraps (tongal tuna, extra-virgin olive oil, onions, slaw)
- Spirulina/Chlorella (5 tablets)
- Macadamia nuts with a handful of raisins
- Organic Greek yogurt with fruit
- Sushi nori strips

Lunch

- Big salad with tuna, chicken, or fish, slaw, bell peppers, extra-virgin olive oil with lemon, apple cider, or balsamic vinegar

- Leftovers (chicken, fish, game meat, baked vegetables, and sweet potato)
- Spirulina/Chlorella (5 tablets)

Dinner

- Chicken, fish, flank steak, buffalo, ostrich, or elk
- Baked, steamed, or grilled vegetables (root, asparagus, broccoli, cauliflower, purple cabbage, spinach, or kale)
- Small salad of greens and slaw
- Sweet, red, or purple potatoes
- Spirulina/Chlorella (5 tablets)

Evening Snacks

- Wheatgrass ice cubes
- Frozen berries or dark cherries with shredded coconut
- Small piece of chicken or fish with bell peppers
- Organic rice cake with extra virgin coconut oil
- Warm water with lemon
- Organic pomegranate, cinnamon, or green tea

Daily Rituals

- Water with lemon or lime (6 ounces per hour)
- Mineral water (3 servings per week)
- Planned sleep (7 to 8 hours per night)
- Breath awareness and diaphragmatic breathing
- Foam roller daily!
- Planned White Space into my day, week, and month
- Dynamic and foundation exercises daily
- Strength training (three-day split, reps of 5-8-13, with planned recovery)
- Cardio exercise (steady state and interval training, 21 minutes)
- Massage two times a month
- 5-finger shoes (wear around the house daily)

Measurements

- Blood work
- Weight

- Clothes/belt
- Resting heart rate and blood pressure
- Sleep
- Energy and mood

These are just a few plans to choose from and will help create a structure to follow. The real key for sustainable success is to make it your own!

THE BOTTOM LINE

1. The American population is obsessed with weight loss, spending over $50 billion a year on weight loss related products and services.
2. Most conventional diets directly address only weight loss, downplaying or ignoring optimal health and performance.
3. Understanding the Art and Science of Dieting is essential for sustainable weight loss.
4. A calorie does not equal a calorie!
5. Develop an eating plan that you can sustain and live with, "The 80/20 Plan."
6. Believing your plan will work is a powerful step to take!

23

How to Feed Your Kids

Lessons Learned Living with the "Health Freak"*

Vision is the art of seeing the invisible.

—Jonathan Swift

People have always asked us, "What was it like growing up with a health freak?" To tell you the truth it seemed normal, but why wouldn't it be normal to have family meals most days of the week? Why wouldn't it be normal to consume cod liver oil, flaxseeds and wheatgrass on the daily? Why wouldn't it be normal to exercise as a family? Looking back neither one of us would change our childhood one bit. Did we have challenges with what we had in the refrigerator? Yes! Did we always like exercise? No. Did we eat birthday cake and ice cream? Yes!

Kristen's Story

"Dad, why can't we eat like normal people? This goat's milk is disgusting and why is this hempseed bread so hard? Do we have to have salmon patties and peas for dinner tonight?" This was my life.

Growing up, flaxseeds, cod liver oil, and oatmeal made up my diet vocabulary. Not only was my dad a "health freak," as I like to call him, but my mom comes from a huge Lebanese family and is a fabulous cook—combined, our meals were not only healthy

*Chapter written by Matt Johnson.

but also delicious. My brother and I grew up liking all foods. We learned to like eating everything my mom prepared and looked forward to our healthy and delicious family dinners around the table.

Not only was healthy eating part of my life, but so was exercise. Growing up with a dad who was a personal trainer and a speaker on nutrition and wellness, I guess I couldn't ask for more. My brother and I practically lived at my Dad's Athletic Club, which felt like a huge playground at the time with all sorts of fun things to do. After a while, Dad stopped taking us with him once we got into all kinds of trouble for using the weight room under age and racking up too many charges of chicken fingers and French fries on his account.

Family vacations consisted of ski trips to Colorado, summer trips to Lake Michigan to swim and climb the sand dunes, and leisure activities like golf and tennis. We also had an outdoor pool growing up and spent most of our time outside. When renting vacation homes on Lake Michigan, we would choose homes that had a long staircase leading down to the beach so we could climb the stairs for *fun*. Now I realize why my friends never returned for a second year on family vacation with the Johnsons.

This life of eating healthy and exercising was all I ever knew. As I got older I realized that my family's way of living wasn't your average family life.

Once I hit high school, I was determined to rebel. Everything my parents did and said was stupid. I started going over to friends' houses more and was fascinated with all of the junk foods in their cupboards. I even got to explore the world of fast food with my friends' families.

Throughout my high school years, I was a pretty good track athlete and was diagnosed with asthma shortly into my first season. Before I knew it I was prescribed a steroidal inhaler, a bronchodilator, and an allergy pill. I didn't think much of it at the time since most everyone on my track team had an inhaler. My current diet consisted of no breakfast, a salt stick and cookie for lunch, and sometimes fast food for my afternoon snack. As I

(continued)

(continued)

got older and more into my track career I realized that I had the potential to be a great track star if I actually tried. I started to eat breakfast, packed my lunch everyday with salads or leftovers from dinner, and worked out year round and not just during track practice. My need for my asthma medications went away and I was running my best times ever. I didn't have asthma at all- I just had a crappy diet and needed to clean up my immune system with pure, wholesome foods. This was my first aha moment.

Off to college I went and into the dorm life I lived. I felt like I was a kid in a candy store the first time I entered the dorm cafeteria. I thought this was the good life until I put on those legendary 10 pounds. I did not like how my body was changing, but most of all I did not like the way I felt. I fell into the freshman trap of eating food that left me feeling tired all the time and interfered with my ability to concentrate in class. I guess I could say I had my fair share of junk and actually craved healthy foods and longed for my old family dinners. I was tired of feeling sick and tired! This was my second aha moment and the gateway into my career.

My lifestyle changed pretty quickly and I started to resort back to my old childhood ways of working out at the gym and eating the right foods. I ended up losing those freshman 10 pounds plus some, effortlessly. This made me realize how powerful nutrition and exercise could truly be. Throughout college I was constantly surrounded by people who ate bad foods, didn't exercise, and took ADHD medication. I knew that I wanted to somehow find a way to teach people just how powerful food and fitness can be!

Eat Healthy, Live Happy!
—Kristen Johnson, Registered Dietitian and Certified Personal Trainer
(Hey, if you can't beat 'em, join 'em!)

Matt's Story

Why is my acne getting worse and my grades suffering? This was my final aha moment.

Let's back up before I begin. Throughout my childhood I was always the most active, joyful kid in the group. Borderline spaz kid, I loved sports, I loved playing outside, and I hated sitting still. Remember the movie *Problem Child*? That was me (okay, maybe I wasn't *that* bad). My childhood was the best, but my teachers always thought I was a little too high-energy and lacked concentration skills. I think most kids who dream of playing in the NBA have trouble focusing on history and language arts! I was diagnosed with ADHD and my only solution was medication, right? Wrong! As you have read in this book, this was not the solution my family was going to live with. What could I do to control my ADHD? Although I was always high-energy, taking control of my eating, exercise, and rest helped me cope with ADHD. As I grew older I learned what I needed to do to perform on a day-to-day basis without medication. This helped me play better golf and get into college. I never made the NBA, but I earned my way to a college scholarship as a golfer for Grand Valley State University. Although I lived it, breathed it, and saw the results, I still needed the aha moment, and to do that, I needed to get into a new environment where I made the choices.

As I left for college, I was 155 pounds, had a mean six-pack and could hit a golf ball 300 yards and straight. That totally flipped upside down in three months. I was 20 pounds heavier, felt like crap, had horrible skin, didn't get good grades, and the worst was I was playing horrible golf. I was eating only two large meals per day at the Fresh Food dining center, I wasn't exercising, I wasn't sleeping, and had a ton of new emotions and hormones going around. Who doesn't?—it's freshman year of college. So what did I do? I started to realize that what I had been taught my whole life really does make a difference. I got to experience eating fast food, late-night pizza rolls, and the freshman 15. The best part was that I had a solution. Since that period of time, my health and well-being are much more than looking good or following what I am told. I know what it is like to feel your best and I know what it is like to lose that feeling in a short period of time. The rest of my college career was amazing: I was first team all-conference, won two conference team titles, was on the dean's list, was in the best shape of my life, my skin got amazingly better, and I met my wife Holly. I used the

(continued)

(continued)

cooking skills from my mom and the knowledge of eating from my dad and finally put them to good use.

My mission is like my dad's: to help people realize what it is like to feel and be your best. Do I have challenges and weaknesses? Yes! But do I know how to take care of myself in a way that gives me an opportunity to succeed? Yes!

—Matt Johnson, Director of Business Development and Health & Fitness Coach for On Target Living

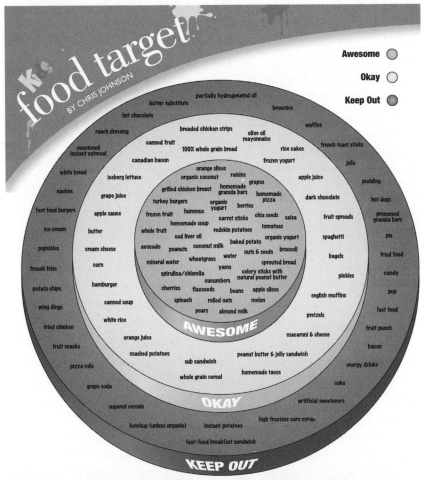

FIGURE 23.1 Kids Food Target

With the explosion of obesity, type 2 diabetes and a long list of other problems our kids are now facing, we felt it was time at On Target Living that our Kids needed their own "Kids food target"—Figure 23.1. The Kids food target was designed by Kids—for kids!

Feeding Your Kids 101

Based on our upbringing along with the knowledge we have gained from our careers in nutrition, we suggest the following tips for feeding your kids.

1. **Be a Role Model**

   Kids learn a lot by observing their parents, and that includes eating habits. If you want your children to eat healthy foods, then you should eat healthy foods, too. The key to life-long healthy eating is to learn how to make correct choices at a young age. Experts say children develop lifelong eating habits between the ages of 6 and 12. Kid's can actually develop taste buds for healthier foods. By teaching your kid's the basics of proper nutrition now, you can *inspire* your children to eat better no matter where they are.

2. **Get the Kid's Involved**

   Involving kids in food choice and preparation is one of the best strategies for helping them eat healthier. Teach your kid's basic cooking skills. If your kid's helped prepare the food they will be more likely to eat it. They will also be more likely to prepare their own meals as they grow older. Try to eat family meals together most days of the week. Family meals can also be much healthier and less expensive than dining out. Research shows that eating together around the dinner table translates into a better diet and less chance of overeating.

3. **Upgrade**

   Everything can be fit into a healthy meal plan in moderation. You don't have to give up anything! You can literally fit any food into your meal plan- just upgrade it and make it healthier. Choose organic dairy products and meats, whole grain chips/crackers/breads, or make your own baked goods using coconut oil or applesauce as the oil/fat replacement. Just improve the quality of the foods you are buying and eating! Less is best when looking at a food label or ingredient list. If you can't pronounce an ingredient or you don't know what it is- back away!

4. Superfoods = Superheroes

Consuming healthy fats, greens, vegetables and fruits can make a tremendous impact on your kids. Epidemic levels of obesity, Type 2 Diabetes, asthma, ADHA, digestive health; acne, low energy and poor sleep habits are at an all time high amongst our kids! As a society, we are becoming more and more nutrient deficient. Ninety-five percent of our kids are deficient in Omega-3 fats necessary for brain development and overall health. Cod liver oil, flaxseeds and chia seeds are powerful Omega-3 fats and necessary for optimal brain health. Kid's with ADHD tend to have lower levels of EPA and DHA which help to support brain function. Cod liver oil is the number one source of EPA and DHA needed to help the brain relax and focus. Start with the problem rather than the symptom and use food, sleep, and movement as your prescription!

5. **Don't Be the Food Police**

Don't force your kid's to eat a certain food or finish their plate. Making kid's clear their plate only reinforces overeating. Unlike adults, kids know when they are full. When kids are truly hungry-they *will* eat. Practice the "one bite" rule where your kid's have to take at least one bite of a new food. If they don't like it- they don't have to eat it- but at least they have tried it. You can also reintroduce foods several times- children's taste buds as well as their attitudes change every few years.

Good luck! Be patient. Have fun and experience the benefits of healthy eating!

THE BOTTOM LINE

1. What your kids eat and drink will have a powerful impact on their health, energy, and happiness!
2. To get your kids to eat healthier, you must eat healthier. Be the leader!
3. Whatever your kids enjoy eating—ask the question, how can you make it better?
4. Work with your kids and experiment with foods and recipes.
5. Start slowly and make small changes.

24

Creating a Healthy Food Environment

Grocery Shopping

When you do what you do best you are helping others.

—Roger Williams

Creating a healthy environment at home, at work, or wherever life takes you is critical for supporting a healthy lifestyle. Whether I am on the road, in the office, or at home, I always try to have healthy food and beverage options available to support my goal of feeling great and performing at my best. Creating a healthy environment begins in the grocery or health food store. Sometimes I have to laugh to myself: What is the difference between a grocery store and a health food store? Isn't the grocery store healthy too? Is everything in the health food store healthy? Learning how to maneuver in the traditional grocery stores along with the health food stores is a learned skill that will help you in your quest for being your best!

I spent over eight years working in grocery stores with Butternut Bread and Frito-Lay, watching people look at labels, ask questions, trying to figure out the healthiest foods available or how to put a healthy meal together while on a budget. Knowing how to grocery shop is not easy. A few times each year, I hold a free shopping trip at our local health food store, Foods For Living. Foods For Living is a beautiful store, pleasing to the senses, and it offers a large variety of fresh produce, meats, bulk items, supplements, and nonperishables. They also have a terrific staff who is extremely passionate and knowledgeable about healthy eating. At the beginning of each shopping trip, I ask if there are any first time shoppers.

211

At least half of the group has never been in a health food store before. I truly enjoy talking with many first-time shoppers. Many are completely overwhelmed standing in a health food store for the first time. When I tell the group to relax, nobody has to eat alfalfa or sea vegetables, everyone laughs, begins to relax, and the learning begins. We begin each shopping tour by breaking down each aisle, what to look for, how to read a label, how to make easy upgrades, and then determine if some of these foods or beverages can fit into their lifestyles. I explain how they can improve their catsup, salad dressings, soup, peanut butter, crackers, mineral water, cacao, nuts, seeds, produce, meats, milk, frozen foods, shampoo, deodorant, lotions, toothpaste, laundry soap, and even food and treats for their pets! I also want them to know why they are making these upgrades. Remember growing up, I was eating Beefornia, bologna sandwiches on processed white bread with mayo, and drinking grape-flavored Kool-Aid.

Take small steps when improving your nutritional plan. Over time these small steps become a permanent part of your routine. Seldom do people like a new taste or texture, especially if they think it is good for them. Switching from a processed, highly sweetened peanut butter to a natural or organic peanut or almond butter, many people may not like the initial change, but within a week or so they get used to it and then they start to like it.

The question I hear in many of my seminars is "how does it taste?" Whenever I talk about cod liver oil and its wonderful health benefits, most people get this disgusting look on their faces. For years I have been trying to get some of my family members to start taking cod liver oil; the cod liver oil is lemon-flavored and tastes like a lemon drop, honestly. I knew how the cod liver could improve their health, so at Christmas a few years ago I poured everyone a shot of cod liver oil. (Don't you wish you could spend Christmas at my house?) Most thought it tasted okay, not as bad as they anticipated, and many decided this was something they could do. My mom now preaches to anyone who will listen the benefits of the cod liver oil and its refreshing taste.

Do you choose foods that taste good or choose foods that are good for you? Can you have foods that are good for you and taste good too? Absolutely! But you need to be willing to try new tastes and be patient. Many people have a difficult time understanding how wheatgrass or lemon-flavored cod liver oil could be part of my daily routine. Maybe my taste buds were out to lunch the first time I tried them. My intention was not that these products were going to taste good; my intention was that I wanted the wonderful health benefits that they bring. Improving the quality of the foods and beverages you eat and drink makes a tremendous difference in how you look, feel, and in your overall health and performance.

When you fill your shopping cart wisely, you are well on your way to a healthier you. If you have unhealthy food and beverages in the house, start cleaning out your pantry and refrigerator and start fresh. Almost all of your healthier food and beverage items can be purchased at most conventional grocery stores. Many now have a natural or organic food section. I would also recommend that you find a natural food store in your community along with a farmers market.

Go shopping with a plan and ask questions.

Making upgrades can be easy. Start slowly and experiment with foods and beverages.

> To help you in your quest for a healthier you, go to www .ontargetliving.com and print the On Target Living "Shopping List" along with our "Brand Favorites."

Healthy Eating on the Run

In our fast-paced lives, it can be difficult to eat in as healthy a manner as you would like, especially when you get busy or while traveling. It is easy to get out of your normal routines, and this is when many people get in trouble.

Out-of-Town Travel

What do you do when you fly? I am on a plane more than 40 weeks per year. I truly love what I do, but flying can beat you up! Busy airports, delays, overbooked flights, cramped seating, recycled air, hydrogenated nuts, crackers, chips, cookies, soda pop, juice, alcohol, and water. You are virtually going into the jungle when you travel, and you have to be prepared. You want to feel and look your best when you arrive at your final destination. You don't want to feel like garbage every time you travel. Come prepared to feel your best.

I never leave home without a bottle of water, wheatgrass, spirulina/ chlorella, chia seeds, my own trail mix, cod liver oil, sushi nori, fruit, carrots, celery, and health bars. It takes me less than 10 minutes to put everything together. I never know how long the trip is going to take and don't want to be stuck having to depend on the airports to feed me. There is good news: many airports are now offering healthier food options.

Last spring I was on my way to New York City from Detroit, and my hub was Detroit. Our plane had been delayed from taking off for one hour due to inclement weather. As everyone boarded the plane, another thunderstorm struck quickly, and our plane was not able to take off. High winds, rain, and lightning: we were all now stuck on the plane. For over two and a half hours, our plane was unable to take off. It was now almost 9:00 p.m. and most people had not eaten since breakfast or lunch. There was not one morsel of food left to eat on the plane. Not a bag of nuts, chips, cookies, nothing! People were beginning to melt down. I was on my way to New York for four days and was armed for battle. So I pulled out everything I had, wheatgrass, trail mix, nuts, dried fruit, health bars, spirulina/chlorella (spirulina/chlorella is a survival food and we were all trying to survive), chia seeds, carrots, celery and sushi nori. I announced that I was open for service. I wish I had videotaped this exchange—but most people were not in the mood to be videotaped at this time. It was like I was doing a mini On Target Living seminar on the plane. I told people what I did, showed them the Food Target and gave away every food item I had. The most interesting of all was the sushi nori (sea vegetable). Many were afraid to try the sushi nori strips, but after one brave soul took a bite, they disappeared in minutes. After the food frenzy exchange, the questions started pouring in. Where do you get some of these food items? How long does it take you to pack all these food items? How do these food items get through security? A few days after I returned home, I received multiple e-mails thanking me for the food, but more importantly showing them that you can eat healthy while traveling.

Travel Items

- **Trail mix** (rolled oats, raisins or organic cherries, dried white figs, macadamia nuts, pecans, organic shredded coconut, cacao nibs)
- **Health bars**
- **Carrots**
- **Celery**

- **Orange or banana**
- **Spirulina/Chlorella**
- **Wheatgrass** (shipped to speaking events)
- **Cod liver oil** (shipped to speaking events)
- **Chia seeds** (do not have to grind, mixes easily with a few ounces of juice)
- **Sushi nori** (comes in thin strips)
- **Bottle of water**
- **Exercise bands** (green/red)

Plan ahead, come prepared, and maybe you can share a healthy snack with a new friend.

Dining Out

Dining out is one of the most popular leisure activities around the world. Almost everything we do in the United States is centered around food. Football tailgating, graduations, weddings, retirements, holidays, entertainment, business meetings, getting together with friends—you name it, we do it with food. Today dining out is an everyday event for most Americans.

From a health standpoint, eating out can be a bit more challenging than eating at home. It is possible, however, to eat out and maintain healthy habits. Most restaurants have healthy choices, and the choices you make have a major impact on your waistline, your health, and your performance. Here are a few tips that you can use when dining out.

Have a plan: Just like grocery shopping, dining out begins with a plan. What do you want to eat? What type of restaurant? What are your options at this restaurant? How much time do you have? Take-out or sit-down? Sometimes you find yourself in situations in which you don't have much of a choice; if that is the case, focus on making the best of what is available to you and let it go.

Make smart menu choices: When dining out with people for the first time, many want to know what I am going to order, then many times they order the same thing. Granted I don't get many invitations to dinner, and I try not to be the "food or exercise police," but I guess it comes with the territory. Many times after we have ordered, I ask if our group would like to learn more about the menu and how to make healthy choices. We go over the menu, discuss options, and how to make upgrades. It generally turns into a fun exchange. Most restaurants allow you to make substitutions and get exactly what you are looking for. Many times I order a plain baked potato with extra-virgin olive oil on the side versus the cheesy potatoes, or clear soup versus the thick cream soup, or a healthier salad dressing option, or a fresh bowl of berries for dessert versus the hot fudge sundae with a cookie. It is the little stuff that makes a big difference over time.

Making better choices: Making better choices when dining out gets down to one thing—focus! You may want to debate me on this statement, but the next time you eat out, take a second and think about what you are focused on. I believe what you are focused on is what you will get. What are you focused on when scanning the menu? Is your focus merely on taste, or are there other factors that you want along with taste? Don't get me wrong, taste is important; I want my food to taste good too! But are you focusing on other factors that will influence your decision making process? Are your health, your energy, your waistline, and your performance areas that you are focused on?

Every time you eat out, you will be faced with these decisions. Focus on what you want. If you know what you want, your decisions will be much easier. Should you choose the diet soda or a glass of mineral water with a slice of lemon? The bread before lunch or dinner? The salad with bacon, croutons, and ranch dressing or the salad with nuts, added vegetables, extra virgin olive oil, and balsamic vinegar dressing? The pasta with Alfredo sauce or the Alaskan salmon and asparagus? The chocolate cake or a cup of raspberries for dessert?

The instant gratification from food and beverages is extremely powerful, and making healthier choices can be challenging at times. As I have said throughout this book, change can be difficult, but you can change! Moving your attention away from just taste to other areas such as health, energy, and controlling your body weight may take time. The thought of a piece of warm bread dipped in olive oil or a slice of chocolate cake with a scoop of ice cream may sound great. We all have had these thoughts, and this is okay. Food is meant to be enjoyed and shared. But can you have your cake and eat it too? Again, a big part of creating healthier lifestyle habits is what you focus on. If you truly want the warm bread or chocolate cake for dessert, then go for it and don't look back. Just be mindful of what you truly want. You may find that if you pass on the bread and cake, you may feel like you have not given anything up because your focus was in a different place. You may start by focusing on drinking mineral water with lemon instead of the diet soda, or eating half your entrée and taking the rest home. Eating out can be a healthy and pleasurable experience all rolled into one.

THE BOTTOM LINE

1. **Create a healthy environment**. One of the first steps on your journey is to set up healthy environments all around you. At home, at work, when traveling.
2. **Grocery shopping made easy**. Learn how to maneuver in the grocery or health foods stores, where your food and beverage choices begin.
3. **Eating on the run**. Buy a cooler for your car. Pack snacks for the plane ride. Developing strategies when eating on the run; they can be simple and extremely effective in your quest for a healthy lifestyle.
4. **Have a plan**. What do you want to eat? Where are you going to eat? Does the restaurant have healthy options?
5. **Scan the menu for healthy options**. Do you have many options to choose from? Can you get what you want? If you don't see it on the menu, ask.
6. **Focus on what you want**. Do you want good taste? Better health? Higher energy? A trimmer waistline? You *can* have it all!

25 Recipes

The shell must break before the bird can fly.

—Alfred Lord Tennyson

The On Target team thought adding a couple sample recipes for different meals would be a good way to show you how to practically apply some of the principles taught in this book.

First rule of thumb: when you have the option to cook with organic produce, meat/dairy, and spices, then we recommend doing that. As you know, this is not always a feasible option, but trying to find a better source is always going to be beneficial. As you look at these recipes, take them as examples; we want to show you how easy and beneficial cooking and preparing food can be.

In the following recipes, if you see "eggs," we are always using a high-quality free-range egg; if it says "honey," we are using a raw organic honey; if you see "oats," we are using 100 percent rolled oats. For more recipes and how-to videos, check out www.ontargetliving.com.

Breakfast

Egg Frittata

6 free-range organic eggs
1 cup almond or coconut milk
1/4 cup fresh organic Parmesan cheese

$^1/_2$ cup small asparagus, chopped
Celtic sea salt
Pepper

Whisk all the ingredients together in a mixing bowl, season with salt and pepper. Spray some extra-virgin olive oil spray on a mini muffin pan and fill each spot with the egg mixture. Cook at 350° for 8 to 10 minutes or until fully cooked through. Serve immediately.

Oatmeal on the Run

$^1/_2$ cup rolled oats
$1^1/_2$ tablespoons fruit (dried, frozen, or fresh)
1 tablespoon slivered almonds, pecans, walnuts, or macadamia nuts
$^1/_2$ cup almond, coconut, or hemp milk

Place all ingredients in a small bowl with lid. Let stand in refrigerator overnight or for 10 minutes prior to eating. No cooking required. Fast, easy, healthy, and tastes great.

Breakfast Smoothie

2 cups water or carrot juice
1 cup organic kale or spinach
1 banana
2 cups frozen or fresh berries
2 tablespoons ground flaxseed
$^1/_2$ cup of organic rice, amaranth, alfalfa, pea, or hemp protein powder

Mix in blender. Makes three servings.

Crockpot Oats with Figs and Apples

1 cup oat groats
1 apple or pear, peeled and chopped
4 dried white figs, chopped
1 teaspoon ground cinnamon
4 cups of water

Rinse oats and soak in cold water for 1 hour. Drain oats and add to small (1.5 quart) crockpot. Add 4 cups of water, apple, figs, and cinnamon.

Stir to mix. Turn on crockpot and cook for 7 to 8 hours. Serve hot with almond milk (optional).

Superhero Breakfast

2 cups traditional quinoa, rinsed and drained
$1/2$ cup natural or organic crunchy peanut or almond butter
2 tablespoons organic honey
1 tablespoons cinnamon
$1/2$ cup raisins

Bring quinoa and 4 cups water to a boil in a large pot. Lower heat to simmer and cook for 10 to 15 minutes or until quinoa is al dente and all water is absorbed. While hot, mix in peanut or almond butter, honey, and cinnamon until well blended. Stir in raisins. Serve warm or chilled.

Scrambled Eggs and Veggies

$1/2$ tablespoon extra virgin olive oil or extra virgin coconut oil
$1/4$ cup sliced or chopped onion
$1/4$ cup sliced or chopped green or red bell pepper
$1/4$ cup sliced or chopped mushrooms (approximately 6)
4 eggs (organic free-range)
1 tablespoon feta cheese (optional)

Heat oil in skillet and sauté vegetables. Pour beaten eggs into skillet. As eggs begin to set, mix the scrambled eggs with the veggies.
Serve with sliced fruit.

Oatmeal Pancakes

2 tablespoons almond or coconut milk
5 egg whites (organic free-range)
2 whole eggs (organic free-range)
$1^1/2$ cups rolled oats
$1/2$ cup organic low-fat cottage cheese
$1/2$ cup natural unsweetened applesauce
$1/2$ teaspoon vanilla extract
$1/2$ teaspoon cinnamon
$1/2$ tablespoon extra-virgin coconut oil

Mix all ingredients except oil in a blender until smooth (add more milk for creamier batter). Pour into large bowl; let stand for 5 minutes. Pour ⅓ cup batter per pancake onto hot, oiled griddle. Cook until bubbles form, then flip. Serve topped with a spoonful of fruit or natural applesauce.

MJ's Salmon Hash

Salmon:
   1 salmon fillet, with the skin on
   Extra virgin olive oil
   Sea salt and freshly ground black pepper
   Fresh dill, for garnish

Hash:
   About 1 cup extra-virgin olive oil
   6 organic redskin potatoes, rinsed in water and diced
   Sea salt and freshly ground black pepper
   2 onions, thinly sliced
   1 red bell pepper, seeds and ribs removed, thinly sliced
   2 cloves garlic, minced
   2 green onions, finely chopped
   3 sprigs fresh thyme, leaves removed
   1 teaspoon smoked paprika
   Pinch cayenne pepper

Egg:
   Water
   White vinegar
   4 to 6 large organic free-range eggs

Preheat oven to 300°.

Place the salmon on a large baking sheet skin-side down. Drizzle salmon with olive oil and season with salt and pepper to taste. Place into the oven and bake for 30 minutes until flaky. Transfer to a cutting board.

Heat a large sauté pan over medium-high heat and add olive oil. Once heated, add the potatoes and shallow-fry for about 8 minutes until evenly browned on all sides. Remove the potatoes with a slotted spoon and place onto a plate lined with a paper towel. Season with salt and pepper and transfer to a large bowl.

Using two forks, flake the salmon, removing it in chunks from the skin, and fold into the potatoes.

Remove most of the oil, leaving only a couple of tablespoons. Place over medium heat and add the sliced onions, sliced peppers, and garlic and allow to caramelize. Add the green onions, thyme leaves, paprika, and cayenne pepper. Season with salt and freshly ground black pepper to taste, and stir to combine. Add the potatoes back to the pan and stir to combine.

Eggs: Place a large sauté pan with high sides over medium heat and fill with a few inches of water. Heat until just below a simmer. Add a splash of white vinegar and, using a wooden spoon, stir the water in one direction to create a small whirlpool. Crack the eggs and add, one at a time, to the spinning water. Allow to poach until desired doneness. Remove with a slotted spoon to a plate.

Lunch

Tuna Salad

2 cans of tongal tuna in water
1–2 tablespoons of organic olive oil mayo
1 tablespoon freshly grated organic Parmesan Cheese
½ cup red pepper, chopped small
½ green onion, chopped
Pinch Celtic sea salt
1 teaspoon black pepper
5 fresh chopped basil leaves

Mix together and let sit in refrigerator.

Awesome Chicken Salad

4 organic chicken breasts (poached in broth), cooled and chopped
1 cup black or wild rice (cooked and cooled)
1 cup chopped celery
4 scallions, chopped
1 cup chopped walnuts
3/4 cup dried cranberries

Mix all ingredients and combine with sauce.

Sauce:

   One 16-oz. jar organic olive oil mayo
   Juice of $1/2$ lemon
   2 tablespoons curry powder (more or less to taste)
   Salt/Pepper to taste

Whisk together and store in refrigerator for one hour to mesh flavors before combining with dry ingredients.

Krissy's Favorite Salad

$1/4$ cup pecans
1 tablespoon organic agave nectar or organic honey
2 organic hearts of romaine lettuce, washed and chopped
$1/2$ cup hearts of palm, chopped
$1/4$ cup organic dried cherries
$1/4$ cup red onion, chopped
$1/2$ cup organic cherry tomatoes, halved

Dijon Mustard Vinaigrette:

   2 tablespoons white wine vinegar
   $1/4$ teaspoon sea salt
   Freshly ground black pepper
   1 tablespoon Dijon mustard
   $1/4$ cup extra-virgin olive oil

Heat a medium skillet over medium heat. Add in pecans and cook for 5 to 10 minutes or until toasted. Turn off heat and drizzle pecans with agave nectar. Let sit for 10 minutes.

Meanwhile, for the Dijon mustard vinaigrette, add vinegar, salt, pepper, and Dijon mustard to a small deep bowl. Slowly pour in the extra virgin olive oil into the bowl, beating constantly with a fork. Salt and pepper to taste.

Combine all salad ingredients and toss to mix. Toss salad with Dijon mustard vinaigrette and mix well. Serve with grilled chicken or salmon.

Serves two.

Minestrone Soup

1 tablespoon extra virgin olive oil
1 pound organic ground buffalo (optional)

1 cup diced onion

2 garlic cloves, minced

1/2 cup sliced organic carrots

2 14.5-ounce cans Italian stewed tomatoes

3 cups beef broth

1 cup finely shredded cabbage

1 15-ounce can cannellini, black or great northern beans, rinsed and drained

1 teaspoon dried oregano

1/2 teaspoon dried thyme

1/2 teaspoon sea salt

Freshly ground black pepper

1 small zucchini cut in 1/4-inch slices

1 ounce whole grain capellini

1 teaspoon dried sweet basil

Parmesan cheese (optional)

In a large skillet, heat olive oil over medium-high heat and brown meat. Add onions, garlic, and carrots and brown another 5 minutes. Transfer mixture to a large soup pot; add tomatoes, beef broth, cabbage, beans, and seasonings. Simmer 30 minutes. Add zucchini, pasta, and basil; simmer for 10 minutes. Sprinkle with Parmesan cheese to serve (optional).

Dinner

Buffalo, Ostrich, or Turkey Burgers or Meatloaf

1 1/2 pounds organic ground buffalo, ostrich, or turkey

1 10-ounce package frozen organic chopped spinach (thawed and drained)

2 eggs whites (organic free-range)

1 1/2 teaspoons Italian seasoning

1 cup rolled oats

1/2 cup chopped organic onions

1/2 cup shredded organic carrots

1 small organic apple, shredded

1/3 cup almond or coconut milk

$^1\!/_2$ teaspoon sea salt

$^1\!/_4$ teaspoon freshly ground black pepper

Preheat oven to 350°. Combine all ingredients in a large bowl and mix thoroughly. Shape into loaf in 9 × 13-inch baking pan. Bake for 45 to 50 minutes or until internal temperature reaches 160°. Let stand 5 minutes before slicing. For burgers, form into patties and broil, bake, or grill as desired.

Optional: spread $^1\!/_4$ cup tomato salsa on meatloaf during last 15 minutes of baking.

Easy Cookie Sheet Dinner

1 large organic sweet potato, peeled and cut into $^1\!/_2$-inch slices

1 tablespoon extra virgin olive oil, divided

8 ounces boneless, skinless organic chicken breast

$^1\!/_2$ teaspoon lemon pepper

8 ounces (combined) cleaned asparagus, green beans, onions, mushrooms and/or other preferred vegetables

Preheat oven to 425°. Lightly coat cookie sheet with some olive oil. Place sweet potato slices on cookie sheet in a single layer; sprinkle with 1 teaspoon of olive oil. Place cookie sheet on bottom rack in oven and roast for 10 minutes. Turn the potato slices over. Sprinkle chicken breast with lemon pepper. Place on the cookie sheet with the potato slices and drizzle with 1 teaspoon of olive oil; roast for an additional 10 minutes. Turn chicken pieces over and check potato slices for browning. Place vegetables on the cookie sheet with potato slices and chicken. Drizzle with 1 teaspoon of olive oil; roast for an additional 10 minutes. Shake the cookie sheet periodically after adding the vegetables to ensure that they don't get overly browned on one side.

Zucchini "Lasagna"

1 pound zucchini (about 3 medium)

$^1\!/_2$ teaspoon freshly ground black pepper

1 tablespoon extra virgin olive oil, divided

2 medium onions, chopped

2 garlic cloves, minced

3 cups "Sauce for Spaghetti or Lasagna"
1 cup low-fat organic cottage cheese or ricotta cheese
1 egg white (organic free-range), slightly beaten
2 tablespoons grated organic Parmesan cheese
1 cup (4 ounces) shredded organic part-skim mozzarella cheese

Preheat oven to 450° with rack at the bottom. Coat a large cookie sheet with extra virgin olive oil. To make zucchini "noodles," wash zucchini and cut ends off; cut lengthwise into $\frac{1}{2}$-inch thick slices. Arrange zucchini slices on cookie sheet; sprinkle with pepper and $\frac{1}{2}$ tablespoon olive oil. Roast for 10 minutes. Turn slices over and roast for an additional 5 minutes or until tender and nicely browned. Remove pan from oven and set aside. Reduce oven temperature to 350°.

Sauce: In a large skillet, heat $\frac{1}{2}$ tablespoon olive oil over medium-high heat; sauté onion and garlic. Add "Sauce for Spaghetti or Lasagna." Simmer uncovered a few minutes to thicken. Remove from heat and set aside.

Filling: In a medium bowl, combine cottage cheese and egg white; stir to mix. Set aside.

To assemble lasagna, brush a 9 × 13-inch glass baking dish with oil. Add a thin layer of sauce just to cover the bottom. Layer half of the zucchini slices, and sprinkle with 1 tablespoon Parmesan. Add half of remaining sauce and spread on all of the cottage cheese filling. Arrange remaining zucchini slices on top of filling. Cover with remaining 1 tablespoon Parmesan and remaining sauce.

Bake uncovered for 20 minutes. Sprinkle mozzarella cheese over the top and bake for an additional 10 minutes or until the edges are bubbly and the cheese is melted and just starting to brown. Remove the dish from the oven and let it rest for 15 minutes before serving.

Cut into squares and lift out with a spatula.

Hawaiian Grilled Chicken with Whole Grain Brown Rice

Chicken:

2 lbs. of boneless skinless organic chicken thighs
$\frac{1}{2}$ cup Bragg's Amino Acids (soy sauce)
1 (13.5-oz.) can of organic coconut milk
1 teaspoon of sesame oil
1 bunch of green onions, chopped (save some for the top for garnish)
$\frac{1}{2}$ teaspoon minced garlic

Rice:

    1 cups multi-color whole grain organic brown rice

    1 quart vegetable broth

    1 tablespoon extra virgin olive oil

    $1/2$ white onion, chopped

Remove visible fat from chicken thighs. Combine all ingredients in a resealable plastic bag. Marinade chicken for at least 4 hours or overnight.

Meanwhile, bring rice, broth, and oil to a boil. Add in onion and turn heat to a simmer. Cook according to package directions. Season with salt and pepper and top with additional soy sauce, if desired.

While rice is cooking, grill chicken at medium-low heat for 5 to 7 minutes per side or until cooked through.

Serve the chicken with rice and top with green onions.

Black Bean and Mango Salad

2 cans of rinsed organic black beans

1 can of golden sweet corn that has been rinsed

1 chopped avocado

1 chopped mango

1 green onion, washed and sliced

1 red pepper, washed

2 tablespoons of extra virgin olive oil

1 tablespoon of balsamic vinegar

Celtic sea salt and black pepper

Mix all ingredients together, store in refrigerator for 30 minutes, and serve.

White Bean Chicken Chili

3 cans of organic mild salsa

2 pieces of organic chicken, chopped, that has been seasoned and grilled
    (seasoned with sea salt and pepper)

2 cups of northern white beans, rinsed

Chopped onions (optional)

Organic chicken broth if you don't want it so thick (optional)

Cook on medium heat for 20 to 30 minutes or until hot.

Chicken, Wild Rice, and Pesto Soup

Chicken Broth:
>   1 organic chicken
>   5 large organic carrots, washed not peeled, rough chop into 3-inch
>   pieces
>   5 large organic celery stalks, washed, rough chop into 3-inch pieces
>   1 large onion, washed not peeled, cut into four pieces
>   1 tablespoon peppercorn
>   2 tablespoon Celtic sea salt
>   10 stalks of thyme
>   1 large stalk of rosemary
>   Handful of fresh parsley

Place all the ingredients in large pot and fill with water (2 inches above the ingredients). Bring to a boil and cook for 1 to 2 hours or until the broth is golden and the chicken is cooked. Strain all the ingredients and keep the broth; dispose of the veggies and set chicken aside to use for other recipes.

Pesto:
>   1 cup walnuts
>   4 cups fresh basil
>   1 cup of spinach
>   2 tablespoon of extra virgin olive oil
>   3 cloves of garlic
>   1 teaspoon of Celtic sea salt

Put all the ingredients but the oil in the food processor; start the food processor and slowly pour the oil in. It is done when it is all mixed into a sauce.

Soup—Wild Rice/Mushroom with Pesto

3 large carrots, peeled and sliced into small pieces
Mushrooms, cut into small pieces
2 cups cooked organic wild rice

Pesto sauce:
>   2 cups organic baby spinach
>   Celtic sea salt and pepper for taste

Fill pot with the fresh broth. Add the carrots and mushrooms, then the rice. Add the pesto, and then the remaining ingredients and cook for 1 hour on medium heat or until the veggies are tender. Add sea salt and pepper to taste.

Desserts and Snacks

Raw Banana Pecan Pie

Pie Shell:
   1 cup raw pecans
   1 cup dates, pitted
   $1/2$ teaspoon vanilla extract

Filling:
   5 dates, pitted
   3 bananas, fairly ripe
   1 tablespoon lemon juice, fresh
   1 banana, ripe
   Pecans for topping

For the shell, grind the pecans, dates, and vanilla in a food processor until finely ground. Press mixture evenly into a pie plate.

For the filling, blend dates, 3 bananas, and lemon juice in the food processor until smooth.

Cut the last banana into $1/4$-inch circles and fold into the filling mixture. Pour filling into the pie shell.

Decorate the top of pie with pecans and sliced bananas if desired. Cover with plastic wrap, and refrigerate for a couple hours.

Serves 8.

Dad's Spirulina Birthday Pie

Recipe provided by: Kristen Johnson

Crust:
   2 cups raw almonds, finely ground in food processor
   $1/3$ cup dried figs, chopped (2–3 figs)
   1 tablespoon agave nectar or raw honey

Filling:
   $3/4$ cup coconut water
   $1/4$ cup raw cashews
   $1/4$ cup extra virgin coconut oil
   1 tablespoon organic agave nectar or organic raw honey
   1 tablespoon crushed spirulina/chlorella tablets
   1 tablespoon cacao nibs

To make the crust, combine ground almonds and figs in a food processor until mixed well and they form a sticky mixture. Transfer almond-fig mixture to a mixing bowl, and add agave nectar; mix well to form a crust-like consistency. Press the crust mixture evenly into the bottom and sides of a 5-inch pie tin.

In a high-speed blender, combine all of the filling ingredients and blend until smooth. Pour the mixture into the pie crust and freeze for approximately 1 hour before serving.

Serves 6.

Banana Ice Cream

3 frozen bananas (take old bananas and freeze them so they don't go to waste)
2 tablespoons natural crunchy peanut butter
2 tablespoons dark chocolate chips or cacao nibs

Cut frozen bananas into 1-inch slices. Place in food processor and blend until creamy—about 30 seconds. Add in peanut butter and blend to mix. Top with dark chocolate chips or cacao nibs and enjoy!

Feel free to enjoy banana ice cream plain or add your own favorite toppings!

Energized Bars

1 20-ounce can crushed pineapple in own juice
$1/2$ cup crushed almonds
2 cups rolled oats
3 scoops organic whole grain rice protein powder
1 cup chopped dried fruit
$1^{1}/2$ teaspoons cinnamon

Preheat oven to 200°. Combine all ingredients. Spread in 13 × 9-inch pan brushed with organic coconut oil. Bake for 90 minutes. Cool and slice. Store in refrigerator. Great snack anytime.

Flax Bran Muffins

$1\frac{1}{2}$ cups white whole wheat flour (unbleached, unbromated)
$\frac{3}{4}$ cup ground flaxseeds
$\frac{3}{4}$ cup oat bran
$\frac{1}{4}$ cup organic brown sugar plus 3 tablespoons Stevia Plus™
2 teaspoons organic baking soda
1 teaspoon aluminum-free baking powder
$\frac{1}{2}$ teaspoon sea salt
2 teaspoons cinnamon
$1\frac{1}{2}$ cups organic shredded carrots
2 apples, unpeeled, shredded
$\frac{1}{2}$ cup raisins
$\frac{3}{4}$ cup chopped walnuts
3 egg whites (organic free-range)
$\frac{3}{4}$ cup almond or coconut milk
1 teaspoon vanilla extract

Preheat oven to 350°. Combine flour, flaxseeds, oat bran, sugar, baking soda, baking powder, salt, and cinnamon in a large bowl and mix well. Add carrots, apples, raisins, and nuts. In a separate bowl, blend egg whites, milk, and vanilla. Add liquid ingredients to dry ingredients; mix until just combined. Do not overstir.

Coat muffin tin with coconut oil. Divide mixture into 12 muffin cups. Bake for 27 to 30 minutes. Allow to cool slightly; remove from muffin tin to finish cooling.

On-the-Go Trail Mix

1 cup rolled oats
1–3 tablespoons slivered almonds, walnuts, pecans, or macadamia nuts
$\frac{1}{8}$ cup raisins
3–4 dried figs
2 tablespoons of organic unsweetened shredded coconut
1 tablespoon of cacao nibs (real chocolate)
Dash of cinnamon

Mix all ingredients and eat as a snack. To save time, make multiple servings; store in airtight container.

Coconut Oil Kettle Corn

1 tablespoon organic coconut oil
$\frac{1}{2}$ cup of uncooked popcorn
1–2 tablespoons organic agave nectar
Hint of Celtic sea salt
Dash of cinnamon

In medium saucepan, heat the oil until hot, add the popcorn, and cover with clear lid. The popcorn will start to pop; listen until it sounds like most of the kernels are popped. Remove from heat and season with Celtic sea salt, cinnamon, and agave nectar. It is best warm, but can stay good for two days in a Ziploc bag.

Move

26 Let's Get Moving

Nobody need wait a single moment before starting to improve the world.

—Anne Frank

For centuries, people have been searching for the Fountain of Youth. Remember the movie *The Wizard of Oz*? One of my all-time favorites (I was always scared of the flying monkeys), when Glinda, the Good Witch, tells Dorothy that her way home was not in her magical ruby slippers or the hot air balloon, but in her ability to focus. The answer was right in front of her the whole time. The same can be said about exercise, quality nutrition, and restorative rest. The magic is in our mind and body, but we sometimes need to be reminded just how powerful the human body can be. If you could put exercise in a bottle, it would be the most prescribed medication on the planet. It can be said that exercise *is* the Fountain of Youth!

Benefits of Daily Movement

The human body is designed to move or exercise on a daily basis. I will use exercise or daily movement in the same context throughout the rest of this chapter. When I speak of exercise, many people immediately say they don't have enough time to exercise on a daily basis. Let's stop right there: first, many people consider the exercise to be time intensive, painful, stressful, no fun, too much work—the list can be long. I want you to view exercise maybe a little differently. Like the slogan "Just Do It," this is how I want you to view exercise—something you do on a daily basis. It could be as simple as a few stretch breaks during the day, yard work, going for a walk over lunch, playing outside with your kids or grandkids, working out with a health and fitness coach or training for some specific event; the key for health of your body and mind is a lifetime of daily movement.

Daily movement can be fun and enjoyable, and there are endless ways to move the human body. Walking, jogging, running, biking, swimming, hiking, climbing, skiing, court sports, ping pong, badminton, yoga, Pilates, strength training, stretching, anything, and everything that gets your body in motion on a daily basis. There is no one right way to move your body; the key is daily movement and then trying to perfect the ordinary. If you have a dog, do you walk your dog every other day? Of course not; in most cases, you walk your dog multiple times a day. Most dog owners know that to get your dog to have a regular bowel movement, your dog needs to move (okay, enough said about bowel movements!)

Exercise has so many wonderful benefits, including improved bone health, better balance and strength, heart health, lower blood pressure, improved brain function, decreased risk of cancer and type 2 diabetes, improved mood, increased energy, better sleep—the list is long, and the return on investment is very powerful! The number one reason I like to move my body on a daily basis is how it makes me feel during and after exercise. My mind becomes clear, my body feels loose and relaxed, and I feel energized and alive. Have you ever had a bad day, lots on your mind, too much stress, nothing seems to be working? Then you move your body and you feel 100 percent better? Movement washes your brain, no longer do things bother you as much, your energy is up, and you feel great! Don't get me wrong; I like the look of a fit, trim physique, but it is the experience and feeling I get when exercising that keeps me coming back.

Why Don't We Move Daily?

The Surgeon General reports that a sedentary lifestyle carries the same health risk as smoking, high cholesterol, diabetes, or high blood pressure. Yet, even with all this information, research, and promotion, the United States remains a sedentary nation. Less than 25 percent of the adult U.S. population exercises on a regular basis. Today, many nations across the globe have begun to follow the United States, not only with the processed food movement, but also lack of physical movement.

Okay, so most know the powerful benefits that come with exercise; then why are we not moving more? With over 25 years of health and fitness coaching experience, speaking all over the world, talking with seminar attendees, friends, family, clients, physicians, and colleagues, I believe there are five major reasons most Americans are not exercising: values and beliefs, instant gratification, knowledge, time, and rituals.

Values and Beliefs

We all have different values and beliefs in all aspects in our lives, and I am not here to make judgments about your values and beliefs. My goal is to get you to think about them. Values differ from beliefs. You may value success, but you may believe that to be successful you have to make over $1 million a year. You may value your health, but may believe that you must spend hours in the gym to become healthy. For a good portion of the American population, exercise is low on the priority list. For many, it is not even on the radar screen. I believe most people recognize that exercise is a good thing, but that is where their exercise wagon ends. Many feel that exercise is not for them. They may feel intimidated, uncomfortable with their body, or fear that they may fail.

Exercise can be magical and life changing. Exercise can improve your fitness and ability to move, decrease aches and pains, prevent injuries, improve your mood and mental clarity, decrease stress, help you sleep better, and improve your health. If you polled your friends and family members, they would all say their health is of great importance to them. They value their health, and why not? When you don't have your health, you don't have much.

How valuable is your health to you? If you believe your health is important to you, what are you willing to do to maintain or improve your health? We all have to put some effort into maintaining our health. Make exercise a priority in your life. Value your health and believe you are worth it!

Instant Gratification

We are a society that wants everything now. We seek instant gratification. Many of the benefits from regular exercise come later, in the form of delayed gratification. Lower cholesterol, lower blood pressure, lower body fat, improved fitness, a better night's sleep, hormonal balance, stronger bones and muscles—you don't reap all of these benefits overnight. There have been many times when I just don't feel like moving my body; I am too busy, too tired. I have all the excuses too. When I feel like this, I focus on how I will feel when I am in the middle of my exercise activity and how I will feel when I am done exercising. For me, these are two powerful motivators. In the middle of my exercise routine, my heart is pumping, my body is sweating, my energy has increased, and my body feels alive. After exercise, my energy is high, my mind is clear, my body feels loose, and my mood is good. The feelings I get from exercising are priceless.

The most difficult time for many is just getting started. Most agree that once they began to exercise it was not too bad and felt wonderful afterwards. In addition, there was a sense of accomplishment.

We can all learn a little from Grandma's and Grandpa's Laws.

Grandma's Law: Eat your spinach, and then you get to have your ice cream.

Grandpa's Law: First do your homework, and then you can go out and play.

In his book *Emotional Intelligence*, Daniel Goleman explains a study he conducted with kids and marshmallows. The study begins by giving each kid one marshmallow. If they can delay eating the marshmallow for a certain amount of time, they are given more marshmallows. The purpose of this study was to compare instant gratification to delayed gratification and the discipline that goes with each. Dr. Goleman wanted to find out if there was a direct correlation between delayed gratification discipline and happiness. The interesting part of the study was that the same kids were monitored for over 20 years. Dr. Goleman concluded that the kids who delayed eating the marshmallow, who had the discipline to delay their gratification, became more successful, happier adults.

Don't fret if you were one of the kids who ate the marshmallow without waiting. The good news is that you can develop the skill and discipline to increase your ability to delay gratification. One of the keys for learning to delay gratification more consistently is to change your focus. Change what you place your attention on. I am going to pass on the fudge brownie with ice cream. My focus is on improving my health and having a smaller waistline.

How many times have we all said to ourselves, why didn't I study enough for that final exam? or why did I overeat when my goal was to lose 10 pounds? In most cases, we lost our focus. Remember, what you focus on is what you will attract into your life.

Knowledge

Just as with the nutritional side of the health equation, most people lack knowledge about what exercises to do, how to start, how much exercise is enough, and how to keep it going. You might want to challenge me. You might say, "Are you kidding me? Everywhere I look there are articles, books, magazines, videos, infomercials—you name it—dedicated to exercise." And as with nutrition, there's so much information that people are overwhelmed. Many people are confused about whether to do high- or low-intensity cardiovascular exercise to lose weight, which specific exercises shape or sculpt a certain body part, whether strength training is really necessary, and how much time should be devoted to what types of exercises. Now I am confused. In addition to these concerns, many people have specific questions about exercise that relate to their personal needs, such as, "If I have bad knees, type 2 diabetes, migraine headaches, a hundred pounds to lose, pain in my shoulder, or a bad back, what exercises should I avoid? What exercises would be beneficial?"

I see evidence of the lack of knowledge and an abundance of misinformation everywhere. When visiting other health clubs, working out in hotels, listening to friends, fielding questions from participants in my seminars, I hear comments and rationales that people have constructed from myriad sources. During a recent television interview with a health and fitness expert on the subject of weight loss, the question came up about exercise and how much is necessary to lose weight. The expert recommended 60 to 90 minutes of cardiovascular exercise per day for weight loss! I almost fell over in disbelief. I thought to myself, "Is this person out of his mind?" Less than 25 percent of the American population move their bodies on a daily basis, and now some expert is telling millions of viewers to exercise for 60 to 90 minutes of cardiovascular exercise a day to lose weight! I think many viewers were saying to themselves, "I might as well sit back on the couch and eat some cookies. There is no way I am going to do cardiovascular exercise for 60 to 90 minutes a day." Pass the remote!

Exercise plays an important role in maintaining a healthy body weight, but it is a combination of lifestyle factors that contributes to healthy weight loss and better health. Having the right information is necessary for your success in all areas of our life. This is one reason I recommend hiring a health and fitness coach for many people to help guide and educate you on developing an exercise plan that works for you. I believe almost everyone could benefit by hiring a health and fitness coach for a few sessions. You don't need to see a health and fitness coach two to three times per week. You may want to use a health and fitness coach weekly, once a month, or three to four times per year to learn new information and help keep your momentum going. Many clients say they wish they had hired a health and fitness coach years earlier and that it was one of the best investments they ever made. Whether you have a bad back, pain in your shoulder, migraine headaches, want to lose weight, improve your numbers, or want to get into the best shape of your life, there are many wonderful health and fitness coaches to help you reach your goals. Give it a try!

Time

Time is a big issue for almost everyone. I want to make this point extremely clear, **you can never out-train a poor diet!** *Most people don't need to spend large amounts of time to stay healthy or get into good shape.* If you are training for a triathlon, marathon or the Olympics, then yes, you do have to invest large amounts of time to reach your goals. If your goal is to become healthier and get in better shape, it is important to understand that to get the most out of your exercise program, you can achieve your goals if you adjust your frequency of your exercise, the quality of the exercise you do, and the amount of time you schedule for exercise.

At the beginning of each New Year, I see so many people desperately trying to get in better shape. "This is my year!" *One of the biggest mistakes people make is believing that the more time they spend on exercise the greater their results will be.* Spending more time on the treadmill or in the gym does not necessarily add up to greater results. What race are you trying to run? Is it the 100-meter sprint or the marathon? What kind of pace can you sustain for a lifetime? This is a large reason most people slowly abandon their exercise program. It is too difficult to sustain over time. I am not saying you can't have greater focus and intensity at certain times with your exercise or nutrition program, but is this something that you can sustain? Do you want to run a sprint or a marathon? How can you incorporate daily movement into your already busy life? Can you carve out 5 or 10 minutes a day for the rest of your life to devote to daily movement? I want you to get into the mind-set that you need to move your body every day. Yes, every day! **The human body is designed to move on a daily basis!**

Years ago I was discussing this concept with a new health and fitness coaching client. He was frustrated with his weight, health, and current exercise program. He said he was currently exercising for 75 to 90 minutes two to three times per week. His program included 30 minutes of cardiovascular exercise followed by 40 minutes of strength training and some light stretching. By the time he arrived at the gym, exercised and showered, he was spending over two hours on his exercise commitment! By listening to him, I thought his exercise frequency might be the problem, so I asked again, "How often are you exercising?" He said, "two to three days per week."

Then I asked him, "How many times did you exercise last year? 100? 150? 200?" This is when he spilled the beans! When he really started to analyze the frequency with which he exercised, he had exercised less than 30 times last year. His life was so busy with his job and family, he just didn't have the time to devote to exercise.

So I asked him, "What kind of results do you think you would get if you moved your body over 300-plus times a year?" Remember, he had been exercising less than once per week, and now I am asking him to move his body on a daily basis. I told him, "The two major changes that you need make are to decrease your time and to increase your frequency." His new program consisted of a five- to eight-minute series of yoga and strength exercises daily. He did these exercises every morning before he took a shower. He also committed to at least 10 minutes of walking every day along with doing six strength-training exercises twice a week.

His frequency of moving his body increased, but the total time investment per week was less than three hours. Similar to eating more frequent small meals, he was exercising more frequently in small pieces of time. An additional bonus was that he could do most of his exercises at home, saving even more time. Six months later he had lost 25 pounds and said he had never felt better. With his new exercise momentum, he also became more in tune with eating healthier foods. He said he never would have believed a little bit of exercise every day could really make that big of a difference. He now believes!

Developing Rituals

What is a ritual? To me, a ritual is something that becomes an automatic part of you. A behavior starts as a thought, and then moves into a habit, and over time may become a ritual. Rituals are similar to habits, but more powerful. A ritual is something you do on a regular basis without much thought. This is one reason it is so difficult for people to quit smoking. It has become a powerful ritual. You have a cup of coffee—you have a cigarette. You read the newspaper—you have a cigarette.

Rituals are powerful. Making my oatmeal the night before has become such a ritual for me that I sometimes don't remember making it; maybe I need more cod liver oil for greater memory? I open up the refrigerator in the morning, and there it is. You just do it, rain or shine, without much thought or energy—like brushing your teeth, taking a shower, drinking more water, or even exercising daily.

If you are not exercising or would like to get greater results, how do you develop an exercise ritual? You must focus on what you want, why you want it, and how are you going to do it. Just like your nutritional changes, take baby steps with exercise. Make it doable and enjoyable for yourself. This is one reason I have most of my clients walk for 10 minutes and do a series of yoga poses for 5 minutes every day. It does not take much time, incorporates balance, strength, flexibility, and fitness all rolled into one, they can do it anywhere, and it makes them feel great. We can always add more to their exercise program later, but first I want them to develop some exercise rituals that will last. Imagine moving your body on a daily basis for the rest of your life. Developing healthy rituals is one of the keys to a healthier and happier you.

Exercise and Weight Loss

Before I explore the specific exercise portion of this chapter, I must discuss weight loss and the mind-set associated with successful weight loss. Many people I encounter have a specific goal of losing weight and believe that they will lose weight if they exercise more. Truth is, it just isn't that simple. You will burn more calories and maybe lose a few pounds by exercising more, but many people who exercise regularly are still overweight due to their poor nutritional patterns. Many folks also believe that long duration, low-intensity cardiovascular exercise is the best method to lose weight.

Cardiovascular exercise is an important component of a balanced exercise program, but long-duration, low-intensity cardiovascular exercise is not the most efficient method for losing weight. A more successful approach to exercise takes into account the **hormonal effects** that occur with daily exercise.

For many years I have competed in Natural Physique Competitions in the Masters Division. That makes me sound as old as Lake Michigan! My daily movement routine does not change a great deal prior to my contest; it's just a little more focused. But nutritionally, everything tightens up. I eat more frequently, have smaller portion sizes, and take no liberties for 13 weeks. I move from the 80/20 rule to the 98/2 rule. This 98/2 eating regimen is very strict and difficult to sustain long term but for 13 weeks, I can do it.

Proper nutrition accounts for 80 to 85 percent of successful weight loss. To get the weight loss you desire, you must begin with nutritional changes. Interestingly, while 80 to 85 percent of initial weight loss begins with nutrition, research shows that maintaining weight loss has to do with a combination of lifestyle factors, namely the Big Three: restful sleep, proper nutrition, and most importantly daily movement. **Remember, you can never out-train a poor diet!**

Posture Alignment

When I was young, my grandmother always told me to stand up straight and tall. She was so right to stress the benefits of good posture. As we age we are in a constant battle with gravity, which is trying to pull us out of ideal alignment. Daily stresses of life, sitting, standing, bending, walking, playing, and exercising, challenge our ideal body alignment. We all make some type of compromise when it comes to our posture. The challenge, and goal, is to identify our own ways of compromising and correct them, trying to improve our posture alignment.

What is ideal posture alignment and why is it so important? Ideal posture alignment happens when the body is perfectly aligned, or in neutral position, starting with the feet and ankles, and moving up through the knees, hips, pelvis, arms, shoulders, neck, and head. The five key points for posture alignment are the ear, shoulder, hip, knee, and ankle.

This is where exercise can be especially beneficial. We all get into repetitive movement patterns, and over time, certain muscles become shorter and stronger, while opposing muscles may become longer and weaker. This creates muscle imbalances that lead to poor posture, injury, pain, and decreased mobility. Proper exercise improves muscle imbalances and leads to better posture alignment. Having good posture is one of the key foundations to a healthier you!

A few years ago a retired, 80-year-old orthodontist, Dr. Bruce Nakfoor, walked into my office complaining of back and neck pain. For years, Dr. Nakfoor had been working in a hunched over position as an orthodontist, and over time, gravity took its toll. As part of my evaluation process, I had Dr. Nakfoor stand against the wall with his heels, glutes, and shoulders touching the wall. I think we were both surprised when his head was more than a 12 inches away from the wall! No wonder he was having major shoulder and back discomfort. His posture alignment needed help! So we worked on his posture, standing, sitting, and incorporated exercises he could do every day (a five-minute series of yoga/strength exercises), added some strength training, cardiovascular exercises, and good nutrition. Within three months, the discomfort started to disappear, his posture improved, he lost weight, and now he has started to play tennis for the first time in 20 years!

The Bionic Woman

Let me tell you about my mother, whom I call the "bionic woman." At 80 years of age, she had suffered through an ankle fusion and replacements of both hips and a knee, all within a five-year time span. She had never been one to exercise, except for our occasional footraces in the backyard when I was a kid growing up. She actually was fairly quick! After going through post-surgical physical therapy, I nagged her about starting a regular exercise program. She resisted, arguing that she was in too much pain and didn't have the energy to devote to exercise. She also believed that exercise would increase her pain and didn't believe that it would help her.

I finally convinced her to work with a health and fitness coach by the name of Todd Yehl. Todd is an expert in body alignment and posture, I believe one of the best in the business. After working with Todd twice a week for six weeks, my mother felt noticeably less pain and had more energy. More importantly, for the first time in many years, she had hope that her physical condition could improve. Along with improved mobility and less pain, perhaps the greatest reward has been the change in my mom's attitude. She is more active, smiles all the time, talks all the time, and has had her vitality restored. She has been exercising regularly for the past 12 years and works out weekly. Mom was also heavily medicated, taking up to seven medications a day, and today at age 79 Mom is medication-free. In addition, Mom is a true believer in taking her frozen wheatgrass ice cubes, spirulina/ chlorella, coconut oil, ground flaxseeds, cod liver oil, oatmeal, and drinking mineral water; she extols the benefits to anyone who will listen.

Getting Started—How Much Exercise Is Enough?

I don't want to suggest that there is only one specific way to move your body, or that the exercises I discuss in this book are the only means to achieve the results you are seeking. My recommendations are meant to be a starting point for someone new to exercise or a way to get back to basics for the experienced, then you can incorporate greater knowledge into your current exercise program. There are endless ways to move your body, and that's all exercise is—moving your body. Pilates, yoga, tai chi, walking, hiking, biking, using cardiovascular exercise machines, jumping rope, swimming, skiing, surfing, strength training with free weights, or rubber tubing are just a sampling of the exercises you can do on your own. Then there are group activities like tennis, basketball, soccer, hockey, squash, racquetball, handball, playing with your kids, and exercise classes of many varieties. Your goal is to find exercises you enjoy. Get a routine; develop your daily movement rituals, then over time experiment with new forms of movement.

Personally, I do a series of foundational movements daily that improves my strength, balance, flexibility, and posture, and they take only five to eight minutes to complete. I also walk daily. These are my everyday rituals. On top of my daily rituals, I like to do 15 to 25 minutes of cardiovascular exercise and a split strength training routine for 40 minutes most days followed by 1 to 2 minutes of stretching. I also enjoy paddleball, pickle ball, tennis, swimming, skiing, and golf. Some days I need to get away from my daily routine and just play. Mixing it up keeps my daily movement fresh.

Remember what race you are in. Start slow, train smart. Choose ways to move your body daily that are fun and enjoyable for you and give you a balanced workout. Invest in yourself!

I have outlined five basic components of a balanced exercise program.

1. Dynamic warm-up: 2 to 3 minutes
2. Foundation exercises: 5 to 8 minutes

3. Cardiovascular exercises: 5 to 25 minutes
4. Strength training: 5 to 45 minutes
5. Stretching and flexibility: 1 to 10 minutes

Although each of these five components will be discussed separately, they may be integrated into one. Yoga is just one discipline or daily movement activity that integrates all five components into one workout. Yoga combines body alignment, balance, flexibility, cardiovascular fitness, and strength together in one form of exercise. This is one reason I believe yoga has become amazingly popular in the United States over the past 10 years.

Before I go further in this daily movement section, I want to mention the Rule of Training Specificity. Training specificity means that you follow a designed exercise program to fit a specific need or goal. If your goal is to become a competitive power lifter or an elite endurance athlete, you will not achieve it through yoga. However, if integrated into an athlete's exercise program, yoga can enhance that program to create better balance, flexibility, strength and focus, and decrease the chance of injuries.

Dynamic Warm-Up: 2 to 3 Minutes

With every form of daily movement, you need time to transition your body from static or sedentary into dynamic or active. This activates the nervous, cardiovascular, and muscular systems. If you did nothing more than walk each day along with a few of these dynamic warm-up exercises, you would be ahead of the game. In my seminars, I always try to get the crowd moving with a few of these exercises, and you can feel the energy in the room jump. You are probably thinking, after listening to me it has nowhere else to go but up! This is one way I get the energy back in the room, and it works every time. *Motion creates positive emotion!* I use the dynamic warm-up exercises at the beginning of all my workout sessions. (See Figure 26.1.) The dynamic warm-up exercises cover the entire body, increase synovial fluid to help lubricate the joints, improve balance and flexibility, and are quick, taking less than two to three minutes. Use slow and controlled movements and gradually increase the range of motion as you warm up. If some of the movements are difficult, let pain be your guide and modify them as needed. Let the motion create positive emotion in your day!

FIGURE 26.1 Dynamic Warm-Up

Dynamic Warm-Up Foundation Exercises

- Arm swings
- Neck (rotation)
- Neck (side to side)
- Side bend
- Trunk twist
- Front leg swing
- Side leg swing

Foundation Exercises: 5 to 8 Minutes

Practice does not make perfect. Only perfect practice makes perfect.

Vince Lombardi

You may choose to modify each movement or add or delete any of the following 12 exercises to fit your current needs. You may choose to do foundation exercises before you play golf, tennis, basketball, bike, walk, jog or run, strength train, or just as your main source of exercise for that day. Hold each exercise for 3 to 10 seconds, and focus on the proper technique for each movement. See Figure 26.2.

FIGURE 26.2 Foundation Excercises

Foundation Exercises

1. Centered Squat
2. Straight Leg Lunge
3. Warrior 3—Half Moon (balance poses)
4. Warrior 1
5. Warrior 2
6. Reverse Warrior
7. Extended Angle
8. Spread Eagle
9. Dancer (balance pose)
10. Standing Wall Extensions (against the wall)
11. Half Moon (against the wall)
12. Standing Up and Down Dog

Cardiovascular Exercise: 5 to 25 Minutes

When most people think of cardiovascular exercise, they think of walking, hiking, jogging, biking, swimming, cross-country skiing—virtually any exercise that is rhythmic in nature and gets you breathing harder. Cardiovascular exercise places demands on the heart, lungs, and muscles. There are many benefits including stress reduction, improved pH balance, improved cellular sensitivity, mood elevation, increased cardiovascular efficiency, decreased blood pressure, improved blood glucose, lipids, weight control, and, most of all, it makes you feel good!

Cardiovascular exercise can be either aerobic or anaerobic or somewhere in between, depending on the intensity level of the exercise. *Aerobic exercise* occurs when the demand of exercise *meets* the supply of oxygen. *Anaerobic exercise* occurs when the demand of exercise *exceeds* the supply of oxygen.

It is important to understand the difference between aerobic and anaerobic exercise and how the intensity of your exercise program can affect certain hormones and, more importantly, help you get the results you desire. Your Fountain of Youth hormones, testosterone, estrogen, and human growth hormone, are stimulated by higher-intensity anaerobic exercise. These three hormones help the body become leaner, stronger, and more youthful for both men and women.

Quality versus Quantity

When educating my health and fitness coaching clients about cardiovascular exercise, I explain that as their cardiovascular fitness levels start to improve, the goal is not to increase the length of time dedicated to cardiovascular exercise, but to slowly increase the intensity level, or difficulty, of that exercise.

I believe many people look at cardiovascular exercise as a way to burn calories and lose weight, assuming more time is better. This is not necessarily true. *If your goal is weight loss, it is far more effective and more efficient to limit the time spent on cardiovascular exercise to 25 minutes, but raise the intensity*. The higher intensity and corresponding stimulation of testosterone and human growth hormone will have a greater impact on weight loss than tracking the number of calories burned.

It sounds simple. To lose weight using cardiovascular exercise, increase the intensity and go like mad! But hold on. There are a few other things you must understand about high-intensity cardiovascular exercise. First, high-intensity exercise day in and day out is tough, and can turn you off to exercise altogether. Personally, I work hard during the cardiovascular section of my workout, but in most cases I am not torturing myself. Second, it is more difficult to maintain good posture with higher-intensity cardiovascular exercise. Pay attention to your posture the next time you go for a walk, jog, jump on the mini-trampoline, ride a bike, or get on your favorite cardiovascular exercise machine. Maintaining good posture will increase the difficulty of each exercise. Poor postural alignment may lead to orthopedic problems and injuries.

The biggest reason that you should not spend excessive time doing cardiovascular exercise is the hormonal changes that begin to occur. Testosterone and growth hormone levels begin to drop after 25 minutes of cardiovascular exercise. These are the hormones that stimulate muscle growth and make the body leaner. *Human growth hormone is the most powerful fat-burning hormone in the body*. So it does not make much sense to exercise longer if one of your goals is weight loss. On the other hand, as the length of your cardiovascular session increases, cortisol, your "stress" hormone, begins to rise. Excessive levels of cortisol can cause bone loss, muscle wasting, thinning skin, hypertension, poor wound healing, impaired immune function, and weight gain. No other hormone in the human body ages you faster than cortisol!

If you are an endurance athlete, you need to put in more time. This is the rule of training specificity. If you enjoy going for a leisurely long walk or bike ride, do it and enjoy all the wonderful benefits that follow. But if your goal is to improve your fitness, improve your health, and control your weight, start adding short bouts of higher-intensity effort throughout your cardiovascular exercise program as you become more efficient with your exercise time. The benefits of cardiovascular exercise do not increase by adding more time to your program; 15 to 25 minutes of moderate- to high-intensity cardiovascular exercise are all that's needed!

Clients tell me that one of the main barriers to regular exercise is a lack of time. Time is precious. Don't waste it with unnecessary cardiovascular exercise. Unless your goal is to participate in endurance activities such as long-distance marathon running or triathlons, stick with shorter duration, moderate- to higher-intensity cardiovascular exercise. Start slowly and progress gradually to allow your body time to adapt to the demands of exercise.

Cardiovascular Exercise Outline

Modality: It's what you do. Find an exercise you enjoy and add variety to your workouts. Walking, biking, swimming, running, hiking, snowshoeing, cross-country skiing, group fitness classes, mini-trampoline, and using cardiovascular machines are just a few of the cardiovascular exercises that many people enjoy.

Frequency: It's how often you do it. Try to develop exercise patterns that fit your available time and schedule. Exercise two to seven times a week.

Duration: It's how long you do it. Even 10 minutes of cardiovascular exercise can have many benefits. Ideally, try to get 15 to 25 minutes and pay attention to posture and intensity level.

Intensity: It's how hard you work. "Intensity" means the level of difficulty in sustaining the exercise. If the exercise is so hard that you can last only a few minutes before you have to stop, your intensity level is too high. If your intensity level is too low, your body will make only minimal adaptations and you will get fewer benefits from the exercise session.

Methods to Monitor Exercise Intensity

Visual: Watch your body language and postural alignment. If the intensity is too high, the body begins to make compensations, leading to a breakdown in postural alignment.

Talk test: As exercise intensity increases, it becomes more difficult to talk. The body is switching energy systems from aerobic to anaerobic metabolism. If you can easily carry on a conversation, your intensity may be too low. If you can say only a few words without stopping to catch your breath, your intensity is too high. Find the balance that is specific to your goals.

Perceived exertion: Assess your level of exertion on a 1 to 10 scale, with 1 to 2 being easy, 4 to 6 moderate, and 8 to 10 extremely difficult.

Heart rate: Traditionally, this is the gold standard for monitoring exercise intensity. As exercise intensity increases, heart rate increases. Use the following formula to find a target heart rate zone: take 220 minus your age and multiply this number by how hard you want to exercise. A beginning level, or lower intensity level, would be 50 to 60 percent. The maximum or highest-intensity level is 80 to 90 percent. Let's figure out a heart rate zone to fit a 40-year-old person's fitness level.

Intensity	Age	Intensity	Heart rate
Easy	220 − 40 (age) =	180 × 50% =	90 bpm (beats per minute)
Moderate	220 − 40 (age) =	180 × 60–70% =	108–126 bpm
High	220 − 40 (age) =	180 × 80–90% =	144–162 bpm

If you are just getting started with exercise, start slowly and keep your heart rate around 90 to 107 beats per minute (bpm). For a moderate exerciser, 108 to 126 bpm would be the goal. For the advanced exerciser or when doing interval training, 144 to 162 bpm is the target. These are just guidelines. Monitor your heart rate further with the talk test and by assessing your perceived exertion to see how your heart rate measures up.

The challenge of monitoring your heart rate is that it uses age as a predictor of fitness level, which can be inaccurate. If you are on any medications, especially cardiac medications, the medication may affect heart rate levels. It's important to use all the methods to monitor the intensity level of your exercise.

It is always a good idea to consult with your doctor or exercise professional before beginning any exercise program. Remember to start slow and let your body slowly acclimate to your exercise program.

Strength Training: 5 to 45 Minutes

If there is one form of exercise that can turn back the hands of time, it is strength training. More and more, people reap its benefits. Even people in their eighties and nineties can improve their strength, mobility, and bone density with strength training. I have seen the benefits of strength training with many of my personal training clients who have trained with me for many years. The benefits of strength training include increased strength, increased bone density, improved mobility and functionality, improved posture, better balance, fewer injuries, improved athletic performance, reduced stress, increased self-esteem, increased metabolism, and weight control.

Strength training is exercise that uses resistance to place demands on the nervous system, hormones, bones, and muscles. Strength training is generally done with a short burst (10 to 30 seconds) of the strength-training phase, followed by a recovery phase. The rest or recovery phase can last 10 seconds to 4 minutes, depending on your goals.

With the right intensity, strength training taxes the anaerobic system and stimulates testosterone and human growth hormone. Women, don't be afraid that you will bulk up with strength training. Men have a great deal more testosterone than women do. It takes a tremendous amount of effort, good nutrition, and the right parents to get larger muscles. I have been trying to build bigger muscles for years, and it is difficult to do!

Recently at one of my seminars, I was asked the question, "How long have you been strength training?" I have been strength training for over forty plus years! When I was younger, my main goal was to build larger muscles and enhance my athletic performance. At age 55, I am still trying to build bigger muscles. But strength training does so much more than build larger muscles. Strength training improves posture and balance, prevents injuries, reduces stress, improves mobility, increases confidence, increases bone density, improves athletic performance, and most of all improves the way you feel. Strength training increases one's *vitality!* After I strength train, my mind is clear, my mood is great, and I feel energized.

Strength training can be done with a variety of equipment. Use your own body weight, push-ups, pull-ups, free weights, kettle bells, rubber tubing, Swiss ball, or strength training machines, to name a few. As you begin your strength-training program, focus on the following five guidelines:

1. **Good posture**: Before the start of each exercise get into good posture and maintain this posture alignment throughout the entire exercise. When your postural alignment begins to break down, stop the exercise.
2. **Focus**: Concentrate on the exercise you are performing. What muscles are you trying to engage? Are you making a connection between the brain and the muscles, using the body's neuromuscular system?
3. **Technique**: Are you doing the exercise correctly? This is a big one. Doing an exercise correctly is everything. The correct strength training technique does matter. I see so many people just walk into the strength training room, jump on a piece of equipment or pick up free weights and go at it, with no idea how to do the exercise correctly. The exercises in this book are just a sample of what's out there. Hiring a health and fitness coach for a few sessions to learn proper exercise technique is money well spent. Invest in yourself!
4. **Proper progressions**: There's more to strength training than repetitions, sets, and resistance. As your body adapts to your strength-training program, start making a few small changes in your program so your body stays challenged and continues to make adaptations. These seven areas of progressions include number of exercises, sets, repetitions, resistance, rest and recovery, speed of movement, and stability and balance.
5. **Breathing**: Do not hold your breath when strength training. Ideally, you should exhale during the exertion phase and inhale during the recovery phase of the strength movement. Most importantly, try to keep your breathing regular.

Number of exercises: The big question is how many exercises to do. If you are just beginning, work the entire body by doing four to six exercises. As you advance, add a few more exercises or divide your routine into splits, upper body on the first day, and lower body on the second day,

I personally do a three-day split routine. Day one is chest/back/core, day two is shoulders/arms/core, and day three is lower body. It is quick, intense, and I enjoy the workouts!

Sets: Start with one set of each exercise. As you advance, move to two to four sets per exercise.

Repetitions: Within each set, do from 5 to 13 repetitions, or "reps." Use reps as a guideline to measure your intensity and progress. More important than the number of reps is your technique and maintaining proper posture throughout each exercise movement. If your posture breaks down, regardless of your desired rep range, stop the exercise. Losing proper posture is how people get injured or develop muscle imbalances and poor movement patterns. Each month, I change my repetition number. For example in the month of January, I do **5 repetitions** of each exercise, and I add more resistance and intensity. The month of February, I do **8 repetitions** of each exercise and drop the resistance a little. For the month of March, I do **13 repetitions**, dropping the resistance. I having been alternating repetition ranges each month for the past five years. It keeps the workouts fresh, helps me stay injury-free and challenges my mind and body to adapt.

Resistance: Resistance is the load used in any given set or rep. Choosing the correct resistance can be a bit challenging at first. Your goal with every exercise is to create and maintain good posture alignment and then add resistance to challenge the muscular system. I tell my clients, "Listen to your body, maintain perfect form, and don't get caught up in just pushing weight." As with the repetition changes, it is important to introduce changes in resistance. The lower the repetitions, the greater the resistance; the higher the repetitions, the lower the resistance. Changing your repetitions and resistance each month makes your workouts fresh and keeps you performing at a high level.

Rest and recovery: The more intensity, reps, and resistance in each exercise set, the more recovery time will be necessary between sets. If your goal is to max out during with a specific amount of resistance, you will need a longer recovery time between sets (one to three minutes). Rarely do I lift my maximal amount of weight in a specific exercise, but if this is one of my goals then I will need much more recovery time between sets. If your goal is to integrate many exercises with a moderate amount of resistance, you will have shorter recovery times (10 to 45 seconds) between sets.

Speed of movement: Speed of movement is an important tool to help monitor the intensity of each exercise. Begin with a two-second count in both phases of the strength movement, making the total time for each rep four seconds. I will use a pushup as an example. Take approximately two seconds to lower your chest to the floor, and two seconds to come up. Experiment with the speed of your strength movements; it is a great way to keep your training fresh.

Stability and balance: As you improve and become fit, start challenging your stability and balance. When you are beginning, it is much easier to strength train while you are stable (sitting at a chest press machine as opposed to doing a pushup while your toes are up on a Swiss ball or step).

Strength-Training Exercises

Lower Body

- Squat
- Step-Back or Step-Up
- Lateral Lunge
- Prone Leg Curls or Psoas
- Tubing Side Step and Monster Walks

Upper Body

- Push-Ups (modified and regular)
- Rows (standing tubing or dumbbells)
- Overhead Lat Pull-Downs or Pull-Ups (bands or bar)
- Side Raise (bands or dumbbells)
- Shoulder Press (bands or dumbbells)
- Wide Pull or Reverse Fly (bands or dumbbells)
- Bicep Curls (bands or dumbbells)
- Tricep Kickbacks (bands or dumbbells)
- Wrist Flexion and Extension

Core

- Scissor
- Bicycle
- Cross Over
- Side to Side
- Prone Back Extension
- Spinal Balance
- Swiss ball Combination

Stretching and Flexibility: 1 to 10 Minutes

There are many benefits of stretching the muscles of the body, from decreasing stress to improving muscle imbalances. But remember that stretching exercises should be performed only after the body is warmed up. You would not want to stretch a rubber band after it was in the freezer, and the same is true with your muscles and connective tissue. So spend some time getting your core temperature up before you begin to stretch. This is one reason dynamic exercises are done at the beginning of your workout, and stretching and flexibility is performed at the end of a workout or after the body is warmed up.

There are hundreds of different stretching exercises from which to choose. I have chosen a few basic stretches that cover the entire body. Don't neglect the stretching portion of your exercise program. Start with just a few stretches and build the habit of stretching. I have three stretches I like to introduce to almost everyone: standing wall extensions, half moon against the wall, and the standing up and down dog with the hands on the wall. They cover the entire body, are easy to perform, feel great, and take less than 90 seconds to perform. Focus on proper alignment and diaphragmatic breathing. Stretching exercises can be performed daily. Three general rules to follow, and some basic stretches:

1. Transition through each stretch slowly, holding each stretch for three to five seconds.
2. Maintain ideal posture throughout all stretches.
3. Do not stretch to a point of pain or discomfort.

Stretches

1. Standing Wall Extensions
2. Half Moon against the Wall
3. Standing Up and Down Dog
4. Cat and Dog
5. Child's Pose

Planned Recovery

If you asked me if I have changed my philosophy on exercise over the past few years, I would say yes. Each month I change the intensity of my workouts by changing repetitions and resistance. Changing repetitions along with resistance each month has really added a spark to my workouts, and I like the results. I have been virtually injury-free while maintaining good fitness and strength. My second change is I now take more days off to recover. I actually plan my recovery days. No longer do I just keep pushing forward: now with planned recovery periods my mind and body stay fresh, and I don't feel guilty by taking time off. For many people my goal is to get them to move their body on a daily basis, but for those chronic exercisers out there—the planned recovery is for you. Taking time off is essential for hormonal balance, decreased injuries, greater health, fitness, and improved performance.

Equipment Needs

Very little equipment is needed for the dynamic warm-up, foundations, and cardiovascular exercises that I recommend. For cardio I use a mini-trampoline on a regular basis; it is inexpensive, is great for balance and strength, and it can really get my heart rate high. For strength training, start by using your own body weight, such as a squat, straight-leg lunge, or modified pushup. Using resistance bands is also an easy way to start strength training. Resistance bands come in many colors, each representing different levels of resistance. I use resistance bands in my own training and also with most of my coaching clients.

It is also a good idea to purchase a few dumbbells. A good starter set includes 3-, 5-, 8-, 10-, 12-, 15-, and 20-pound dumbbells. Dumbbells can be purchased in most sporting goods stores.

I also recommend purchasing a Swiss ball and a foam roller. Swiss balls come in different sizes, 55 cm for people five feet eight or under and 65 cm for those five feet nine or taller. Foam rollers are 36 inches long and 6 inches in diameter, great for improving your posture and massaging tired muscles. I use my foam roller daily!

Go to www.ontargetliving.com to learn more and order your bands, Swiss ball, or foam roller.

Frequently Asked Exercise Questions

1. **If exercise is so good for us, then why don't more people do it?**

For many, exercise may be a time element: people feel they just don't have the time to exercise. But exercise is an investment in YOU. Plan some daily movement into your schedule and make it a priority. Also, exercise needs to be fun and enjoyable. Experiment with your exercise program and try to include activities you enjoy.

2. **How much exercise is enough?**

This depends on your personal goals. If you want to achieve a very high fitness level, then the time needed for exercise will be greater than someone who wants to develop basic conditioning. One of the magical things about the human body is that it gets better with use. You do not have to spend a lot of time to keep your body in good condition. Small doses of exercise on a consistent basis are very beneficial. Developing consistent exercise habits will give you the greatest long-term benefits. Start slowly with your program and begin to develop good exercise habits.

3. **Do I need to buy special exercise machines and equipment to get a good workout?**

Not at all. The only exercise tool that is necessary is your own body. You may want to supplement your program with other equipment, but it is not necessary.

4. **Is it expensive to start an exercise program?**

No. If you would like to get started in your own home, you can start without spending any money. Or you may elect to outfit your home with some exercise equipment at a very low cost.

5. **How should I breathe when exercising?**

Never hold your breath during exercise. Holding your breath during exercise may increase your blood pressure. When strength training, exhale during *exertion*.

6. **Does exercise have to be painful to get results?**

Many times you may experience some discomfort when exercising. For instance, you may be out of breath or feel some burning in your muscles. If you are experiencing true pain, your body is signaling you to slow down or to stop. Exercise should not be painful to perform. It may become difficult at times, but it should never be painful.

7. **Can exercise be fun and enjoyable?**

Fitness professionals agree that for people to stay with any exercise program, it *must* be fun and enjoyable. Find activities that get your body moving and that you enjoy. Finding an exercise program or daily movements activities that you enjoy is critical to sustainability!

8. **When is the best time to exercise?**

The core body temperature for most people reaches its peak during the late afternoon and early evening. This is the easiest time for the body to perform at its best. Many people, however, exercise when it fits their schedule. Depending on your goals, schedule time for your exercise program that fits best for you and stick with it. Plan your exercise time.

9. **Should I eat before I exercise?**

If you are exercising first thing in the morning, you may want to eat something small or eat after you exercise. My morning snack prior to exercise is two tablespoons of ground flaxseed mixed with two ounces of organic pomegranate juice. A small balanced snack or meal approximately 1 1/2 hours prior to and after exercise is recommended. If you find you don't have much energy to exercise, focus on eating better, good sleep habits, and finding more balance in your current lifestyle.

10. **What causes muscle soreness and what should I do about it?**

Muscle soreness is caused by micro-tears in the muscle. Most muscle soreness reaches its peak 48 hours after exercise (commonly referred to as *delayed onset muscle soreness*). Activity that overloads muscle in ways it is not accustomed to can cause muscle soreness.

11. **Is muscle soreness good?**

It depends on how severe the soreness is. If you are so sore you can hardly walk, this is an indication that your activity level was too severe, and that your progression into the activity was too quick. A small amount of muscle soreness can be beneficial. This slight soreness is an indication that your activity is progressing in the right direction. You are achieving a training effect.

Active rest, such as walking, stretching, using a foam roller, easy swimming, taking sauna, hot tub, or massage, is an excellent way to help recover from muscle soreness. Remember to enjoy your fitness program and make gradual yet continuous improvements.

12. **How important are rest and recovery?**

Adequate rest and recovery times are essential for good, long-term health and fitness. Give each muscle group a day off between workouts to allow the muscle fibers to rebuild. To perform at your optimum level, you need adequate sleep, relaxation time, active rest, and good nutrition. If you do not allow for adequate rest and recovery, your potential for injury and burnout increases.

13. **Should I exercise every day?**

Moving the body on a regular basis is an important ingredient in keeping the body healthy. However, strength training can put great demands on the body. Adequate recovery between strength-training sessions is important for achieving the greatest benefits. Get one to two days of rest between body parts if you are splitting your training sessions into specific body parts. For example, if you are training the chest muscles on Monday, you can train your back muscles on Tuesday. Cardiovascular and flexibility training can be done on a daily basis. Start slowly; listen to your body, and plan recovery days into your exercise program.

Exercise Considerations

1. You may wish to consult your physician or health professional before you begin your exercise program. I highly recommend hiring a health and fitness coach for three to five sessions to get you started on the right track.
2. Make sure you are well hydrated before, during, and after exercise.
3. Exercise greatly increases body temperature. Be careful when exercising in a warm environment.
4. Wear comfortable, breathable clothing when exercising. Buy a good pair of shoes to wear during exercise.
5. Make the exercise experience enjoyable!

Your Exercise Hierarchy of Needs

As I stated earlier in this chapter, there is no one right way to exercise or move your body, but following the exercise hierarchy of needs will give you a structure to follow. Proper body alignment and posture are at the base of the pyramid. Having correct body alignment and posture is essential for injury prevention and optimal performance in all aspects of your life.

THE BOTTOM LINE

1. Motion creates positive emotion!
2. Move your body daily.
3. Schedule time to exercise.
4. Planned recovery is critical for injury prevention and being your best!
5. Make the exercise experience enjoyable!

V

Your Final Journey

27 Your Body Is Always Talking to You!

Where there is love there is life.

—Mahatma Gandhi

One day while getting dressed at my local health club, a guy a few lockers away asked me if I had a Motrin; he said he had a headache. I told him no, then I thought to myself, should I let this conversation go or should I go deeper and ask a few more questions about his headache? In most cases, I try not to be the food or exercise police, but sometimes I can't help it so I asked him a few more questions. Are you drinking enough water and staying hydrated? Are you consuming any healthy fats? Maybe you are deficient in magnesium or vitamin D? How is your sleep? You should have seen this guy scrambling to get away from me; I think he set a speed record for getting dressed!

What started with a simple question, "do I have a Motrin for his headache," led to a battery of questions! If you have a headache, do you have an ibuprofen deficiency? The answer is no! How did we get so numb to our body and mind? If you had a plant that was wilting, what would you do? Water, sunlight, and soil! Sounds simple, but somewhere along the way many people have lost touch with their bodies and the curiosity of asking better questions.

Your body is always talking to you—but are you listening? For many, the thought of learning how to listen to your body is completely new; that is perfectly okay—self-awareness is the first step in making any change. Nobody knows your body better than you, and it is imperative that you take ownership in your own personal health. This is what this chapter is all about: helping you learn what your body is saying and how to listen. One thing I have learned and am so passionate about after being in the health and fitness industry for almost 30 years is the magic is in you! Your body will try to heal itself if you just give it a chance. There are multiple ways your body is always talking to you:

- Eyes
- Teeth and gums
- Breath
- Digestion and elimination
- Energy and fatigue
- Muscle, tendons, and ligaments
- Bone health
- Resting heart rate
- Blood pressure
- Sleep
- Skin, hair, and nails
- Blood test

Eyes

Just last year I had my first eye exam at age 54 by one of my best friends, Dr. Edward Peters, O.D. He ran me through a battery of tests, took a few pictures of my eyes, and then sat down to discuss what he had found. He then proceeded to show me sample pictures of eyes indicating macular degeneration, type 2 diabetes, high blood pressure, and inflammation, along with a picture of a pair of healthy eyes. I was like a kid in a candy store; it was fascinating to me that the eye showed so much. He explained how the tiny vessels inside the eyes could become damaged by type 2 diabetes or high blood pressure and in most cases showed up much earlier than through traditional blood tests.

I never realized how important getting your eyes examined could be. I now recommend getting your eyes examined as a baseline measurement for everyone and that you continue to get regular eye exams. Dr. Peters is a huge proponent for prevention and explains to all his patients the benefits of daily movement, sleep, and quality nutrition. Dr. Peters is a prevention leader: he even offers his patients shots of cod liver oil in his office.

Teeth and Gums

Seniors that have great teeth and gums always fascinate me. I need to be careful here because technically at age 55 I have moved into this category—now having my own AARP card. Seriously, how many people do you know over the age of 80 that have healthy gums and teeth? How many 80- or 90- or 100-year-olds have all their original teeth? Having healthy teeth and gums tells a great deal about the quality of one's health.

Your dentist or dental hygienist can instantly recognize healthy teeth and gums as soon as you open up your mouth. Growing up I was always told that if I ate too much sugar that I would get cavities; I did not want cavities, but I really liked sugar. It never dawned on me that what I was eating or drinking made that much of a difference in the health of my teeth and gums. I figured if I just brushed my teeth and flossed, I would be okay. I think many people had similar experiences growing up. Today I have a much greater appreciation for the health of my teeth and gums and how powerful a role quality nutrition plays in keeping them healthy for life.

If you go back in time, Weston Price, a dentist from Cleveland, Ohio, whose 1939 book, *Nutritional and Physical Degeneration*, describes the fieldwork he did in the 1920s and 1930s in various world cultures. The book contains numerous photos of the people he studied and includes comparison photographs of the teeth and gums of people who lived on their traditional diet and people who had adopted or grown up on industrialized food. Dr. Price's research and photos are powerful reminders how much a healthy lifestyle impacts your teeth and gums.

Having regular dental check-ups, daily brushing and flossing, keeping your pH in balance, eating high quality foods and beverages, daily movement, along with proper rest and rejuvenation—all play a role in keeping your teeth and gums healthy for a lifetime!

Breath

Your breath is an amazing sign that what is going on inside your body is working—or not. Do you have bad breath? I think we all have had our occasional case of bad breath. But could it be more than just an occasional case of bad breath? I remember years ago my wife, Paula, telling me, "Your breath smells funny again." This was usually after working a 14-hour day for Butternut Bread and getting less than five hours of sleep. I now look back and realize I had acetone breath, due to metabolic acidosis.

What causes acetone breath? In many cases, it could be a form of *metabolic acidosis*. Metabolic acidosis is a condition when the body produces too much acid or when the kidneys are not removing enough acid from the body. The body then moves into ketosis, and what you smell is acetone breath. It is a little more complicated than this, but for simplicity's sake this is the big picture. If left unchecked over time, metabolic acidosis can lead to severe health problems, including death. What causes this excess acid in the body? It could be linked to working long hours without enough rest, too much stress, going too many hours without eating, dehydration, eating a high-protein low-carbohydrate diet, consuming too much coffee or too many energy drinks, taking too many aspirin or ibuprofen, not getting enough sleep, overtraining in the gym, not getting the proper nutrients from your diet, or even diabetes. Acetone breath is not normal and is another way in which the body is talking to you.

Scientists are now developing tests to diagnose a growing list of diseases based on breath such as asthma, diabetes, lung cancer, kidney and liver disease, irritable bowel syndrome, and lactose intolerance—to name a few. The concept of analyzing breath goes back to Hippocrates, who wrote a treatise on breath aroma and disease around 400 BC. Now, scientists are identifying thousands of chemical compounds that create those distinct odors. Many of these breath tests are still in the research stage—but this type of noninvasive technology is exciting and is coming soon.

Digestion and Elimination

Much was said about digestion and elimination in Chapter 13, So What Is Nutrition? I am not going to go into detail, but I want to remind you that the health of the human body begins in the gut. It is not only what you put into the body that makes a difference in your health but also how you break down, absorb, and eliminate. If you are not having a regular bowel movement or your bowel movement does not look like a soft banana, your body is talking back to you to tell you that something is not right.

The mineral magnesium is nature's laxative, so foods high in magnesium such as tahini, figs, raisins, oranges, grapefruit, oats, avocados, coconut, spinach, broccoli, cacao, and wheatgrass will keep your bowel movements regular. If you are dehydrated, your urine will not look like chardonnay or if you pinch the skin on your hand the skin will not bounce back. I used to pinch the skin on my dad's hand to remind him to drink more water. If your skin does not look healthy, you are having poor digestion and it also shows up in the skin. Remember I had terrible skin problems for almost 20 years and nobody ever mentioned that my skin problems were a direct reflection of my poor diet.

Energy and Fatigue

Having great energy is precious, and learning how to recognize ways to build and protect your energy is critical for optimal health and performance. When I am on the road, I know it is essential for me to eat right, take my superfoods, stay well-hydrated, stretch, get plenty of sleep, take a cold shower, and get my workouts in: without these I will not be my best. With energy drinks being the fastest growing beverages in the United States today, it is not a shock that people are constantly complaining about their lack of energy. I had to laugh when I Googled the word "energy," and the first thing that popped up on the screen was an advertisement for Low T (low testosterone). Not one word was mentioned about lack of sleep, poor nutrition, or too much stress?

I believe we can all use more energy now and then, but what about a constant lack of energy and fatigue? The answer cannot be found in an energy drink! What does a lack of energy or chronic fatigue tell us? Let's begin by asking where we get energy from. Our main source of energy comes from the foods and beverages we consume, followed by getting a good night's sleep, planned white space, daily movement or exercise, and controlling our stress. Is your lack of energy and increased fatigue due to your poor lifestyle habits or medications or maybe it runs deeper? If your energy is not what you think it should be, begin with the basics and build energy habits into your day, strategies you do on a daily basis to maintain great energy.

Muscle, Tendons, and Ligaments

One of the areas that I think many people recognize but may be confused is why their muscles, tendons, and ligaments ache. Do you feel stiff, have you lost flexibility, do your muscles ache more than you think they should?

Or has your strength slowly declined? What could be the problem? This is a complaint I receive almost daily! The answer is not more ibuprofen or pain medications. The answer lies in you. Maybe your pH is out of balance, and you are too acidic; too much acid leads to more inflammation and joint pain. Maybe your diet is crummy, and you are deficient in valuable nutrients such as B vitamins, zinc, magnesium, or omega-3 fatty acids? Do you get a good night's sleep on a regular basis? Are your stress levels out of control? Are you getting enough exercise and is strength-training part of your current exercise program? Some of the ways I help keep my muscles and connective tissues strong and flexible and keep pain and discomfort under control without ever using ibuprofen is consuming high quality foods and beverages, white figs and raisins, frozen wheatgrass, cod liver oil and ground flaxseed, regular exercise with strength training, daily foundation exercises, stretching, foam roller exercises, planned down time, sleep, and cold showers. Also I like to get a massage on a regular basis.

If I have an acute inflammation such as a sore joint or muscles, I increase my dosage of omega-3 fats (cod liver oil and flax) and also take bromelain. Bromelain comes from the stem of a pineapple and can be purchased at your local health food store. I consume dried pineapple on a regular basis: I like the sweet taste, and I believe it helps with decreasing inflammation.

Bone Health

Each day people ask me about taking a calcium supplements to improve their bone health. New bone medications hit the market each year! Think about this for a minute: Why do we have such poor bone health in the United States when in fact we have some of the highest intake of calcium in the world and have all these bone medications at our fingertips?

Calcium in the American diet is perceived as almost synonymous with the use of dairy products. Unfortunately, dairy products are not a good quality source of calcium. I rarely recommend taking calcium supplements or consuming dairy to improve a person's bone health.

Then where am I going to get my calcium from if I don't take calcium supplements or consume dairy? Let's set the record straight. Most calcium supplements are difficult for the body to absorb, leading to high levels of calcium in the blood stream and increased calcification in our vessels. Second, dairy is a poor source of calcium: 32 percent of available calcium is destroyed when food is heated above 150 degrees F, making pasteurized milk a limited source of calcium. In Petaluma, California, known as "the egg capital of the world," the egg farmers all know if they want to have a hard eggshell so the eggs don't break, they feed the hens kale, not dairy! So what are some of the other factors that contribute to having healthy bones?

- **Improve pH balance:** High levels of sugar, soda pop, alcohol, processed foods, and stress can all leach out valuable minerals from the body. A more alkaline pH will protect you from losing your valuable buffering minerals such as calcium and magnesium.
- **Vitamin D:** Get outside and get some natural sunlight. Cod liver oil is also high in vitamin D3.
- **Magnesium:** It is common knowledge that vitamin D is essential for calcium utilization, but what we also need to know is that the mineral magnesium must also be available. Magnesium stimulates the hormone calcitonin, and calcitonin is a hormone that increases calcium absorption in the bones and keeps it from being absorbed into soft tissues. Many forms of arthritis are characterized by excess calcium showing up in the soft tissues while skeletal calcium is lacking. If magnesium is not present, then you will have compromised calcium absorption. Foods high in magnesium include tahini, apples, avocados, bananas, beet greens, Brazil nuts, cabbage, coconut, figs, dates, prunes, sea vegetables, lentils, oats, pecans, walnuts, broccoli, spinach, spirulina/chlorella, and wheatgrass.
- **Calcium:** Calcium is necessary for multiple roles in the human body such as digestion, movement, structure, and bone health. Calcium contracts the muscles while magnesium relaxes them. Without calcium, the body would be like a jellyfish! Foods high in calcium include almonds, avocados, kale, spinach, wheatgrass, spirulina/chlorella, broccoli, brown rice, brussels sprouts, cabbage, carrots, sea vegetables, chia seeds, coconut, oats, millet, figs, walnuts, and goat's milk.
- **Exercise and strength training:** Bones are live and adapt when added stress is applied. Regular weight-bearing exercise—along with strength training—stresses the bones and connective tissue and makes them adapt and get stronger.

Resting Heart Rate

One of the best indicators for improved fitness and health is a low resting heart rate. As your fitness level improves, your resting heart rate begins to slow down. For most healthy adults, you should have a resting heart rate under 60 beats per minute. To get an accurate resting heart rate, find your pulse in your wrist, take your pulse for 10 seconds, and multiply by 6. Do this first thing in the morning before you get out of bed. If your stress levels are high, you are lacking in sleep, are eating and drinking too many unhealthy foods and beverages, your resting heart rate will begin to rise. When I am training for a physique competition, I closely monitor my resting heart rate, and I can always tell when I am pushing too hard as my resting heart rate begins to climb.

One of the best ways to improve your resting heart rate is by improving your fitness level through exercise, diaphragmatic breathing, eating and drinking high quality foods and beverages, consuming a few superfoods, adding some all important "white space," and getting enough sleep.

Blood Pressure

For many people, high blood pressure can be debilitating. Many are not even aware they may have high blood pressure. High blood pressure stresses the arterial walls, which may lead to stroke or damaged arteries. High blood pressure also puts more demand on the heart muscle creating a thicker heart, leading to a lower stroke volume and a compromised cardiac output, thus limiting daily activities over time.

My mother was on high blood pressure medications for most of her adult life. Her doctors told her that she would be on her blood pressure medications the rest of her life, and there was nothing that would change this. Today Mom is medication-free and has been off her blood pressure medications for over 10 years. At age 79 Mom has outstanding health along with healthy blood pressure readings. Twelve years ago, Mom began her health journey when she began exercising regularly, consuming cod liver oil, flax, mineral water, spirulina/chlorella, wheatgrass, eating healthy, and quitting drinking alcohol. Remember, everything you need you already have: there is no secret.

So what causes high blood pressure and what can be done about it? There can be multiple reasons for high blood pressure, such as obesity, poor nutritional habits, stress, lack of sleep, poor fitness and lack of exercise, pH imbalance, mineral deficiencies, dehydration, and medication side effects—to name a few.

One of the fastest ways to improve blood pressure is through diaphragmatic breathing. Diaphragmatic breathing or belly breathing stimulates the vagus nerve, which in turn stimulates the parasympathetic nervous system, the nervous system that slows everything down including your heart rate, brain waves, and your blood pressure.

High quality nutrition, consuming healthy fats, such as extra-virgin olive oil, avocadoes, macadamia nuts, cod liver oil, flaxseeds or chia seeds, along with foods high in the mineral magnesium (the relaxer)—all can make a difference in improving your blood pressure. Regular exercise, especially cardiovascular exercise, getting enough rest, and rejuvenation can all make a difference in having a healthy blood pressure.

Get your blood pressure checked every three months; there are many home blood pressure kits that are easy to use and effective. Do you know what your blood pressure reading is?

Sleep

I always know when my body is out of whack because it shows up immediately in my sleep patterns. When life starts getting out of balance, my sleep begins to suffer. My energy level drops, my immune system becomes compromised, and my brain is not sharp. The answer to a better night's sleep is not found with a sleep aid but in learning to listen to your body.

For more information on sleep and how to get a good night's sleep see Chapter 12, Building Your Rest and Rejuvenation Tool Box.

Skin/Hair/Nails

From age three into my early twenties, I had horrible skin, greasy hair, and brittle nails. My parents were always told by the doctors, "Your son has sensitive skin." I did not have sensitive skin, though. I had an extremely unhealthy diet. I took oral medications, topical creams, special shampoos, but nothing made a dent in improving my skin, hair, or nails until I changed my diet. No doctor or health professional ever told me that what I was eating and drinking made a difference in the health of my skin, hair, and nails.

If you have skin rashes, psoriasis, dandruff, brittle hair or are losing your hair, have cracked or discolored nails, your body is telling you something is not right and it is time to take notice. The first signs of poor digestion, poor elimination, deficiencies in vitamins, minerals, or omega-3 fats will show up in your skin, hair, or nails.

One of the questions many people want to know is how long it takes to see results when starting on their journey of having a healthier lifestyle. I tell most people they will see their skin improve, their hair become shiny and full of life, and their nails begin to grow faster and look healthier! One of the first things we teach our health and fitness coaches at On Target Living is to check a person's skin, hair, and nails: the body will be talking to you!

Blood Test

For many having a blood test gives you and your doctor or health professional a meaningful look into your health. A blood test does not keep secrets. If something is not working right inside of you, a blood test may reveal what may be ailing you.

I find that most people have little understanding what the blood test numbers mean, they just hope they are in the "normal" range. If their numbers are not in the normal range and their doctor wants to prescribe a medication, they sometimes feel helpless due to their lack of education.

Each week I receive multiple e-mails and phone calls asking me to further explain their blood test. My goal is to help you have a better understanding of **Knowing Your Numbers** and strategies to help you improve your numbers. Remember, a blood test is just one method of evaluation; your body is always talking to you in a variety of ways. The next chapter will help you understand your numbers and give you strategies to improve your numbers.

THE BOTTOM LINE

1. Your body is always talking to you—but are you listening?
2. Nobody knows your body better than you and it is imperative that you take personal ownership of your own personal health.
3. Your body will try to heal itself if you just give it a chance.

28

Know Your Numbers and Improving Your Numbers

A ship in a harbor is safe, but that is not what ships are built for.

—Unknown

When I first entered into the health and fitness profession almost 30 years ago, I was naive about the world of traditional medicine. My schooling and experience had been geared solely on the prevention side. Fresh out of college with a Master's degree in exercise physiology (along with multiple certifications), I began my career as an intern working for a hospital-based wellness program. My mornings were spent stress testing at the hospital, and afternoons were spent going into companies and educating their associates on the basics of cholesterol, type 2 diabetes, and blood pressure. My role was to help people understand their numbers and show them a few strategies to improve their lifestyle and impact their numbers.

A few years later, I went to work for a family practice physician, Dr. Barry Saltman. Dr. Saltman was a wonderful man, extremely hard-working, seeing on average up to 40 patients per day—40! Dr. Saltman built a small 4,000-square-foot exercise facility in the basement of his practice and wanted me to help design, pick out exercise equipment, and develop exercise and nutritional programs for many of his high-risk patients. This was a wonderful opportunity for me to work with a seasoned physician like Dr. Saltman, but I quickly realized I was in over my head. There were not just a few high-risk patients, but hundreds, and most needed one-on-one attention. I had never seen so many unhealthy, highly medicated people in my life. I kept thinking, "How did all of these folks become so unhealthy? Is this kind of daily interaction with heavily medicated, high-risk people normal for doctors in the United States?"

After two years of this intense hands-on training, I went to work for one of the largest clubs in the world, the Michigan Athletic Club, as the Director of Fitness and Personal Training. My role was to recruit, hire, train, and retain the best and brightest personal trainers, along with developing health and fitness programs for the members. As time went on, I realized our personal trainers were not trained or skilled in dealing with high-risk, highly medicated members, people who were in dire need of our personal training services!

What we needed was a systematic training program to help teach our personal trainers how to interact with our members and their growing needs. Step by step, we looked at body alignment, injuries, nutrition, sleep, breathing, health history, and medications and developed a personal training program that was not centered just on exercise, but the entire person. Members were seeing wonderful results, doctors and health professionals started referring more and more of their patients to our program, the word began to spread, and within a few short years we were one of the highest revenue producing personal-training programs in America.

After more than 17,000 one-on-one personal-training sessions, hiring and training over 300 personal trainers, and speaking around the world to thousands of people in my On Target Living seminars, I felt a need to share this information with more and more people.

Know Your Numbers/Improving Your Numbers

For many, having a blood test gives you, your doctor, or health professional a meaningful look into your health. A blood test does not keep secrets. If something is not working right inside of you, a blood test may reveal what may be ailing you. Yet I find that most people have little understanding what the blood test numbers mean; they just hope they are in the "normal" range. If their numbers are not in the normal range and their doctor wants to prescribe a medication, they sometimes feel helpless due to their lack of education.

My goal for this chapter is to help you have a better understanding of your numbers, to learn strategies to help you improve your numbers, and to give you enough information to converse with your doctor or health practitioner. Remember, a blood test is just one method of evaluation; your body is always talking to you in a variety of ways.

Cholesterol

Let's begin with the big kahuna, cholesterol. Cholesterol is a hot topic wherever you go, and why not?—the cholesterol scare has been rampant for decades. But there is so much misinformation about cholesterol among Americans. I survey my audiences on how many have had their cholesterol checked in the past two years. Almost 100 percent of the audience members raise their hands and say yes. Then I ask how many have had their homocysteine checked, a risk factor for a heart attack, stroke, inflammation, Alzheimer's, and Parkinson's diseases. Very rarely do I get more than one or two hands that go up; most have never heard of such a blood test. Most people believe having high cholesterol is the most important risk factor for predicting a heart attack or stroke. What if I told you that 60 to 70 percent of all heart attacks occur with normal cholesterol levels? How can this be?

Cholesterol may play a role in your risk of having a heart attack or stroke, but there are many other factors besides having unbalanced cholesterol that affect your risk. Most people believe that having low cholesterol is good and having high cholesterol is bad. Let's go deeper and start by having a better understanding of cholesterol.

What Is Cholesterol and How Is It Measured?

Cholesterol is a waxy substance produced by the liver and is essential for optimal health in the human body. The most common way to measure cholesterol is through a fasting blood test. Cholesterol is measured in total cholesterol, HDL cholesterol, LDL cholesterol, and the cholesterol/HDL ratio. Most doctors and medical literature state the "good" cholesterol is HDL and the "bad" cholesterol is LDL. I like to look at HDL and LDL cholesterol a little differently, neither being labeled "good" or "bad"; both are types of cholesterol and are doing what they were designed to do. LDL cholesterol is the "brick layer," patching up holes, and HDL cholesterol is the "sweeper," the one cleaning up after the work has been done. The real key for risk is the balance of your cholesterol profile along with other risk factors that will be discussed later in this chapter.

When looking at a cholesterol profile, the first item to look for is the cholesterol/HDL ratio. The cholesterol/HDL ratio gives a better overall picture of the balance in the cholesterol profile. For example, if a person's total cholesterol is 220 and their HDL cholesterol is 65, their cholesterol/HDL ratio is 3.38 (220 divided by 65). For women, the recommended range is 3.5 or less and for men 4.5 or less. For both women and men, this would be an ideal balance. Many times people are put on cholesterol-lowering medication just because their total cholesterol is over 200, when in fact they could be over 200 like in this example and have virtually no risk! The key to a healthy body and mind is having a balanced cholesterol profile: not too high or too low.

What Does Cholesterol Do?

I believe when most people discuss cholesterol they think of it as something bad or are proud that their cholesterol is so low, believing the lower the cholesterol the better. Let's change that thinking right now! First, cholesterol is the raw material for the building of all steroidal hormones, the sex and healing hormones in our bodies. Second, cholesterol is necessary for the production of CoQ10, a powerful antioxidant coenzyme involved in the energy production of every single cell in our body. CoQ10 is most famous for keeping the heart healthy. In fact, if you live in Canada and are prescribed a statin medication to lower your cholesterol, you are also prescribed a CoQ10 supplement. Remind me again why I am supposed to be taking a statin medication if it blocks the production of one of the most powerful antioxidant coenzymes that keeps my heart healthy?

On top of having healthy hormones, high levels of energy, and a powerful antioxidant coenzyme for the heart, cholesterol is also necessary to maintain cellular integrity. If you did not have cholesterol, your cells would look like a jellyfish, with no structure to the cellular wall. Cholesterol is an amazing substance, and without it we would not have life!

Why Is My Cholesterol High or Out of Balance?

This is a great question to ask. If your cholesterol is too high or out of balance (having a balanced cholesterol profile is what we should all be striving for), you need to ask the question why, why is it out of balance? Remember, cholesterol is the raw material for your healing hormones and helps keep your cells energized and healthy. Maybe your stress levels are too high, your body has too much inflammation, you lack sleep, eat too many processed foods, drink too much soda pop or alcohol; your body may be talking back and trying to help. The body goes into healing mode trying to repair, and the liver begins producing more cholesterol to create hormonal balance and heal the cells. The body is trying to fix itself and does this by producing more cholesterol. Some people may also have a genetically predisposition to produce more cholesterol than the average person, and in most of these cases the goal again is to create balance within the cholesterol profile.

Should I Take a Statin Medication to Improve My Cholesterol Balance?

Before I get too far, I want you to understand that I am not your doctor. My intention is to empower you with greater knowledge and understanding, so you can make a more informed decision about your health along with working with your doctor. With that being said, hang on, because I am going to give you my thoughts and beliefs about how to improve your cholesterol profile—and it is not with statin medications.

What is a statin medication? Statin medications have been on the market for over 20 years and are the most prescribed medication in America and now around the world to help lower cholesterol. Statins are big business, a multibillion-dollar business, and it continues to grow.

The statin class of drugs is very effective at reducing cholesterol. They do their work in the liver by suppressing an enzyme called HMG-CoA. When you block the enzyme HMG-CoA, you also block the production of CoQ10 as I mentioned earlier, a powerful antioxidant coenzyme. A deficiency in CoQ10 can lead to multiple problems, such as leg pain or cramps, impotence, depression and memory loss, type 2 diabetes, shortness of breath or fatigue, cardiac palpitations, and liver enzyme abnormalities: it sounds like these statin medications can have many side effects, and I am not done yet!

Remember earlier I discussed the role of cholesterol and its importance for having healthy hormones. Cholesterol is the raw material for all steroidal hormones, meaning all of your healing hormones such as androgens, estrogens, progestins, mineralocorticoids, and glucocorticoids, your body's sex and healing hormones, are made from cholesterol. If your cholesterol production is blocked by a statin medication, you will have compromised these hormones.

Every week I receive copies of blood work from people wanting to learn more and have a better understanding about their blood work. They want to be more in control of their own health and have better conversations with their doctors. One area I see on a regular basis is an extremely low cholesterol reading followed by an extremely low reading of testosterone. Immediately I know this person most likely is taking a statin medication. The statins block the cholesterol production and compromise the production of sex hormones. We have to ask why the erectile dysfunction class of medications is skyrocketing. Now you know: taking a statin medication blocks the production of cholesterol and many times compromises the production of our sex and healing hormones in the body. I might be oversimplifying this to some extent, but my point is why are we seeing epidemic levels of erectile dysfunction in America? Could it be from our overconsumption of statin medications?

Another concern we are seeing in America and around the world is the epidemic increase in brain and nerve diseases such as dementia, Alzheimer's, Parkinson's, and multiple sclerosis. All of these diseases are based on the breakdown of the myelin sheath, the protective coating that surrounds every nerve in the human body. The thicker the myelin sheath, the faster and stronger the nerve signal becomes. If the myelin sheath begins to break down around the nerve, the signal may become disrupted, similar to the old telephone cord that begins to fray: the signal may be disjointed or sometimes lost. One of the possible side effects of statin medications is the breakdown of the myelin sheath.

As you can tell, I am not a fan of statin medications due to their powerful side effects. If you want to improve your cholesterol profile, I believe there is a safer and much more effective way to go.

How Do I Improve My Cholesterol Profile?

Step 1: Take one tablespoon of cod liver oil each morning for the first two to three weeks, letting your body acclimate. Then move to two tablespoons per day. Try to spread out your intake of cod liver oil, taking one tablespoon in the morning and another tablespoon in the late afternoon or evening. I recommend the lemon-flavored cod liver oil right off the spoon; this will give you approximately 1,500 to 3,000 mg of EPA/DHA per day.

Step 2: Take two tablespoons of ground flaxseed or chia seeds per day.

Step 3: Vitamin C is a natural cholesterol reducer. Try to get some vitamin C into your diet on a daily basis through berries, oranges, grapefruit, lemons, limes, watermelon, pineapple, broccoli, kale, asparagus, and sweet potatoes. You may also wish to supplement that with at least 500 mg of vitamin C per day.

Step 4: Cut out the crap and start eating higher quality foods and beverages using the Food Target: eat leafy greens, spirulina/chlorella, wheatgrass, hemp seeds, pumpkin seeds, walnuts, squash, broccoli, oatmeal, and beans.

Step 5: Drink more water, six to eight ounces of water *per hour*!

Step 6: Move your body on a daily basis.

Step 7: Get a good night's sleep.

How Do I Get Off or Lower the Dose of My Cholesterol Medications?

Do not change one thing with your medications for the first month or two. Get your new habits in place (cod liver oil, flaxseeds, citrus, cut out the crap and upgrade your food and beverage choices, start moving your body on a daily basis, and work on getting a good night's sleep). Then set up an appointment and get your doctor on board with your new plan. Discuss with your doctor your intentions to slowly get off your cholesterol-lowering medication. In three months, get another blood test to monitor your cholesterol profile. For example if you are currently taking 40 mg of your statin medication, cut the dosage to 20 mg and get another blood test in three months. As your cholesterol profile improves, cut your dosage again to 10 mg and follow the same protocol until you are off your statin medication.

I am very passionate about helping people get off of their statin medications because I know it is possible and I know what I am sharing with you works. By slowly working with your doctor and improving your lifestyle habits, your need for cholesterol medications can disappear.

Triglycerides

Triglycerides are another fat in the blood similar to cholesterol. Triglycerides are also produced in the liver and are extremely sensitive to the foods and beverages you consume. Your cholesterol profile may take months to be impacted by your new healthier lifestyle habits, but triglycerides are impacted almost immediately. Triglycerides are like looking in a mirror to see what you are eating and drinking—and the mirror does not lie! So when people tell me they are eating healthy and their triglycerides are over 150, I may not be getting the whole picture. A target triglyceride reading should be under 100.

Why Are My Triglycerides Too High?

In most cases, eating and drinking unhealthy foods or beverages are the biggest cause of having high triglycerides. Too much fast and processed foods, soda pop, energy drinks, and alcohol. Stress and a sedentary lifestyle can also contribute to high triglyceride levels.

Step 1: The fastest way to reduce your triglycerides is by consuming omega-3 fats such as cod liver oil and ground flaxseeds or chia seeds.

Step 2: Foods high in chlorophyll such as spirulina/chlorella, wheatgrass, and greens will also be very beneficial in improving triglycerides.

Step 3: Simple sugars raise triglyceride levels, so cut back on the sweets, alcohol, soda pop, and processed foods.

Step 4: Eat hemp seeds, pumpkin seeds, walnuts, and more vegetables.

Step 5: Drink more water.

Glucose/Hemoglobin A1c

There are two screening measurements for diabetes: glucose and Hemoglobin A1c. Blood glucose is an immediate measurement whereas A1c looks at an average spread over time. Both are effective screens for diabetes. Blood glucose is often measured as part of a group of tests during a routine physical as a screen for diabetes; it reflects your current glucose levels. Since diabetes is a disease that affects your body's ability to use glucose, let's begin by having a better understanding of what glucose is and how your body controls it. Glucose is a simple sugar that provides energy to all cells in your body. The cells take in glucose from the blood and break it down for energy. Glucose in the blood comes from the food that you eat.

When you consume food or beverages that contain calories, glucose is absorbed into your intestines and distributed into the blood stream to all cells in your body. To maintain a constant blood-glucose level, the pancreas produces two opposing hormones, insulin and glucagon. The major role of insulin is to open up the cell for glucose to enter and feed the cell. After a meal, blood glucose begins to rise, the pancreas releases insulin, insulin opens the door of the cell, and glucose enters the cell. Without insulin, glucose cannot enter the cell. Glucagon on the other hand is the opposite of insulin and is released by the pancreas when blood glucose begins to drop, almost as a safety net for maintaining steady flow of glucose to your cells. Glucagon does this by releasing stored reserves of glucose.

There are two types of diabetes: type 1, where the pancreas does not produce insulin and type 2, where insulin is produced but has a difficult time opening up the cell door. With type 1 diabetes, you must take insulin because the pancreas is not producing insulin. Type 1 diabetes is something you are usually born with or have high genetic tendencies for. Type 2 diabetes, on the other hand, is a **lifestyle disease** in which the cells become stiff and rigid and over time, making it extremely difficult for insulin to open up the cell for glucose to enter.

Hemoglobin A1c is a blood test that measures the average level of glucose in a person's blood over the past 6- to 12-week period and is used in conjunction with blood glucose monitoring. Hemoglobin A1c results are expressed as the percentage of hemoglobin molecules that have glucose molecules bound to them. A person with type 1 diabetes needs insulin injections to allow the cells to receive glucose. If there is not enough insulin for the amount of glucose, the person's Hemoglobin A1c will rise. A normal Hemoglobin A1c test is between 4 and 5.6 percent. Hemoglobin A1c levels between 5.7 and 6.4 percent indicate increased risk of diabetes, and levels 6.5 percent or higher indicate diabetes!

In 1970 there were less than 500,000 type 2 diabetics in the United States, but today there are over 26 million—with over 40 million prediabetics waiting in the wings. Genetics play a role in our health—but this is not genetics. One of the fastest growing groups of medications in the world today is for type 2 diabetes. Countries such as Mexico that have adopted the fast and processed food environment seen in the US, have now climbed to number two in the world for type 2 diabetics, just behind the United States.

Why Is My Glucose or Hemoglobin A1c Too High?

Throughout this entire book, I have stressed the importance of getting healthy at the cellular level. Type 2 diabetes is a disease that begins at cellular level. As the outer rim of the cell becomes stiff and rigid, like an M&M candy shell, insulin has a difficult time opening up the cell. Most type 2 diabetics are told not to eat foods high in sugar, and this is true—sugar may have contributed to the problem, but the real problem is the cell membrane, the outer rim of the cell. The first stage of getting a type 2 diabetic on their road to recovery is to educate them about the cell membrane. What is causing the cell to be too stiff and rigid, and what makes it soft and permeable?

Processed foods, fast foods, soda pop, energy drinks, alcohol, high fructose corn syrup, trans fats, nutritional deficiencies, and lack of sleep all contribute to our skyrocketing increase in type 2 diabetes around the world.

How Do I Improve My Glucose and Hemoglobin A1c Levels?

The first step in improving type 2 diabetes is getting the cell membrane soft and more permeable to glucose. Let's get busy making the cells healthy!

Step 1: Omega-3 fats such as cod liver oil, flaxseeds, and chia seeds help make the cell membrane soft and permeable. One of the keys for type 2 diabetes is to improve cellular sensitivity. Take one to two tablespoons of the cod liver oil and two tablespoons of the ground flaxseeds or chia seeds each day.

Step 2: Avoid trans fats, fast food, and processed foods and beverages. Trans fats (partially hydrogenated oils) make the cell membrane hard and brittle, decreasing sensitivity to insulin and making it extremely difficult for insulin to open up the cells to allow the cells to be fed. Processed foods and beverages gum up the cell membrane and also make the cell membrane lose sensitivity.

Step 3: Hydration! Drink more water, ideally half your body weight in ounces per day. Replace other beverages with water; a slice of lemon or lime will also help make your water more alkaline.

Step 4: Superfoods such as wheatgrass and spirulina/chlorella are one of the most powerful ways to help type 1 and type 2 diabetes.

Step 5: Bring on the mineral magnesium! Magnesium also increases cellular sensitivity. Avocados, asparagus, beans, beets, Brazil nuts, brown rice, cacao, coconut, sea vegetables, figs, fish, ginger, oatmeal, prunes, spinach, tahini, and walnuts are all good sources of magnesium.

Step 6: Vitamin D is a powerful healer. If you get 30 minutes of sunshine daily, you receive about 10,000 IU of vitamin D. Sunshine makes vitamin D in your body, and vitamin D protects the body from a host of diseases such as cancer, bone disease, heart disease, and type 2 diabetes. Vitamin D helps type 2 diabetes by improving cellular sensitivity. You can also get vitamin D from the foods you eat, such as wild cold-water fish and cod liver oil. Another reason to take

(continued)

(continued)

one to two tablespoons of cod liver oil daily! If you wish to take a vitamin D supplement, make sure you are taking vitamin D3 (cholecalciferol). Avoid vitamin D2 (ergocalciferol), which is common in many supplements and in prescription drugs containing vitamin D; this is not a natural form of vitamin D.

Step 7: Cinnamon. Using cinnamon on a regular basis is a powerful way to improve diabetes. Cinnamon is high in antioxidants, activates essential enzymes in the body, helping the cells to become more sensitive to insulin. Cinnamon also contains calcium, chromium, copper, iodine, manganese, phosphorus, zinc, and many vitamins that help in the prevention of diabetes. Try to get one to two teaspoons of organic cinnamon in your daily food plan. I like to use cinnamon on my oatmeal.

Step 8: Regular exercise and strength training improve cellular sensitivity.

Step 9: Get a good night's sleep. Nothing is better to boost your immune system than having healthy sleep practices.

Homocysteine

Take a deep breath and pay attention: this is some good stuff I am going to share with you. With all the research on heart disease, we have recently learned that approximately 60 to 80 percent of all heart attacks occur with normal cholesterol levels. So the mere presence of cholesterol does not cause heart disease—oxidation and inflammation also have to occur. So things that cause oxidation and inflammation are risk factors too? Yes! This is why before anyone ever takes another statin medication to lower cholesterol you need to look at all the risk factors involved.

Homocysteine is an amino acid that can be measured by taking a simple blood test. Homocysteine measures oxidation? What is oxidation? You know, it rains outside and metal begins to rust, or you bite into an apple and it immediately begins to turn brown: this is oxidation. Homocysteine that is not cleared in the blood and left intact enters the bloodstream and begins attacking blood vessel walls, creating havoc throughout the entire body.

Homocysteine levels above 13 are a risk factor for heart disease, stroke, inflammation, cancer, Alzheimer's, and Parkinson's diseases, to name a few. So why have most people not had this test before if it is a risk factor for so many diseases? I recommend getting your homocysteine checked every time you get your cholesterol checked.

Why Is My Homocysteine Too High?

For most people, an essential amino acid (methionine) found in meat is an indirect source of homocysteine. There are many circumstances in which homocysteine may become a deadly problem if not broken down and cleared out of the bloodstream. The two biggest are a lack of key B vitamins such as folate B9, pyridoxine B6, and methylcobalamin B12.Lack of these B vitamins can impair homocysteine metabolism. Also, a high acid diet, namely from eating too much meat, processed foods, and beverages can increase homocysteine levels.

While interviewing a new personal training client (a very lean 52-year-old woman) a few years ago, the subject of cholesterol came up. My new client stated that she was concerned about heart disease due to her mother and sister both having a history of heart problems, but she felt good because her cholesterol numbers were low. I proceeded to ask if she knew what her homocysteine level was. She had no idea what homocysteine was or why she needed it to be checked due to her doctor never mentioning it. I informed her it was another measurement to monitor your risk factor for heart disease. So I recommended the next time she was going to get a blood test to ask to get her homocysteine checked. She said she was going to get her annual physical the next week and would make sure to get her homocysteine checked. I also asked her to do a three-day sleep, nutrition, and exercise log. A few weeks later she returned for her second training session, and she returned with her new blood test and three-day logs. When I looked at her blood test, I was shocked to see her homocysteine level at 52. I told her homocysteine should be between 3 and 13, but hers was 52. When I looked at her food log, she had been on the Atkins Diet for over a year, eating lots of meat and cheese, very little carbohydrates, and was drinking three to four cups of coffee along with three to four artificially sweetened beverages throughout the day. Her entire diet was extremely deficient along with being highly acidic. Her hair was brittle, her skin was dry, her breath had the smell of acetone, but she was very lean and that was her goal, to stay lean. After our second session, she never came back; I don't think she wanted to hear what I had to say.

How Do I Improve My Homocysteine Level?

Step number one is to get your homocysteine measured. The amount of oxidation you have in your body plays a role in your risk for heart disease, cancer, type 2 diabetes, arthritis, and aging of the body.

Step 1: Folate—vitamin B9. Folate plays an extremely important role in clearing homocysteine out of the body. Foods high in folate include leafy greens, asparagus, broccoli, beets, cucumbers, sweet potatoes, squash, strawberries, flaxseeds, spirulina/chlorella, and wheatgrass. Just one more tip: if you wish to take folate in a supplement form, take folate, not folic acid. Folic acid is a synthetic form of folate.

Step 2: Pyridoxine—vitamin B6. Vitamin B6 is involved in the metabolism of proteins and carbohydrates. Low levels allow homocysteine to increase. Foods high in vitamin B6 include beans, nuts, bananas, cabbage, cauliflowers, potatoes, and whole grains such as amaranth, millet, and oatmeal.

Step 3: Methycobalamin—vitamin B12. Vitamin B12 is also essential during the metabolism of protein, carbohydrate, and fat. As with folate and vitamin B6, vitamin B12 must be present to rid the body of harmful amounts of homocysteine. Foods high in vitamin B12 include Brussels sprouts, kale, parsley, whole grains, nuts and seeds, legumes, sea vegetables, spirulina/chlorella, meat, and fish.

Step 4: Choline—another essential B vitamin. Choline is a building block for fats, necessary for building cell membranes. Choline is also important for brain function and memory—I better make sure I get enough choline! A few of the highest food sources of choline are beans, peas, and lentils.

Step 5: Antioxidants—decrease oxidation! Homocysteine is a measurement of oxidation. One of the best ways to decrease oxidation is to consume foods that are high in antioxidants, omega-3 fats, colorful fruits, and vegetables.

High-Sensitive C-Reactive Protein

High-sensitive C-reactive protein (CRP) measures inflammation throughout the body. It was not until 2000 that the role of inflammation in heart disease gained momentum. Paul Ridker, MD, of Harvard Medical School, developed a blood test known as high-sensitive C-reactive protein (CRP). He reported in the *New England Journal of Medicine* that women with elevated levels of CRP were four times more likely to suffer a heart attack, compared with women who had normal CRP levels.

CRP is an indicator of inflammation, and high levels of inflammation damage blood vessel walls. Now you know the other risk factors for heart disease, imbalanced cholesterol levels, high glucose, high levels of homocysteine, and high levels of high-sensitive C-reactive protein. The US Centers for Disease Control and Prevention have defined risk groups as follows for high-sensitive C-reactive protein:

- Low risk: less than 1.0 mg/L
- Average risk: 1.0 to 3.0 mg/L
- High risk: above 3.0 mg/L

Why Is My High-Sensitive C-Reactive Protein Too High?

There are many reasons that contribute to high levels of inflammation throughout the body. First and foremost is a high level of acid or an imbalanced pH. Processed foods, fast food, alcohol, soda pop, energy drinks, too much animal protein, too many processed omega-6 fats such as corn and soybean oils, trans fats, stress, lack of essential nutrients, dehydration, lack of sleep, and lack of movement all add up to high levels of inflammation.

How Do I Improve My High-Sensitive C-Reactive Protein Level?

As with homocysteine, step number one is to get your High Sensitive C-Reactive measured. The amount of inflammation you have in your body attributes to your risk for heart disease, cancer, type 2 diabetes, arthritis, poor bone health, pain, and a decrease in your immune system.

Step 1: Adopt an anti-inflammatory diet. Start by cutting out some of the processed, acidic, highly inflammatory foods and beverages. Foods in the red area of the Food Target are highly processed, acidic, and extremely inflammatory.

Step 2: Bring on the healthy fats! Omega-3 fats such as cod liver oil, ground flaxseeds, chia seeds are extremely anti-inflammatory. Also, healthy fats such as extra virgin coconut oil, olive oil, avocadoes, and hemp seeds, most raw nuts and seeds are also anti-inflammatory. Cut out all processed oils such as corn, soy, and canola.

Step 3: Move to the green area of the Food Target. Foods in the green area of the Food Target are more alkaline, more nutrient-dense, and decrease inflammation.

Step 4: Super greens are extremely alkaline and decrease inflammation. Spirulina/chlorella, kale, spinach, broccoli, and wheatgrass are high in chlorophyll and decrease inflammation.

Step 5: Hydration! Being well hydrated is the first step for almost anything related to having a healthy body and is extremely important in decreasing inflammation. Ideally try to drink half your body weight in ounces per day or drink six to eight ounces per hour to improve absorption.

Step 6: Rest and rejuvenation. I have had clients that eat very healthy, but their stress levels are out of control. When their high-sensitive C-reactive protein level comes back and is high, they are confused. Lack of rest and too much stress can contribute to an imbalanced pH and create too much inflammation throughout the body. Some people have a hard time believing *how they think* can make them sick, but I am here to tell you most of our diseases in the United States are attributed to too much stress and not enough rest and rejuvenation. Getting enough rest and rejuvenation is key for improving inflammation.

Prostate-Specific Antigen Screening (PSA)

Prostate-specific antigen, or PSA, is a protein produced by cells of the prostate gland. The PSA test, a screening for prostate cancer, measures the level of PSA in a man's blood. Prostate cancer screening can help identify cancer early on, when treatment is most effective. A normal PSA test combined with a digital rectal exam can help reassure you that it's unlikely you have prostate cancer. Professional organizations vary in their recommendations about who and who shouldn't get a PSA screening test, but most agree to encourage the screening in men between the ages of 40 and 75, and in men with an increased risk of prostate cancer. Whether you have a PSA test is something you should decide after discussing it with your doctor and considering your risk factors. A normal PSA reading is 00. to 4.00ng/ml.

Why Is My PSA Too High?

Consuming processed foods, drinking too much alcohol, soda pop or energy drinks, smoking, high levels of stress, and living a sedentary lifestyle all contribute to increased cancer risk, including prostate cancer. Being deficient in valuable nutrients such as iodine and zinc can also contribute to an increase in prostate cancer.

How Do I Improve My PSA Level?

For all men over the age of 50 it is a good idea to get your prostate checked on a regular basis, especially if you have a family history of prostate problems. Daily rest and rejuvenation practices, regular exercise, and high-quality nutrition all play important roles in keeping the prostate healthy.

Step 1: Consume foods that are high in gamma-linolenic acid (GLA) and omega-3 fats. GLA is an omega-6 and essential fatty acid that helps in the production of prostaglandins (PGE1). PGE1 helps boost the immune system, activate t-cells, which destroy cancer and unwanted substances in the cells of the body. Foods high in GLA include pumpkin seeds, evening primrose oil, black currant seed oil, borage oil, and spirulina/chlorella.

Step 2: Sea vegetables! Sea vegetables such as sushi nori, kelp, kombu, and many others are very cooling and help reduce tumors and other unwanted growths. Sea vegetables are the highest source of iodine, and iodine supports the prostate gland.

Step 3: Cereal grasses such as wheatgrass are high in minerals and chlorophyll and contain unique digestive enzymes that help break down toxic substances in other foods and highly destructive "free radicals" formed by bad air, chemicals, and other toxins that may damage the body. Cereal grasses also contain anti-inflammatory properties that help protect the prostate.

Step 4: Zinc! Zinc is a trace mineral and is essential for many life-sustaining biochemical reactions in your body. Zinc is tied directly to your immune system, and for many people zinc levels can quickly decline with age. Foods high in zinc include chicken, lamb, spinach, beef, squash, broccoli, asparagus, greens, oatmeal, millet, amaranth, pumpkins seeds, and beans.

Step 5: Learn more about how prescription and over-the-counter medications deplete the valuable mineral zinc. Ibuprofen, aspirin, acid reflux, blood pressure, antacids, cholesterol, and hormonal replacement therapy all have a leaching effect of zinc.

Thyroid-Stimulating Hormone (TSH-Ultra Sensitive)

The thyroid-stimulating hormone (TSH) is often the test of choice for evaluating thyroid function, symptoms of hyperthyroidism or hypothyroidism. There are two common conditions of imbalance in the thyroid. In hyperthyroidism, the thyroid is speeded up beyond normal and uses iodine rapidly. In hypothyroidism, the thyroid is functioning below normal, often because a lack of the mineral iodine. The hyperthyroid person is going faster than a speeding bullet while the hypothyroid person is moving like a turtle with sore feet! A normal reading for TSH-Ultra Sensitive is .35 to 5.50 ulu/ml.

What Causes the Thyroid to Get Out of Balance?

You need iodine to make thyroid hormone, so a lack of iodine can cause havoc to the body, leading to a host of problems such as a compromised immune system, breast cancer, prostate cancer, diabetes, heart arrhythmias, diabetes, low energy, little or no sex drive, depression, and weight gain. A nutrient-deficient diet, a high acid diet, too much stress, lack of sleep, along with a host of medications that may rob the body of the valuable mineral iodine can easily put the body out of balance.

How Can You Bring Balance Back to Your Thyroid Gland?

Having a balanced pH is critical for bringing your thyroid back into balance. Planned recovery strategies, coupled with daily movement and high-quality nutrition, all play a role in having a healthy thyroid!

Step 1: I believe one reason we are having an epidemic increase in thyroid gland problems is due to stress and not getting enough rest and rejuvenation. Adrenal exhaustion has become widespread with millions suffering "stress diseases" based on the number of physicians prescribing

(continued)

(continued)

medications for many of these illnesses. Many people believe having rest and rejuvenation strategies plugged into their life is a luxury. I can't tell you how many times I have talked with women who are having thyroid problems and want some advice on how to improve their thyroid. When I ask them about their current rest and rejuvenation strategies, they look at me like I have a third eye. If you want to improve your thyroid, start with getting enough sleep, deep breathing, using a foam roller, massage, and soft music, creating more white space—simple strategies that can truly make a difference.

Step 2: One of the first steps in bringing balance back to your thyroid gland is to consume foods that are high in iodine. You need iodine to make thyroid hormone. Foods high in iodine include asparagus, Brussels sprouts, carrots, coconut, fish, kale, oats, green onions, sweet potatoes, squash, strawberries, tomatoes, and watermelon. The highest food source of iodine is seaweed or sea vegetables such as kelp or dulse. I eat two sheets of sushi nori each week.

Step 3: Zinc! Zinc is not only essential for prostate health but also for a healthy thyroid gland. Zinc is involved in the creation of thyroid hormone. With low levels of zinc, you may develop hypothyroidism that could lead to hair loss, weight gain, fatigue, a feeling of being cold, depression, low sex drive, insomnia, dry skin, and brittle nails. Foods high in zinc include chicken, lamb, spinach, beef, squash, broccoli, asparagus, greens, millet, amaranth, pumpkin seeds, and beans.

Step 4: A clean liver equals a healthy thyroid gland. If the liver is stagnant and sluggish due to consuming too much food, alcohol, or processed foods and dehydration, the thyroid may also become sluggish. Foods high in chlorophyll such as wheatgrass, spirulina/chlorella, greens and broccoli along with drinking enough water keep the liver clean. Also, many of these superfoods are extremely high in minerals that support the thyroid gland.

Step 5: Sleep! Focus on getting a good night's sleep. Sleep is critical for thyroid gland health. Turn off the TV and computer one to two hours prior to going to bed. Get outside during the day, plan your sleep, eat right, drink less alcohol, get some regular exercise and create a habit of diaphragmatic breathing and breath awareness throughout the day and at bedtime.

25-Hydroxyvitamin D Total

The 25-hydroxyvitamin D total is a blood test used to determine if bone weakness, bone malformation, or abnormal metabolism of calcium is occurring as a result of a deficiency of vitamin D. Once ingested, vitamin D turns into a powerful hormone that help build strong bones, move muscles, lower cancer risk by increasing immune function, and lower the risk of Type 2 diabetes by improving insulin sensitivity. Vitamin D is necessary to help absorb important minerals such as calcium and phosphorus, both necessary for having healthy bones. Vitamin D is powerful, and today more and more are people becoming vitamin D deficient. A normal 25-hydroxyvitamin D total is 25.0 to 80.0 ng/mL.

What Causes a Vitamin D Deficiency?

Lack of sunlight is one of the greatest reasons for being vitamin D deficient. Lack of consuming wild cold-water fish along with taking medications that leach out vitamin D also greatly contribute to having a vitamin D deficiency.

How Can You Improve a Vitamin D Deficiency?

Let's get busy bringing more vitamin D3 into your life!

Step 1: Sunlight! By getting just 30 minutes of sunshine daily you will receive approximately 10,000 to 20,000 IU of vitamin D. Getting more sunshine in your day will also improve your mood and stimulate your pineal gland for a better night's sleep. If you are sensitive to the sun, start with smaller exposures to the sun. If you wish to use sunscreen, choose a paraben-free, organic brand if possible.

Step 2: Cod liver oil! At almost every one of my seminars, I bring the lemon-flavored cod liver oil. Cod liver oil is the highest source of vitamin D3 (cholecalciferol) from any food source. One tablespoon of the cod liver contains 1,200 IU of vitamin D3. I personally take two tablespoons of the cod liver each day, giving me approximately 2,400 IU of vitamin D3 per day or 17,000 IU of vitamin D3 per week. If you wish to use a supplement, choose the real-deal vitamin D3 and avoid vitamin D2 (ergocalciferol) supplements.

Step 3: Chlorophyll! All plants touched by sunlight contain chlorophyll, and green plants contain the highest amount of chlorophyll. Fortunately, chlorophyll foods act as a form of stored sunshine, performing like vitamin D in the body to regulate calcium. Foods such as wheatgrass, spirulina/chlorella, spinach, kale, collard greens, romaine lettuce, broccoli, and sea vegetables all contain high levels of chlorophyll.

Step 4: Having a better understanding of how many medications can leach out vitamin D may be a powerful incentive in getting you on a healthier path. Medications such as those used to treat acid reflux and blood pressure, and antacids, cholesterol agents, and antibiotics, along with consuming too much coffee, soda pop, and alcohol—all of these rob the body of valuable nutrients including vitamin D.

Testosterone

Rarely does a day go by when you don't hear something about testosterone, Low T, Ageless Male, Androgel, or a growing number of prescription pills, gels, and patches aimed at boosting testosterone levels of men struggling with symptoms of growing older such as low sex drive, weight gain, and fatigue. The amount of advertising targeting testosterone is everywhere and has become a billion dollar business and is growing fast. This problem has been around for years and is part of life, part of the aging process. Why do we think a pill, gel, or patch is going to fix the problem? Should we first ask how we got here? Could it be too much stress? Not enough rest or down time? Too much alcohol? Lack of sleep? Poor diet? Lack of exercise? Is it possible if we improved our lifestyle habits, our testosterone levels could improve?

Last year at age 54, I had my total testosterone checked and it came back at 926. The doctor asked if I was taking anything to elevate my testosterone level, and I said yes, cod liver oil, flaxseeds, wheatgrass, spirulina/chlorella, deep breathing, planned down time, regular massages, foam roller, strength training, sunlight, sleep, and regular vacations. After a few minutes, I think he had enough and stopped asking questions. The magic is in you; just give it a chance!

It may surprise most people that men don't have a monopoly on testosterone. Testosterone belongs to a class of male hormones called androgens, but women also have testosterone. Testosterone is a powerful hormone that keeps the body young and is involved in many processes in the body such as growth, muscle, bone, repair, sex drive, weight control, skin, hair and nail health, energy, and mood. As we age, testosterone levels may begin to drop, leading to a host of problems such as muscle wasting, weak bones, dry skin and hair, brittle nails, low energy, depression, low sex drive, erectile dysfunction, and weight gain. Having a baseline testosterone blood test for both men and women can be very helpful in monitoring the aging process. The National Institute of Health outlines the normal testosterone ranges for men and women:

- 30–95 ng/dL for women
- 300–1200 ng/dL for men

Keep in mind that testosterone levels vary with age.

What May Be Causing My Testosterone to Become Low or Out of Balance?

I frequently get calls whether to begin hormone replacement therapy (HRT). Many men have had their testosterone checked, it came back low, and now their doctor suggests hormone replacement therapy. Hormone replacement therapy may be an option, but let's begin by asking some better questions. What may be causing your testosterone to drop or become out of balance? How is your stress level? Are you getting a good night's sleep? Are you on a statin medication that blocks the production of cholesterol (cholesterol is the raw material to make testosterone)? Are you drinking too much alcohol? Is your diet too acidic? Are you deficient in omega-3 fats? Are you doing any strength-training exercises? The list of questions can be long, but let's first try to uncover the *why* behind the problem before you head down the hormone replacement therapy (HRT) path.

How Do I Improve My Testosterone Level?

How many, both men and women, know their testosterone level? Get your testosterone measured. It is important to have a baseline measurement and a great indicator of the aging process!

> **Step 1:** Reduce stress! Too much stress can produce too much of the stress hormone cortisol, and cortisol can steal from your healing hormones and that includes testosterone.
>
> **Step 2:** Sleep! Getting a good night's sleep is imperative for having hormonal harmony and healthy testosterone production. When you are sleeping, you are making testosterone. If you are taking a sleep medication, this is not the answer for improving your testosterone levels. Creating daily rest and rejuvenation strategies is essential for having a healthy testosterone level.
>
> **Step 3:** Increase omega-3s! Omega-3 fats are the raw material to make healthy hormones including testosterone. Cod liver

oil, flaxseeds, and chia seeds are a must for hormonal harmony.

Step 4: Increase zinc! Zinc is another raw material for building testosterone. Foods high in zinc include chicken, lamb, beef, spinach, pumpkin seeds, broccoli, asparagus, greens, beans, oats, amaranth, and millet.

Step 5: Begin strength training! I am a huge fan of strength training for both men and women, as I like to call it the Fountain of Youth. Strength training stimulates testosterone and growth hormone production. If you are currently not strength training, start slowly with a few easy exercises like a body weight squat and a pushup. If you are currently strength training and feel like you are doing the same old thing, change your rep ranges each month. For example, month one, choose reps of 5, higher resistance with greater intensity. Month two increase your reps to 8, a little less resistance, and month three move to reps of 13, less resistance but very challenging. Maintain your body alignment and posture with each exercise, and at the end of each month take a few days off for recovery.

Step 6: Avoid statin medications! Statin medications block the production of cholesterol, the backbone for building steroidal hormones, including testosterone. When you block the production of cholesterol, you compromise hormonal balance, including testosterone. I am a huge fan of the book *Drug Muggers* by Suzy Cohen, RPh. Her book does a terrific job outlining which medications are robbing your body of essential nutrients.

This is a sample **Know Your Numbers** form to copy and take to your doctor. They are many other blood tests available, but here is a list of the basics. It is imperative to take ownership in your own health.

Work with your doctor or health professional and remember, *your body is always talking to you!*

Know Your Numbers

Test	Results	Date	Norms	Goal
Cholesterol			125–220 mg/dl	
HDL Cholesterol			30–80 mg/dl	
LDL Cholesterol			60–130 mg/dl	
HDL/ Cholesterol Ratio			<3.5f/<4.5m	
Triglycerides			<150 mg/dl	
Glucose			65–99 md/dl	
Hemoglobin A1C			4-5.6%	
Homocysteine			3.7–13 umol/l	
High-Sensitive C-Reactive Protein			<1.0 mg/l	
Prostate-Specific Antigen Screening (PSA Screening)			00.–4.00 ng/ml	
Thyroid Stimulating Hormone (TSH Ultra-Sensitive)			.35–5.50ulu/ml	
25-Hydroxy Vitamin D Total			25.0–80.0 ng/ml	
Testosterone			30–95 ng/dl for women, 300–1, 200 ng/dl for men	
Blood Pressure			<120/80	
Resting Heart Rate			<65 bpm	

THE BOTTOM LINE

1. Having a blood test gives you and your doctor or health professional a meaningful look into your health.
2. 60 to 70 percent of all heart attacks occur in people with normal cholesterol levels.
3. Take ownership of your health. Become informed and ask better questions!

29 Why and Why Not?

You Can Do It!

Change starts when someone sees the next step.

—William Drayton

Are you pumped up and excited? Are you ready to go? Are you willing to take that next step? The challenge truly facing most people is how to make healthy lifestyle changes a reality. I talk to so many people who say they want to be healthier, have more energy, lose weight, get off their medication wagon, or get the juice back in their life back, but feel like Mount Everest is staring them in the face! The task at hand seems so overwhelming, and many believe they don't have the necessary tools or willpower for success. You need to stop right there! This type of thinking will paralyze you in reaching your dreams. What I do know is you can make a change. You can be successful if you take small steps! Change is a process and, in most cases happens in increments.

The concept of On Target Living might initially be overwhelming. It may seem too difficult to implement into your life because there is just so much information to absorb at one time. This is why it is important to break it down into small steps that you can easily build into sustainable habits. The first step is to decide if you are ready to change any of your lifestyle habits. You might read this book and find a few small things you are ready and willing to change, or perhaps you have already made some changes and are ready to tackle the next level. Either way, you will experience success because you have taken a step toward a healthier way of life.

Once you have determined your level of commitment, start making On Target Living your own. Take a part of the program that you feel you can handle and begin to make changes. For example, study the Food Target and see where your current foods fall. Instead of trying to head straight for the center, gradually move one ring closer. After you have made a few small changes and are ready for more, go back, read another chapter, and begin to make a few adjustments. Perfecting your habits takes practice, and making mistakes is part of the process. The key for improved performance and long-term success is building habits!

Expect Bumps in the Road

We all have times in our lives when we get off track. Don't let one meal, day, week, or even a month of poor eating, sleeping, or exercise habits get you down. Everyone has lapses now and then. Don't give up. Get your mojo back. Look at your successes and how you have made improvements along the ladder of health. Even if you have a lapse occasionally, rarely will you go back to where you started. Monitor yourself weekly. Are you making good nutritional decisions? Are you getting enough rest? Are you moving your body regularly? If you have slipped a little, recognize the early warning signs and get back on track toward better health.

Why?

In all of my seminars, I talk about finding your Why? Your why is your emotional connection to change—your desire, your need—it is your fuel for change to take place! Finding your why is a powerful concept, so powerful that many books have been written specifically on this subject. Not long ago during a Q&A segment of one of my seminars, I was asked about my own personal why or why's. I always enjoy Q&A, but this question took me a little off guard; nobody had ever asked me about my why before.

I have many why's that keep me motivated to live a healthy lifestyle. My family is a big why in my life. I want to be there for my entire family. I would like to have the same relationship with my kids and grandkids that I had with my parents and grandparents. I want to enjoy staying active, walking in the woods, lifting weights, working out, snow skiing, golf, paddleball, hiking, fishing, climbing mountains, swimming in Lake Michigan, and enjoying all the wonders this world may bring. I want to be medication-free the rest of my life! I want to look and feel great! I want to have great "juice." I want to stay curious and continue to learn and strive to get better. Last but not least, I want to share my passion for health and fitness with the world. I want to educate, motivate, and inspire people to become healthier, hopefully making the world a better place!

Why Not?

Both of my parents have had a great impact on my life. I have learned so much from both of my parents and wanted to share with you a couple of things that may help you as they have helped me. Today my mom is a very healthy and fit 80-year-old; I call her a fitness machine. Mom does not drink alcohol, drinks plenty of water, exercises regularly, consumes cod liver oil, flaxseeds, wheatgrass, spirulina/chlorella, oatmeal, greens, coconut, eats healthy—and, by the way, is medication-free at age 80. Mom was the "rock" of our family; she was our guiding light. When the going got rough, Mom was always there to help. Mom inspires me daily, and I love her so much for all the sacrifices she made for her family.

My dad passed away just over a year ago and for those of you who have lost one of your parents or a loved one, you know how tough it can be. My dad was not a healthy guy; in fact, his lifestyle habits were almost comical. Dad skipped breakfast, drank too much coffee, rarely exercised (unless you call playing cards or hitting the golf ball exercise), and ate whatever he felt like. My dad always said to me that he never truly experienced what being healthy felt like. For many years, I kidded Dad about how good he could feel if he just took a few steps. But Dad never really got on track with his health. I think he truly wanted to be healthier, but I believe he waited too long to start on his journey!

What I learned from my dad had nothing to do with health; what I learned from my dad was about life. Dad was a fun guy; in fact, at his funeral everyone came up to my brother, sister, and me and said this was the most uplifting funeral service they had ever experienced—a true celebration of a man's life. Most said they hoped their funeral would be something special like his. My dad inspired me in so many ways that I never told him about, so I wanted to dedicate this last piece to my dad.

My dad's greatest quality was his giving of his time; he always made time for his kids and those closest to him. Dad was an amazing listener, always attentive and nonjudgmental: you could tell Dad anything and you always felt safe. And fun, boy, was Dad a fun guy: Dad loved to have fun and laugh; he was always laughing. So as you begin your On Target Living journey, I ask the question *Why Not*? Why not be a better listener? Why not be a better parent? Why not smile or laugh more? Why not be a better spouse? Why not be a better friend? Why not perform better, be a better leader, boss, or associate by having greater energy and vitality? Why not take better care of yourself? If I could say one thing to my dad or to you, this would be it, "To the world you might be one person, but to one person you might be the world."

Enjoy the Journey!

I hope you have enjoyed *On Target Living*. As with any challenge, the journey is as rewarding as the outcome. Put your back-burner dreams on the front burner. You may be surprised at what you can accomplish. Wishing you a life full of health and happiness!

Visit us at www.ontargetliving.com for more information on our products and services and to find out more information on how to consult or hire Chris to speak. Or call (517) 641-4711.

Also don't forget to sign-up for our free newsletter and check out our free videos of recipes, exercises, and restful activities you can start implementing.

Index